The object of nature is man

the object of man is style

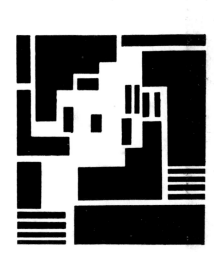

5671

De Stijl: 1917-1931
Visions of Utopia

■

Introduction by Hans L.C. Jaffé

Essays by
Manfred Bock, Kees Broos
Martin Filler, Kenneth Frampton
Martin Friedman, Ger Harmsen
Joop Joosten, Rudolf W.D. Oxenaar
Sergio Polano, Nancy J. Troy
Robert P. Welsh

Mildred Friedman, editor

Phaidon · Oxford

Published on the occasion of the exhibition *De Stijl: 1917-1931, Visions of Utopia,* organized by Walker Art Center. Following its opening at Walker Art Center, the exhibition was shown at the Hirshhorn Museum and Sculpture Garden, Smithsonian Institution, Washington, D.C., and divided chronologically into two presentations at the Stedelijk Museum, Amsterdam and the Rijksmuseum Kröller-Müller, Otterlo, The Netherlands.

Phaidon Press Limited
Littlegate House, St. Ebbe's Street
Oxford, 0X1 1SQ
First published in Great Britain 1982
Second impression (paperback) 1986
Copyright © 1982 by Walker Art Center.

ISBN 0 7148 2250 7 (hardback)
ISBN 0 7148 2438 0 (paperback)
Printed in Spain

Dimensions are in inches and centimeters; height precedes width precedes depth.

(page 2)
1. Piet Mondrian
Composition with Red, Yellow and Blue, 1920
oil on canvas
20½ x 23⅝
52.1 x 60
Collection Stedelijk Museum, Amsterdam

Contents

Foreword

What began as an isolated effort to publish the ideas and images of a small group of Dutch artists has become one of the keys to Modernism. From 1917, when the multi-talented Theo van Doesburg published the first issue of *De Stijl* magazine, until his death in 1931, "The Style" was a focus for wide-ranging invention in painting, architecture, furniture and graphic design. Central to the group's development was Piet Mondrian's speculative imagery. His theories about color and space were the basis for De Stijl's language that carried Cubism's abstraction into a new non-figurative realm. It was van Doesburg and the designer Gerrit Rietveld who transformed the De Stijl idea of "pure plastic art" into the third dimension, with their furniture design and architecture. Other primary participants were the painters Bart van der Leck and Vilmos Huszar, who applied De Stijl's energetic geometry to typography and graphic design. Many architects played important roles in the growth of De Stijl, among them Robert van 't Hoff, Jan Wils and J.J.P. Oud, whose early contributions to the movement reside somewhere between the traditions of the Amsterdam School and the birth of European Modernism. Gerrit Rietveld and Cornelis van Eesteren, who joined the group in the early 1920s, initiated an architecture in which windows and walls become transparent, movable planes.

The movement included a number of participants in and out of Holland who entered the De Stijl circle because of van Doesburg's persuasive advocacy of its ideas in the magazine and in his lectures and teaching in Germany and France. These "fellow travelers" published in *De Stijl* and in some cases contributed to group projects. In most cases their contacts with others in the movement were brief and specific. Among the early artists were the futurist Italian painter Gino Severini, Belgian painter/sculptor Georges Vantongerloo, Dutch poet Antony Kok and the Dutch graphic designer Piet Zwart. As van Doesburg went further afield, his proselytizing efforts attracted Russian constructivist El Lissitzky and architect/sculptor Frederick Kiesler, whose *City in Space* construction for the Austrian pavilion in the 1925 Paris Exposition des Arts Décoratifs was a further exploration of the space-time concepts seen in De Stijl's 1923 Paris architectural exhibition at the Galerie L'Effort Moderne. Movement through time was also the inspiration for Hans Richter's "filmmoment" experiments in abstract animation published in *De Stijl* in 1922. The multi-disciplinary nature of this roster is consistent with the movement's oft-stated goal—the creation of a world of universal harmony. Now, some 50 years after the magazine's final issue, we begin to comprehend the truly revolutionary social and

2. Theo van Doesburg
Composition XXII, 1920-22
oil on canvas
18 x 16
45.7 x 40.6
Collection Stedelijk Van Abbemuseum

aesthetic attitudes it represented: the transcendent purity of Piet Mondrian's geometric painting; the radical simplicity of Gerrit Rietveld's celebrated red/blue chair; the seamless relationship between painting and architecture represented by collaborative efforts such as the Café Aubette.

This loose confederation of artists was held together for approximately 15 years by deeply rooted, shared attitudes about the arts and society that were at the basis of its utopian visions. Fundamental to these visions was a search for essential truths in the arts and in social forms. These truths could be revealed only through the use of the most direct, elemental means: primary color, rectangular form and asymmetrical composition were those means. Finally, the "decomposition" of the closed volume into varied configurations of color planes opened the cube, allowing elements to extend beyond the confines of a two or three-dimensional form. De Stijl's artists resolutely took abstraction to its outer limits and beyond. Pure color and elemental form engendered this art, and then became its subject matter.

Today, De Stijl's place in the evolution of Modernism is clear. Mondrian's "new image in painting" expressed life's fundamental duality through the opposition of the Horizontal and Vertical, and through the use of primary colors to reveal "perfect harmony." For Mondrian this was the essence of reality. Throughout De Stijl's history, its various collaborations between painters and architects can now be understood as efforts to bring harmony to all areas of the environment. In keeping with its fusion of ethics and aesthetics, De Stijl architecture also sought to transcend divisions of social class in order to provide egalitarian space, accessible to all. De Stijl participants worked toward a total cultural

program. These artists were reacting to a Europe in social upheaval at the end of World War I, and to the Russian Revolution that was then in its infancy. These outside pressures were soon felt in the Dutch intellectual and artistic communities and, together with aesthetic concerns, produced De Stijl philosophy in Holland.

The publication of this book coincides with the presentation of a major exhibition devoted to De Stijl painting, architecture and design. It was organized by Walker Art Center with the participation of the great Dutch museums whose collections form the exhibition's core. Since 1952, when the last De Stijl presentation in America was held at New York's Museum of Modern Art, a generation of scholars has developed new material and attitudes based upon firsthand research. In addition, new materials are available for study and exhibition that had remained in little-known or inaccessible collections for many years. The most important of these, the van Doesburg archive, is now in the State-Owned Collections in The Hague. Only this year, it was retrieved from storage in Paris where it has been since the death of van Doesburg's widow, Nelly, in 1975.

To the excellent group of senior De Stijl scholars—several have contributed essays to this publication—we have added a number of younger critics and historians whose work in this field is only beginning. These authors are European, Canadian and American, thus providing important links between the major European holdings and the important works from museums and private collections in the United States that constitute the exhibition. Hans L.C. Jaffé introduces the De Stijl idea with the movement's probable sources—the rectilinear Dutch landscape, the Calvinist theology of puritanism and

iconoclasm that banished the representation of nature from art, and the Spinozistic philosophy whose geometric method frees the artist from arbitrary decisions. Robert P. Welsh provides a general overview of De Stijl, introducing the creative spirits who formulated the ideas behind its search for universal harmony. The impact of the Russian Revolution on the intellectual and social life of Holland is historian Ger Harmsen's subject. He discusses early socialism and the subsequent disillusionment that led to the isolation of the artist from society familiar throughout much of the 20th century.

Joop Joosten's essay on De Stijl painting and sculpture analyzes the derivations of the neoplastic idea in works by van Doesburg, Mondrian, Huszar and Vantongerloo. The early contributions to the De Stijl aesthetic by the painter Bart van der Leck is Rudolf W.D. Oxenaar's subject: his research is based on letters and other documents in the artist's estate. In his contribution, Italian historian Sergio Polano describes De Stijl architecture as the synthesis of all the arts. It was, he contends, the means through which De Stijl could have realized its search for universal harmony. The relationship between De Stijl architecture and other European movements, and its influence on European and American architecture today are considered in Kenneth Frampton's essay. Gerrit Rietveld is discussed as cabinetmaker and as "form giver" by Martin Filler. In his survey of Rietveld's furniture, he analyzes the "plastic" characteristics of these objects whose apparent simplicity belies their daring originality. De Stijl's ambition to create art that touches all aspects of daily life was pursued in the areas of typography and graphic design. Kees Broos describes the development of De Stijl typography especially in relation to Dadaism and Constructivism.

Another of De Stijl's goals was to create art that would involve all aspects of the environment. In addressing this major topic, Nancy J. Troy speculates about a series of abstract, coloristic interiors that were the embodiment of the De Stijl ideal, by such artists as Theo van Doesburg, Piet Zwart and Piet Mondrian. Approaching the question of the larger environment, Manfred Bock applies De Stijl ideas to city structure, as illustrated in the exemplary 1928-34 Expansion Plan of Amsterdam. The spirit of De Stijl is with us, Martin Friedman contends in his concluding essay. He traces its continuing influences through his discussions with a number of contemporary painters and sculptors whose recent works reflect or "echo" De Stijl attitudes.

In three sections of this publication, classic examples of De Stijl architecture, illustrated in vintage photographs, are given particular attention. In 1926, André Kertész photographed Mondrian's Paris atelier. His telling images are combined with photographs by P. Delbo, from the Mondrian archive in the Haags Gemeentemuseum, to create a precise evocation of Mondrian's living and working environment. From the Hagenbach-Arp archive in Meudon and the Musée d'Art Moderne in Strasbourg, we have included 1928 photographs of the Café Aubette. They are shown with drawings for a number of its rooms by van Doesburg and Sophie Taeuber-Arp, and with floor plans of the 18th-century building into which these astounding coloristic interiors were introduced. The Rietveld/Schröder house in Utrecht, the only extant De Stijl structure, is shown in images from the 1920s and in a series of photographs that were commissioned for this publication in 1981.

Artists and architects associated with De Stijl believed that when their ideas were implemented, harmonious relationships would pervade all aspects of the visual environment. Piet Mondrian summarized their utopian vision in this extraordinary statement: "Art is only a substitute while the beauty of life is still deficient. It will disappear in proportion as life gains in equilibrium." Although the De Stijl ideal of a universal harmony that would create a visual environment in perfect balance with the social climate remains unrealized, the attitudes it represents can now be understood in terms of the movement's history and continuing influence.

Mildred Friedman
Design Curator, Walker Art Center

3. Theo van Doesburg (standing), Nelly van Doesburg and sculptor Richard Scheibe in van Doesburg's Weimar atelier, 1922. On the right-hand wall, one-half of the stained-glass window for the Drachten agricultural school; behind van Doesburg, his *Composition in Gray*, circa 1918. Vintage photograph

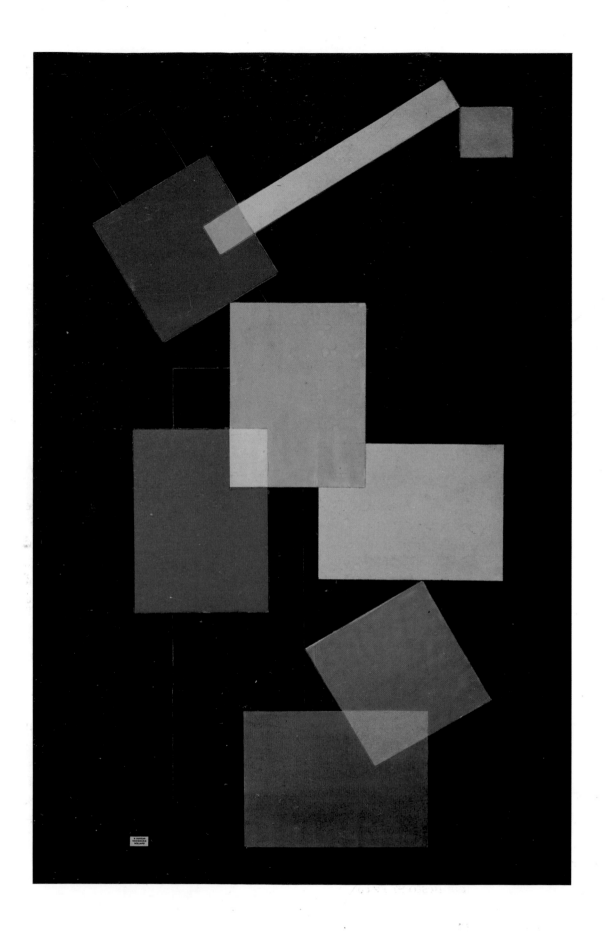

Introduction ■

Hans L.C. Jaffé

What was De Stijl, and why has this loosely organized, mercurial group had a sustained influence on the visual arts—not only painting, but architecture, typography and furniture design—throughout this century? Never a cohesive movement, in the beginning it included three painters, two architects, a sculptor and a poet, who came together to exchange ideas in a public forum. The vehicle for this exchange was a monthly magazine, *De Stijl*. Founded in mid-1917 in Leiden, Holland, it ceased publication in 1931 after the death of its founder, Theo van Doesburg, who was publisher and editor of the magazine and the movement's primary spokesman. Without van Doesburg, De Stijl as a movement fell apart.

In visual terms, the group had a shared point of departure: the principle of absolute abstraction—that is to say, the complete elimination of any reference to objects in nature. Its means of visual expression were limited to the straight line and the right angle, to the horizontal and the vertical, to the three primary colors—red, yellow and blue—with the addition of black, white and gray. But this initial description reveals only the method of De Stijl, not its scope or its philosophical outlook.

In order to discover what these artists wished to render with their new, revolutionary language, a series of facts about De Stijl's genesis and history must be reviewed. In rejecting perceptible subject matter, the artists of this movement did not abandon content or meaning in their work. The essential content of De Stijl works is harmony, a harmony that for these artists could only be rendered by abstract means, through compositions unhampered by associations with objects in the external world. This search for harmony was the springboard and constant goal of De Stijl. Yet De Stijl artists were not solely concerned with aesthetics. The movement was an effort to renew the links between life and art. In creating a new visual style it attempted to create a new style for living.

This unity between art and life was stressed even in De Stijl's first manifesto in 1918:

4. Vilmos Huszar
Figure Composition for a Mechanical Theater,
circa 1923
gouache on paper mounted on cardboard
48 x 31
121.9 x 78.7
Collection Herbert F. Johnson Museum of Art,
Cornell University
Gift of Silvia Pizitz

5. P.J. Saenredam
*Interior of the Church of St. Odulphus,
Assendelft,* 1649
wood panel
17 x 30
48.5 x 76.2
Collection Rijksmuseum, Amsterdam
(not in exhibition)

1. Redactie, "Inleiding Bij De Tweeden
Jaargang," *De Stijl,* II, 1 (Nov. 1918), p 2. From
the facsimile reprint, 2 vols. (Amsterdam:
Athenaeum and Polak & van Gennep; The
Hague: Bert Bakker, 1968), I, p 236.

There is an old and a new consciousness of time.
The old is connected with the individual.
The new is connected with the universal.
The struggle of the individual against the universal is revealing
itself in the World War as well as in the art of the present day.
The War is destroying the old world with its contents:
individual domination in every state.
The new art has brought forward what the new
consciousness of time contains:
a balance between the universal and the individual.
The new consciousness is prepared to realize the internal life as
well as the external life.[1]

De Stijl was founded during World War I. Though its origins were in a
then neutral country, it came out of a period of utter chaos, when
harmony and balance were longed for by the majority of Europeans. But
it was clear that future harmony implied changes in the traditional ways
of life. De Stijl artists discovered these changes everywhere in
contemporary life: in industrial production, in the organization of
politics and trade unions, in the growth of large cities. In all of these
domains, a general plan, a conception was established to replace
individual, often arbitrary decisions. A blueprint, a formula, stood at the
base of all modern, progressive creation. The blueprint, therefore,
became the model for artistic creation as well. Just as a building is
complete in its ground plan and elevations, before a single wall is
constructed, or a symphony exists in its score, before a note is played,
the conception of a visual work of art gains priority over its execution.
And in the execution of their conceptions, the De Stijl group was striving
for a precision such as that found in the products of the machine. They
determined that precision and exactitude can only be realized with
strictly determined geometrical elements, which do not include the
arbitrary forms of perceived objects. Abstraction requires precision and
precision is—as in music—the only way to render harmony. For the De
Stijl artists, harmony did not only mean a restful, reassuring balance:
harmony for them was the law of the entire universe. This law and the
rules derived from it were only veiled and obscured by the arbitrary
forms of objects. Nature presented only variations of this law, and what
the artists had to seek and reveal was the theme behind these
variations.

De Stijl was founded in a country with a tradition that corresponded with
the movement's central aspiration: the domination of nature by human
thought and inventiveness. It seems absurd to think that the Dutch
landscape with its rectangular fields and straight roads and canals should
have been the hidden subject matter in De Stijl paintings; but one can
establish a common goal in De Stijl work and in the will of the Dutch
people to control nature. The Dutch landscape is, in fact, man-made,

using the means of geometry and precision. This precision has been highly valued in The Netherlands, and the De Stijl group made use of it in order to show, in a visual language, the triumph of the human spirit over the capriciousness of nature. When van Doesburg wrote, "Gradually the old dream of primitive man becomes reality: to be the master of his surroundings," he formulated a centuries-old Dutch aspiration. It may, therefore, not be a mere accident that De Stijl was founded in The Netherlands: its scope and characteristic features coincide with what historian Johan Huizinga called ". . . the hallmark of Dutch spirt."

De Stijl is closely linked with The Netherlands in another way as well—in its history. The artistic purism of De Stijl is synonymous with the tradition of Dutch puritanism. A peculiarity of the Dutch language throws some light on this relationship. In Dutch, the word "schoon" means "clean, pure" as well as "beautiful." This double meaning appears again in the works of De Stijl. Their beauty consists in their purity, in their utter sobriety. In their structure, parallels can be found with works of such masters of the 17th century as Saenredam (fig. 5), de Hooch and Vermeer. But the most significant parallel in the 17th century, and in Dutch tradition, seems to be with philosophy, in the great work of Baruch Spinoza, *Ethica, Ordine Geometrico Demonstrata*. Spinoza chose the geometrical method of presentation in order to free his arguments from arbitrary or casual interpretation—so did the De Stijl group. They strove for precision, for the unchangeable elements of the visual language. Their preference for abstraction also can be placed within Dutch tradition. The Dutch national character owes a great deal to the influence of 16th-century Calvinism. As a matter of fact, almost the first act of the early Calvinists was the destruction of the images of worship in their churches. They felt that any representation of a religious image was a detraction from the absolute sanctity of God. The De Stijl artists, who can be regarded as descendants of these earlier iconoclasts, had similar reasons for their banishment of every representation of nature: any representation of a natural object was, for them, a distortion of the divine purity of the laws of creation. Abstraction was the only way to maintain their faith in universal values.

Universal values, the absolute harmony, were the goals of De Stijl's work. To this end an absolute purification of the vocabulary and grammar of the arts seemed necessary. Abstraction and strict limitations on the elements of visual language were the consequences. Purification of the arts meant, in the first instance, the autonomy of the various arts, their independence from each other and their obedience to their particular laws. Independence had a double meaning: on one side it meant liberation from the arbitrary subjective temperament of the artist and the

13

beholder, on the other, it involved the dissolution of every link with the perception of objects in nature. Abstraction granted freedom from external reality; the limitation of the means of expression excluded, by its elementary character, individualistic tendencies. It was a vital step towards ". . . a true vision of reality." This step was deemed necessary and logical to the history of art which was leading gradually from the representation of things to a rendering of the essential laws of creation. The arts ceased to be the handmaiden of any other field of creative activity and became—like science, philosophy and religion—another way to approach universal truth in strict objectivity. Only an "art of pure relationships" could fulfill this demand, could render a visual image of the laws of harmony, which dominate the entire creation and are related to every single appearance in reality as the theme in music is related to the variations based upon it. This conception of reality, parallel to ancient philosophical views of the world, brought with it far reaching implications.

The art of De Stijl starts from and aims at conceptions that are not only artistic, but that pertain to the formation of a new style of life. De Stijl's paintings and buildings do not want only to purify the work of art, but the "gates of perception," the spirit of the beholder, as well. De Stijl's art aspires to be a "model" for future life. Mondrian's dedication of his pamphlet "Le neo-plasticisme," of 1920, "to future man," is one of the proofs of this fact. In De Stijl's outlook on contemporary life, the arts—and first of all painting—were able to free themselves from the oppression of everyday irrelevancies, which prevented man from pursuing his true purpose: to seek truth and to find harmony. Where daily life was still working in the dark, the arts had already seen the light. Art is therefore ahead of life, and hence its task is to show life the way towards the realization of that harmony. Art could be capable of guiding mankind toward a brighter future, a new and revolutionary utopia.

Mondrian felt at home in this future world, but he realized that if this concept were carried to its ultimate conclusion, the visual arts would be doomed to disappear. He did not worry about this fate. As long as universal harmony was not a reality in daily life, painting would offer a temporary substitute. And once harmony had found its way into every domain of life, painting—as a guide toward harmony—would have played out its part. It would no longer be needed. The art of De Stijl cannot be looked at adequately without considering this utopian vision, this newly created task for the visual arts, which exceeds the boundaries of aesthetics and sets itself moral and ethical aims.

It was primarily Mondrian who prophesied this great utopian dream. But a different personality was needed to make the dream a reality. Theo van

Doesburg succeeded in allowing reality to dominate the dream, the spirit of architecture to prevail upon that of painting. And van Doesburg, the gifted painter, turned toward architecture after 1923. He had brought a number of architects into the collaborative work of De Stijl. First, J.J.P. Oud, who had, in 1918, given three-dimensional form to the principles of De Stijl, and very soon after, Gerrit Rietveld and Cornelis van Eesteren. As a team, van Doesburg and van Eesteren studied the new possibilities of architecture on the occasion, in 1923, of a commission to design an artist's house and a private residence for an exhibition in Paris. In the same year, Rietveld designed a house in collaboration with Mrs. Truus Schröder-Schräder in Utrecht, which has become the most significant monument of this phase of De Stijl architecture. And van Doesburg continued to work in this vein. The internal reconstruction of L'Aubette, a Strasbourg café—alas destroyed not long after its completion—was one of his major works, completed in 1928. This building, and his 1929 house in Meudon, were landmarks of a new spirit in the old city. And the city assumed a new harmonious shape with the planning of van Eesteren who succeeded, in his master plan for the enlargement of Amsterdam, in applying the principles of De Stijl to urbanism, to the organization of a large city, realizing them in daily life and on a large social scale.

The artists and architects of De Stijl not only redefined the vocabulary and the grammar of the visual arts, they assigned a new task to painting, architecture and the other arts: to serve as a guide for humanity to prepare it for the harmony and balance of a "new life;" to serve mankind by enlightening it.

Hans L.C. Jaffé is Professor of Modern Art History, University of Amsterdam.

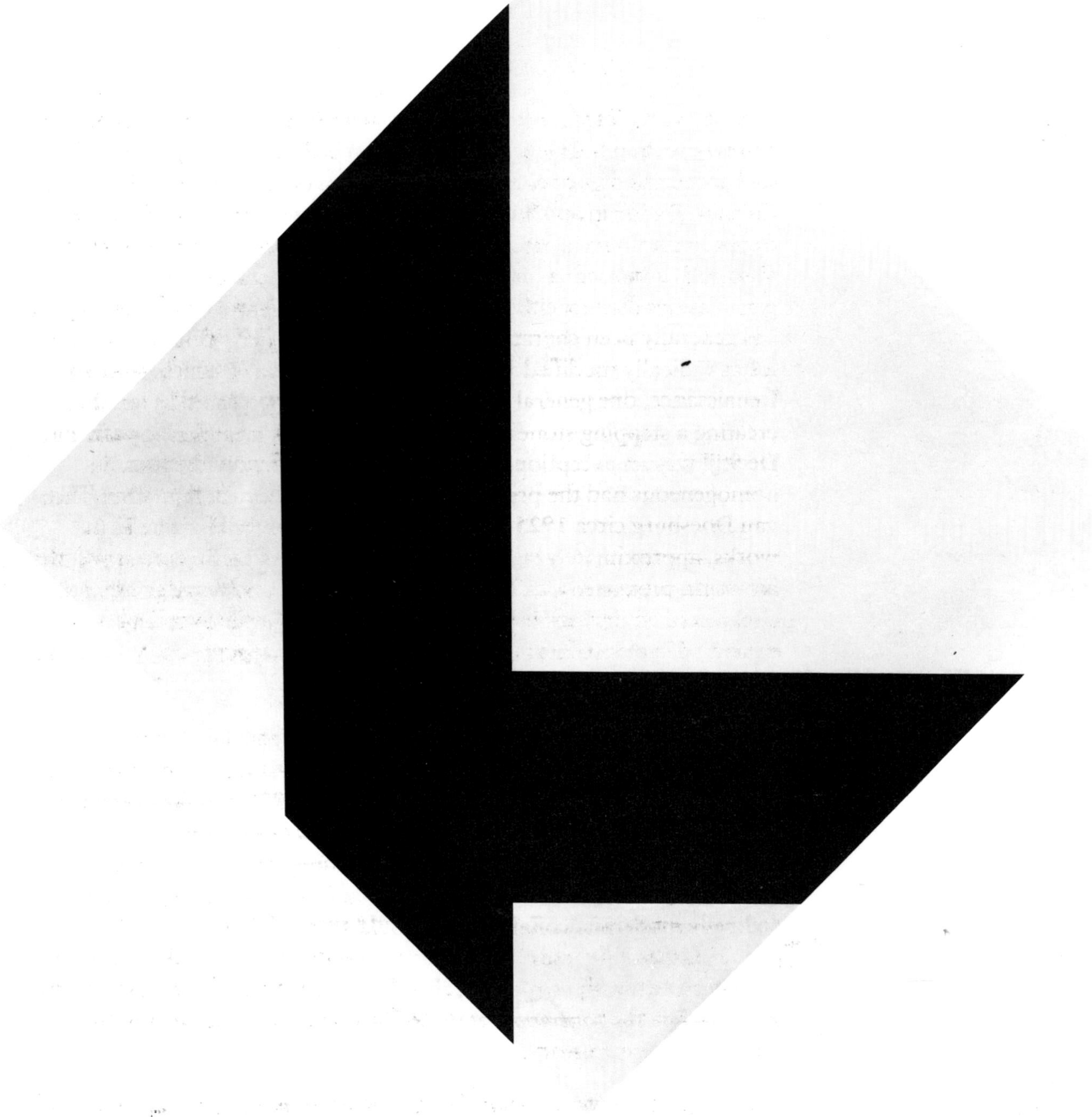

A Reintroduction

De Stijl

Robert P. Welsh

Among the major innovative developments in 20th-century Western art, none more than the De Stijl phenomenon is thought to have embodied such a consistent, not to say obdurate, form of art. Although Fauvism, Cubism, Dadaism and Surrealism did experience brief periods when a common group style predominated, these movements sooner or later dissolved as individual artists sought to establish identifiable personalities distinct either within or outside the group. 20th-century art has generally been characterized more by multiplicity than uniformity. It has radically modified Western artistic tradition in which, since the Renaissance, one general mode was successively replaced by another creating a stepping stone in a single if sometimes meandering path. But De Stijl was an exception to the century's rule of individualism. So homogeneous had the production of its artists seemed, that when Theo van Doesburg circa 1925 introduced diagonal linear elements in his works, approximately eight years after he initiated *De Stijl* magazine, the art world presumed that De Stijl was defunct as a cohesive group. How circumscribed or flexible the thinking of De Stijl artists was will be examined in this collection of essays, so it seems appropriate to pose this question at the outset.

The issue of group solidarity was of primary importance from the years 1915-17, when Theo van Doesburg was proselytizing for an avant-garde association of Dutch artists, until his death in 1931 and the publication early the following year of the *dernier numéro* of *De Stijl* commemorating his work. From the beginning there was very real uncertainty that van Doesburg's efforts to form a cohesive group of radically modernist collaborators would succeed. Both the precariousness of these efforts and van Doesburg's eventual achievement have been variously explained; therefore, a review of the circumstances surrounding the formation of the Stijl group is necessary to a sound knowledge of its history.

In retrospect the founding of De Stijl seems to be a logical consequence of Cubism, yet the circumstances leading to its emergence during 1917

6. Theo van Doesburg
Countercomposition VIII, 1924
oil on canvas
39⅜ x 39⅜
100 x 100
Collection The Art Institute of Chicago
Gift of Miss Peggy Guggenheim

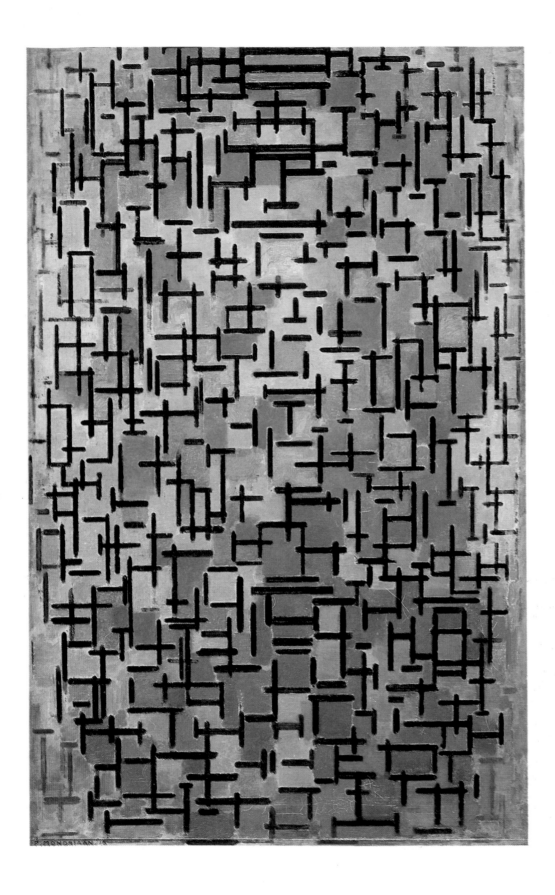

in The Netherlands were often more fortuitous than inevitable. Above all else, World War I and Holland's neutrality were the overriding pre-conditions to the consolidation of a Dutch group of abstract artists. Mondrian, caught in Holland by the war between 1914 and 1919, hesitated to join forces with van Doesburg, in part because he hoped that hostilities would cease quickly and allow him to return to Paris where he had resided from 1912-14. Had Mondrian remained in Paris throughout the war, it is quite uncertain that he would have continued to exhibit his most advanced work in his home country or that he would have become personally acquainted with those artists who joined together in De Stijl.[1] The crucial meeting in 1916 between Mondrian and Bart van der Leck is hardly conceivable without Mondrian's wartime residence in his native country, and it is equally possible that van Doesburg would have continued his involvement with less than fully geometric forms of abstraction had he not been able to establish personal contact with Mondrian. In addition, during van Doesburg's military service in Tilburg he developed a friendship with Antony Kok, a poet who became an art theorist in the Stijl cause; and Georges Vantongerloo never would have come into contact with De Stijl except for his presence in The Netherlands as a Belgian war refugee.[2]

The paucity of surviving correspondence between Mondrian and van Doesburg previous to May 1917, when agreement was reached in principle to found an art periodical, reflects Mondrian's hesitation to join forces with someone whose thoughts on art he knew more from published writings than from paintings, which were exhibited, if at all, in The Hague or in Leiden. Though Mondrian may have had little ongoing firsthand knowledge of van Doesburg's development as a painter before 1917, his own work was doubtless seen by van Doesburg and the Hungarian born Vilmos Huszar in several exhibitions in Amsterdam and in the Kröller-Müller collection then housed in The Hague, where van der Leck was also generously represented.[3]

Symptomatically, Mondrian, as late as in a letter of 21 May 1917 to van Doesburg, admitted to not knowing the work of Huszar, who, in the January 1918 issue of *De Stjil*, analyzed *Composition with Color Planes* by Mondrian, while admitting to knowing it only through a black and white reproduction and to being unaware of what motif in nature was its point of departure.[4] More remarkable still, it was only in 1920 in Paris that Mondrian finally met another Leiden-The Hague situated friend of van Doesburg, the architect J.J.P. Oud, whose designs and executed projects Mondrian and van der Leck are unlikely to have known except through illustration in *De Stijl*. Vantongerloo, too, met Mondrian only in 1920 in Paris.

1. See Oxenaar, p 69.
2. In a 1961 autobiographical sketch, reprinted in *Georges Vantongerloo* (Washington, D.C.: exh. cat. Corcoran Gallery of Art, 1980), p 22, the artist gives his arrival in The Hague as 1914, but his exhibited work of 1916 (*ibid.*, illus. p 20) comprised loosely pointillist paintings and naturalistic figural sculptures. His intial contact with the De Stijl movement may well have occurred only after seeing an issue of *De Stijl* magazine and he apparently returned to Brussels immediately upon war's end (*ibid.* p 22).
3. See Rudolf W.D. Oxenaar, "The Birth of De Stijl, Part II: Bart van der Leck," *Artforum* XI: 10 (June 1973), pp 42-43, and R.P. Welsh, "Theo van Doesburg and Geometric Abstraction," in *Nijhoff, van Ostaijen, De Stijl*, ed. F. Bulhof (The Hague: M. Nijhoff, 1976), pp 81-85.
4. Vilmos Huszar, "Aesthetic Contemplation II," *De Stijl*, I, 3, pp 33-35. Illustrated in color in *Piet Mondrian 1872-1944* (New York: exh. cat. S.R. Guggenheim Museum, 1971), no. 74.

The issue of whether or not architects were to be included as De Stijl members doubtless was another factor contributing to Mondrian's and van der Leck's initial reluctance to join in van Doesburg's plans. Mondrian's pre- and early De Stijl period correspondence with van Doesburg deals almost exclusively with painting, and on several occasions he expressed the thought that developments in architecture lagged behind those in painting. Van der Leck, perhaps because of difficulties he had experienced with H.P. Berlage over a color scheme for the art room of a Kröller-Müller residence at Wassenaar (fig. 150), clearly shared Mondrian's viewpoint. This was stated in the only two articles that van der Leck contributed to *De Stijl*.[5] In one he included a list of five differences between the most advanced form of contemporary painting and the traditional character of architecture, and he pleaded for architects to respect this difference and to grant painters the right to decorate buildings according to their own principles and aims. Van der Leck had been preoccupied with painting as a form of mural decoration from early in his career, and he continued to manifest this interest during the two year period, mid-1917 to mid-1919, in which he participated in the De Stijl movement. Yet despite written appeals from Huszar and van Doesburg to join in presenting a common front, van der Leck felt himself isolated enough from the De Stijl program that he refused to sign the first manifesto published in November 1918. By 1920, he had abandoned contact with the group altogether.[6]

In sum, it can be inferred that from some time before its first public manifestation as a journal, De Stijl was composed of individual artists holding distinct, sometimes antithetical viewpoints. Bifurcation took several forms. First, from 1916 there was the geographical distinction of the Leiden-Hague group surrounding van Doesburg, including the painter Huszar, the poet Kok, the sculptor Vantongerloo and the architects Oud and Wils, and then there was the pair situated in Laren, Mondrian and van der Leck. This distinction from the beginning carries with it the greater enthusiasm of the Leiden-Hague artists to advocate and, as evident in several collaborations involving Huszar, Wils and van Doesburg and Oud, to practice the integration of architecture with painting and the applied arts. In contrast, the Laren artists remained cool to a blurring of the distinction between painting and architecture, considering painting more advanced than architecture in its historical evolution. One result of this reservation was the joint decision of Mondrian and van der Leck that van Doesburg would be the principal editor of *De Stijl*, and that they thus would not be held responsible for his choice of authors and illustrations.[7] Ultimately this would mean the inclusion of material by Russian constructivists and dadaists within the pages of *De Stijl*. Mondrian obviously tolerated such "outsiders" in the name of fraternal support for more or less related tendencies in art.

5. "The Place of Modern Painting in Architecture," *De Stijl*, I, 1 (Oct. 1917), pp 6-7, and "Theory of Painting," *De Stijl*, I, 4 (Feb. 1918), pp 37-38. These and many cited articles from *De Stijl* to follow are translated into English in either or both Joost Baljeu, *Theo van Doesburg* (New York: Macmillan Publishing Co., Inc., 1974) and, Hans L.C. Jaffé, *De Stijl* (New York: Harry N. Abrams, Inc., 1971).
6. Oxenaar, p 77.
7. Oxenaar, p 73.

However, he would hardly have classified these artists as participants in the De Stijl movement itself.

A case could be made for defining the movement largely in terms of the interests manifested in *De Stijl*. This interpretation of course would not only cast van Doesburg as the driving force behind the movement but also identify the periodical as the fundamental vehicle for its definition. Such a conclusion is supported by a number of considerations. The foremost of these is that during van Doesburg's lifetime not a single comprehensive exhibition of De Stijl art was held.[8] Even the most loyal among De Stijl artists retained individual career outlooks despite allegiance to the universalist principles stated in the manifestoes and articles published in the magazine. In addition, many artists joined and then abandoned the De Stijl cause throughout the life of the magazine. It was chiefly by reference to *De Stijl* and the several associated publications in languages more widely read than Dutch that a knowledge of De Stijl art and theory could be acquired.[9] In this sense, the original decision by Mondrian and van der Leck not to share in editorial responsibilities ensured that van Doesburg's involvements in diverse art forms and styles would be seen as reflective of the De Stijl movement by both participants and outside observers. Yet this view of a cohesive art movement subject to the vagaries of the interests of its self-appointed ringmaster has its weaknesses, and it is necessary to return to the years of incubation in order to understand how the Stijl group was induced to work together in the first place.

A number of positive factors affected the founding of De Stijl. A basic instance was the Dutch cultural tradition into which all but Huszar and Vantongerloo among the original membership were born. As H.L.C. Jaffé has persuasively argued, the Dutch physical environment, its dominant religious and philosophical system and a major tendency within its artistic heritage may be characterized as "abstract," and the De Stijl movement can be seen as the ultimate form of Protestant iconoclasm, with not only saints and holy legend but all naturalism banned from the realm of art.[10]

Although none of the De Stijl artists had met previous to the war years, several of them had experimented in various ways with anti-naturalistic or proto-abstract modes of expression. In his successive involvements with Art Nouveau, Pointillism and Cubism, Mondrian had developed a personal style, which by 1913 he himself, like the critic Apollinaire, had begun to describe as "abstract."[11] Circa 1912-14 Theo van Doesburg had begun to examine the modernist tradition in European painting in a series of critical reviews which included discussions of Cubism, Futurism and the "abstract expressionist" art of Kandinsky as he termed it and to

8. The most inclusive De Stijl group exhibition was held in 1923 at the Galerie L'Effort Moderne, Paris; it was exclusively devoted to architecture. Until the present exhibition the sole comprehensive De Stijl retrospective was held at the Stedelijk Museum, Amsterdam, 1951, and The Museum of Modern Art, New York, 1952.

9. Apart from various foreign language articles, certain manifestoes and other important articles appeared in translation in *De Stijl* or elsewhere. Yet, Mondrian's booklet, *Le Neo-plasticisme* (Paris: L'Effort Moderne, 1920) and its German translation, *Die Neue Gestaltung* (published by the Bauhaus in 1925 and also containing other translated articles by the artist), plus various articles written for French language journals made him the most accessible De Stijl spokesman to non-Dutch readers.

10. H.L.C. Jaffé, *De Stijl, 1917-1931: The Dutch Contribution to Modern Art* (Amsterdam: J.M. Meulenhoff, 1956), p 78 ff.

11. The term appears frequently in Mondrian's cubist period sketchbook annotations (see *Two Mondrian Sketchbooks, 1912-1914*, eds. J.M. Joosten and R.P. Welsh, Amsterdam: Meulenhoff International, 1969). The Apollinaire reference to Mondrian's painting as "très abstraite" occurred in *L'Intransigent* 21 March 1913 in reference to the then current *Indépendants* exhibition.

a degree exploited in his own painting.[12] Van der Leck, too, had developed a quasi-abstract style, which by the years 1913-15 featured flattened figural images painted increasingly with the three primary colors plus black against a white ground (fig. 9). It cannot be claimed that a common style of painting existed by the year 1915 when van Doesburg first proposed the idea of a periodical, but if these three painters had not already been advancing in a similar stylistic direction by this date it is unlikely that the final group coalescence would have occurred.

Another basis for collaboration was the widespread idea within late 19th- early 20th-century Dutch art circles that some form of cooperative interaction among the fine arts was desirable. Basic to Art Nouveau, and the Arts and Crafts movement as well, this tendency in The Netherlands is exemplified in the architecture of H.P. Berlage, whose buildings typically included sculptural and pictorial decoration while often evidencing a concern with abstract mathematical formulas. Not only is Berlage's architecture generally viewed as a necessary precedent for the work of Oud, Wils and van 't Hoff, but his own debts to and publications by 1912 of the work of Frank Lloyd Wright help explain the latter's widespread influence on early De Stijl architecture. Van der Leck worked for several years with Berlage (circa 1912-19) under the patronage of Mrs. Kröller-Müller, having met him as early as 1905 in connection with his own work as a glass painter. Less known is the fact that Berlage was an editor of the monthly periodical, *De Beweging*, where van Doesburg published from May to September 1916 his "The New Movement in Painting."[13] In this series of articles, van Doesburg made a plea for putting the various art forms, including poetry and music, on an equal footing, with none being an "applied art" to another.

While it remains unsettled to what extent Mondrian's principles of design derived from architecture, a penchant for painting architectural motifs was manifested from early in his career.[14] The prevalence of church and Parisian building themes in the late and post-cubist years testifies to the sympathy he had for the concept of painting as a form of mural decoration (fig. 28). Doubtless as opposed as van Doesburg or van der Leck to any subservience of painting to architecture, Mondrian had progressively abandoned traditional perspective and modeling in favor of a two-dimensional form of painting. This development likely derived in part from an interest in the interrelationship between painting and architecture and certainly helps explain the early rapport he felt with van der Leck. The single most important event leading to the foundation of the De Stijl movement was undoubtedly van der Leck's move to Laren in April 1916. Previous to this, in a letter of 20 November 1915, Mondrian had explicitly rejected van Doesburg's proposal for an

8. Piet Mondrian
Tree, circa 1912
oil on canvas
37 x 26½
94 x 67.3
Collection Museum of Art, Carnegie Institute
Patrons Art Fund

9. Bart van der Leck
The Storm, 1916
oil on canvas
46½ x 62½
118.1 x 158.8
Collection Rijksmuseum Kröller-Müller

12. A complete bibliography of writings by van Doesburg is found in Sergio Polano, *Theo van Doesburg, Scritti do arte e di architettura*, (Officina Edizione, 1979).
13. i.e., "The New Movement in Painting," which appeared as an illustrated booklet only in Oct. 1917 (Delft: J. Waltman).
14. Churches, house facades and windmills figure prominently among Mondrian's subjects during most phases of his pre-cubist career and are treated in monumental isolation during the years 1909-11.

10. Theo van Doesburg
Still Life, 1916
oil on canvas
13½ x 15½
34.3 x 39.4
Winston-Malbin Collection
(Dr. and Mrs. Barnett Malbin)

11. Piet Mondrian
Pier and Ocean, 1914
charcoal, white watercolor on buff paper
34⅝ x 44
87.9 x 111.7
Collection The Museum of Modern Art,
New York
Mrs. Simon Guggenheim Fund

association of artists with its own periodical, on the grounds that his manner of working was unique to himself and that there did not as yet exist enough written or visual material to justify a periodical.

Whereas van Doesburg's painting style in 1916 largely involved an attempt to achieve a form of Cubism based on geometry with the still life and landscape subject references remaining readable, Mondrian and van der Leck through mutual influence produced such works as Mondrian's *Composition 1916* (fig. 7), *Composition with Line (Pier and Ocean)*, 1917 (fig. 24), and *Composition[s] in Color A* and *B*, both of 1917, (figs. 30, 31), and van der Leck's 1916 *Mine Triptych* (fig. 38).[15] In these canvases, the subject reference is scarcely discernible and the proximity of abstract geometric style so close that they deserve to be recognized as the breakthrough paintings of what became the De Stijl movement. Indeed, when first seen by van Doesburg and Huszar in The Hague, there followed an unrestricted outpouring of praise from van Doesburg to van der Leck, and almost immediately thereafter both of the painters in south Holland were working in the manner of those based in Laren.[16]

Following several spring 1917 visits by van Doesburg to Laren, both Mondrian and van der Leck accepted van Doesburg's invitation to contribute to the "modest periodical" he planned to publish under the title *De Stijl*.[17] As would be announced on the cover of the first and subsequent issues, the journal was to be issued monthly and to contain articles from both Dutch and foreign contributors. Along with suggesting the Dutch Theosophist-Christophist Dr. M.H.J. Schoenmaekers as a writer, Mondrian recommended reproducing illustrations of work by Picasso, Braque and Léger, since none of these would wish to submit an article. Ultimately, apart from Vantongerloo's contributions, Severini's "Avant-garde Painting" was the only foreign article to appear in the first year of *De Stijl*.

Mondrian was decidedly less enthusiastic about Futurism than was van Doesburg. Van Doesburg, in fact, had first wished to call the periodical "The Straight Line" perhaps following a source in Futurism. However, indebted to Berlage and others, the idea of "style" as an absolute concept does occur in the theoretical articles written by Doesburg in 1915-16.[18] Moreover, when prefaced by the definite article "De" this word takes on an assertive quality that suggests it is at least the best, and quite possibly the only, style appropriate to modern art and culture.

The implications of the chosen name are thus many and varied, but above all it refers to the claim that this group of artists had evolved a collective, which is to say anti-individualistic form of art. This was to be based upon what van Doesburg in his introduction to the first issue of *De Stijl* calls

15. See Oxenaar, "Birth of De Stijl," pp 42-43. Mondrian's acknowledgment of his own indebtedness occurs in the van Doesburg commemorative issue of *De Stijl* (dernier numéro, 1932, p 48).
16. Oxenaar, p 72.
17. The title "De Stijl" and description as "modest" appear, apparently for the first time, in a van Doesburg letter of early May to van der Leck.
18. Baljeu, *Theo van Doesburg*, pp 24-25.

"the new consciousness of beauty" and explains as ". . . the pure relationship between the spirit of the times and [an appropriate] means of expression." In terms of art historical consciousness these and other statements reflect the common Hegelian view of historical development which permeates the various articles by the Dutch contributors to *De Stijl*.[19] Sources and nuance of outlook vary with individual writers, but from the beginning, the pages of *De Stijl* reflect a preoccupation with the question of the relationship between painting and architecture. In the very first issue a considerable difference of opinion is apparent. Van der Leck calls for a strict distinction between architecture and painting, while Oud cites Berlage as his point of departure for a new form of monumental architecture in keeping with the character of city streets and modern building materials.[20] Yet differences may be exaggerated, and Oud's insistence upon flat roofs and no picturesque ornamentation nonetheless accepts in principle van der Leck's separate roles for the two art forms. Thus one could hardly imagine a more appropriate environment than Oud's Strandboulevard housing (fig. 12) in which to show the first van der Leck painting illustrated in *De Stijl*, namely, *Composition 5, 1917 (Donkey Riders)* (fig. 13). Clearly it was thanks to van Doesburg that this first *De Stijl* issue aimed at establishing the journal as relevant to both architecture and painting. It also included an article by Huszar on "Modern Painting and the Interior" and coincided with the period of cooperation by van Doesburg on projects undertaken with Oud and Wils. It was nonetheless the long series of articles by Mondrian, "The New Image in Painting," that dominated the first year of *De Stijl*, and in the French resumé of 1920 and the German version of 1925 this statement of principles made Mondrian's De Stijl-period art theory available across the European continent.[21] Despite the fact that Mondrian's writings were philosophically elaborate and somewhat obscure, they carried great authority within the Stijl group, since he clearly was senior to all in terms of international contacts and recognition. Yet when the first manifesto appeared in the initial issue of volume II, its nine-point program barely mentions the actual stylistic principles upon which the movement was based, referring merely to its harmony with a "new consciousness of the times" and "universality" in opposition to the individualism of past culture. Perhaps a strictly uniform program was impossible to formulate, given the occasional use of green by van Doesburg and Huszar and of diagonals by van der Leck, who did not sign it. Moreover, the manifesto obviously was principally intended as a means of attracting non-Dutch members and contributors, being issued in four languages upon the cessation of hostilities in November 1918. Clearly, foreign artists would have had scant previous opportunity to learn about the wartime emergence of the Stijl movement let alone experiment in their own work along lines similar to those illustrated in the Dutch-language periodical. It is also significant that the

19. Mondrian, for example, refers to Hegel several times in his initial series of articles for *De Stijl*, "The New Image in Painting," and van Doesburg's essay, "Klassiek, Barok, Modern," published in 1920, clearly incorporates the Hegelian thesis-antithesis-synthesis chain of historical causation.
20. For van der Leck as in note 5; the Oud article is "The Monumental Townscape," *De Stijl*, I, 1, pp 10-11.
21. i.e., "Neoplasticism in Painting," *De Stijl*, I, 1-12 (Oct. 1917-Oct. 1918) plus II, 2 (Dec. 1918); see also note 9.

ecumenical call for "critical, philosophical, architectural, scientific, literary, musical" articles along with "reproductions" conspicuously omits politics as a topic to be included. This might be thought merely tactful considering the moment in history, except that in an article of May 1918 by Oud concerning the social function of architecture, he specifically rejects the proposal by a socialist faction at a housing congress that favored building working class houses along traditional and therefore presumably economical patterns.[22] Instead, Oud saw the inventive use of mass production (doors, windows, bricks and so forth made in a very limited number of standard types) combined with a style of varied scale relationships and rhythmic dispersal of design components as producing a new form of urban architecture suitable to the contemporary industrial age. To this degree he was adopting the "form follows function" aesthetic. His further observation that, unlike painting, architecture has to be a compromise between practical necessity and free creativity, indicates an early unwillingness to accept unqualifiedly the goal of an "art of pure relationships" as appropriate to architecture. This middle of the road approach to town housing may explain why Oud never produced quite so pure or extreme an example of De Stijl architecture as the Schröder house by Gerrit Rietveld. But Oud's view did represent a radical break with the still dominant arts and crafts orientation of the Dutch Art Nouveau movement in architecture.

The distinction between a two-dimensional art of painting and the three-dimensional nature of architecture as stated so frequently by the artists of De Stijl did not prevent the realization of a variety of projects, some as models, others as realized structures, in which the two arts were intimately combined. Although the fullest attempts to integrate architecture and painting were to occur in the 1920s, already in "De Vonk," the Oud-designed and van Doesburg-"painted" vacation house at Noordwijkerhout of 1917-18, there is a partial breakdown in the distinction between the two arts thanks to the elimination of or de-emphasis on architectural moldings and, most striking, the painter's asymmetrical design of colored floor tiles (fig. 148). Inadvertently or not, these designs are related to the numerous grid paintings by van Doesburg, Mondrian, Huszar and Vantongerloo. All produced circa 1918-19, these canvases are analogous to a modular conception more commonly associated with architecture or interior design. Moreover, the partial "dematerialization" of the walls produced by the use of so much white paint in later De Stijl architecture was anticipated by van der Leck's project for the decoration of the "art room" of the Kröller-Müller residence in Wassenaar.

Whatever the conceptual interaction between painting and architecture within De Stijl, when one reviews the production of sculpture and other

22. In "Standardization in Architecture Through Mass Production," *De Stijl,* I, 7 (May 1918), pp 77-79.

12. J.J.P. Oud
Strandboulevard apartments
as illustrated in *De Stijl*, I, 1, 1917

13. Bart van der Leck
Composition No. 5 1917 (Donkey Riders)
oil on canvas
23¼ x 57⅞
59.1 x 147
Private collection
as illustrated in *De Stijl*, I, 1, 1917

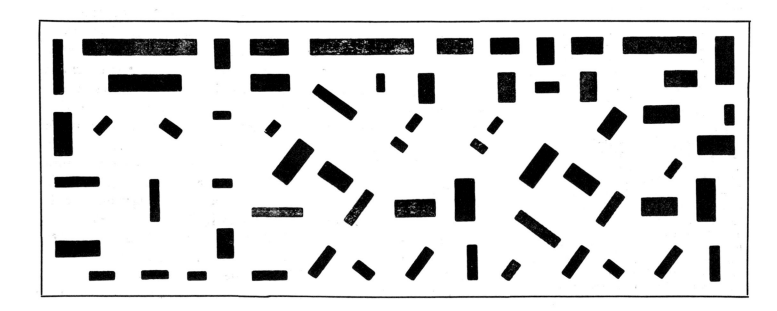

23. The term "trappaal," (stepped column) is apparently a eulogism in Dutch intentionally rendering ambiguous its architectural function, if any. In his accompanying comment to the illustrations (*De Stijl*, I, 6, pp 71-72), van Doesburg further insists that the work embodies an identification between the nature of architecture and sculpture. This hermetic approach to function is also present in van Doesburg's own 1918 design for a concrete *Monument for the City of Leeuwarden* (illus. in Baljeu, *Theo van Doesburg*, p 110).

24. Ankie de Jongh, "De Stijl," *Museumjournaal*, XVII, 6 (1972), p 275, has demonstrated how one of the rectilineated "interrelation of volumes" sculptures, circa 1919, derives ultimately from a figural study. This indeed would seem to be the case for his three-dimensional work until 1922-23 (e.g., nos. 2, 3, 5, 6, 8, 9, 13, 14 and 26 in the recent Vantongerloo exhibition. See note 2). Similarly, his sculpture of the late 1920s (illus., *ibid.*, p 59 ff.), appears to fuse architecture, furniture design and sculpture, indicating the survival of this De Stijl attitude in his post-De Stijl work.

25. This example is the exception to the illustration of Rietveld's early De Stijl furniture without color, since his own explanation (*De Stijl*, II, 9, 1919, p 102) to the triple illustration (Bijlage XVIII) describes a green-red complementary color opposition as basic to his conception. In reference to the illustrated, non-colored forerunner of the famous red/blue chair by Rietveld (*De Stijl*, II, 11, Bijlage XXII), van Doesburg again posits a breakdown in functional distinctions among the plastic arts, in this case identifying the chair simultaneously as a piece of sculpture.

"intermediary" arts, the attempt to reach common means of expression is even more apparent. The first illustrated example of what might best be called functional ambiguity was recorded in the April 1918 issue of *De Stijl* in a double illustration of what was termed an example of "space-plastic interior architecture" (a stepped column) designed by Robert van 't Hoff (fig. 15). Given the ambiguity of scale, heightened by the absence of any base or horizontal pediment, one is left at sea as to the intended function of this wooden model. It could as easily be a piece of sculpture as an architectural design for a skyscraper; if it had been colored in the De Stijl primaries, the confusion would have been even more complete.[23]

This same ambiguity was inherent in the sculpture of Vantongerloo. Until shortly after he returned (circa 1919) to Brussels, his small creations in plaster, wood or stone exhibit not only an abandonment of rounded for cubical form, but a tendency to take on the appearance of an architectural experiment in complexly equilibrated structural components (fig. 16). Although apparently all based upon the theme of a single figure either standing, squatting or kneeling, they uniformly embody an asymmetry in keeping with this firmly established tendency in De Stijl painting. In later examples of Vantongerloo's rectilinear sculpture, the interpenetration of volume and void and the extreme asymmetry of design assumes an even greater architectural character, testifying to the survival and extension of De Stijl principles in his work despite his defection from organized group activity early in the 1920s.[24]

Another special case of the amalgamation of visual disciplines is provided by the furniture designs of Rietveld. First illustrated in the years 1919-20, with the wood not yet painted, in these largely rectangular designs Rietveld appears to have been concerned with attaining a satisfying balance of abstract structural components more than with serving a primarily functional purpose. The child's chair, for example, while still recalling a stylized tendency in Art Nouveau furniture similar to that of Charles Rennie Mackintosh, at the same time suggests the structural grid of a skyscraper or another form of open architectural framework (fig. 14).[25] An analogy with Russian constructivist principles might also be made, although this movement would not yet have been known to Rietveld. The artist's sideboard appears equally architectural in character, with its cantilevered horizontal planes recalling the work of Frank Lloyd Wright or the middle section of the Wright-influenced 1919 model for a factory at Purmerend by J.J.P. Oud which was illustrated on an adjacent sheet in the same March 1920 issue of *De Stijl*. Only three months later, the magazine carried a photograph of the American steel and glass-clad factory interior, "Bethlehem Shipbuilding." Like the reproductions of futurist architectural examples

14. Gerrit Rietveld
Child's chair, 1919
as illustrated in *De Stijl,* II, 9, 1919

15. Robert van 't Hoff
Stepped Column, 1918
as illustrated in *De Stijl,* I, 6, 1918

16. Georges Vantongerloo
Construction in a Sphere, 1917
painted wood
3¼ x 2½ x 2
8.2 x 6.3 x 5.7
Collection Philadelphia Museum of Art
A.E. Gallatin Collection

in the period 1919-20, this photograph demonstrates that the "machine aesthetic" earlier propounded by Oud had been solidly grafted onto the main body of De Stijl theory and practice.

As for painting, the above mentioned occurrence of grid compositions in 1918-19 provides the equivalent approximation in this medium of the tendency towards repetition of standardized elements championed by Oud in architecture. Whether or not inspired to some degree by the experiments with floor tiles and related decorations on the facade of De Vonk or by related stained-glass window designs by van Doesburg and Huszar (fig. 17), as a collective tendency the grid paintings symbolized a profound breakthrough within the tradition of Western painting. Most essentially, they signified the final denial of the figure-ground dualism which had dominated European painting since the Renaissance. Certainly with Cubism and particularly in Mondrian's use of this style, the figure-ground relationship often barely survives. Within De Stijl it was further compromised by the 1916-17 experiments of Huszar and van Doesburg in which a background grid division undermines any normal sense of illusionist picture space for the figural content.[26]

It was nonetheless Mondrian who by early 1918 introduced to De Stijl painting proper the encasement of color planes within a uniform grid of modular rectangular units. In his 1919 *Lozenge with Bright Colors*, for example, the analogy with stained-glass windows and hence with an architectural function must have occurred to him (fig. 18). Unfortunately, he does not refer to this usage directly in his writings, but it is significant that in the January 1918 issue of *De Stijl* he credits no less an authority than Aristotle with "identifying abstraction with mathematics."[27] It is therefore all the more surprising to learn from a 1 August 1919 letter to van Doesburg that this same 1919 lozenge painting was recommended for illustration ". . . precisely because a configuration of stars was the original inspiration for me to make it." Doubtless referring to the "popping effect" optical illusions that rhythmically appear and disappear at the line interstices of the lozenge grid paintings, Mondrian hereby also demonstrates why he continued to describe his paintings as "abstract-realist" even after no concrete figural imagery could be evoked by the specifics of his compositions. Ironically, whereas Mondrian by 1921 had abandoned the regular grid format as a foil for his otherwise asymmetrically dispersed compositional elements, van Doesburg, albeit sometimes using intentionally covert formulas, retained a modular grid as the substructure of his paintings until the end. Perhaps not by chance, then, throughout the years 1919-24 the majority of paintings and certain related art forms illustrated in *De Stijl* were those employing a grid format, a fact that increases the likelihood that it was widely thought to be the basis of De Stijl composition.[28]

26. See Welsh, "Theo van Doesburg," pp 85-86.
27. *De Stijl*, I, 3, p 29, note 1.
28. One of these, van Doesburg's *Composition in Gray*, a painting circa 1918, was shown in 1922 in the artist's Weimar studio (fig. 3), where his use of a grid principle is likely to have been known to his "students."

In any case, these grid paintings clearly represent the final manifestation of what could be considered common stylistic practice within the Stijl movement. Quite possibly its introduction by Mondrian may be one reason why van der Leck subsequently refused to sign the first De Stijl manifesto and thereafter drifted away from group activities. Van der Leck's allegiance to the figural tradition in Western art ultimately proved too strong to allow for lasting conversion to a fully abstract mode, and his disaffection with De Stijl was all but inevitable.

Despite the abandonment of De Stijl by several of its early members, in particular van 't Hoff and van der Leck, the third annual volume of *De Stijl* betrays little evidence of discontinuity of purpose or activities. Mondrian's autobiographical "trialogue" series of articles, "Natural and Abstract Reality," began in the December 1919 issue and finished only the following August. Also in this latter issue, the first installment of the novel *The Other Face* appeared, which van Doesburg published pseudonymously as I.K. Bonset. This literary effort followed upon the second De Stijl manifesto that was devoted to literature and signaled van Doesburg's willingness to link the cause of De Stijl in literature—a style that combined abstract or anti-naturalistic elements—with a new found interest in the international Dada movement. This reflected his new friendship with Jean Arp and Tristan Tzara, with whom he would participate in the 1922 Weimar "Constructivist Congress," and to a surprising variety of Dada involvements.[29] These include a Dada "concert tour" of Holland with his wife, Nelly van Doesburg, and Kurt Schwitters, and personal experiments in both literature and the collage medium. While it is known that Mondrian remained skeptical of the contributions to *De Stijl* of Bonset, he was co-signer with van Doesburg and Kok of the second manifesto, and on occasion signed letters to van Doesburg as "Dada Piet." In general he saw in Dada a De Stijl ally in the fight to destroy the surviving forces of naturalism in art (the same reason for which he sometimes wrote approvingly of Futurism). It remains true that van Doesburg encouraged Dada in *De Stijl* in a somewhat clandestine manner, and it is doubtful that Mondrian would have seen this movement as "the other face" of De Stijl as for a time did van Doesburg.

With the post-war departures of Mondrian for Paris and Vantongerloo for Brussels, followed finally in 1921 by van Doesburg's travels to Germany and elsewhere, a stable basis ceased to exist in The Netherlands for continuing coordinated group activity—to the extent that this had existed outside the pages of *De Stijl*. Van Doesburg, doubtless acutely aware of the real possibility of complete dissolution of the movement, transported De Stijl in his own person to wherever he sensed an opportunity for proselytizing new members or associated causes.

29. Already in letters of 24 Feb. and 2 June 1920, van Doesburg mentions to Oud his contacts with Francis Picabia and Tristan Tzara (these and all other herein mentioned letters from van Doesburg or Mondrian to Oud are located at the Fondation Custodia, Institut Néerlandais, Paris). In an undated letter of late 1920, van Doesburg explained to Oud his appreciation of Dada and his use of the pseudonym "Bonset," a secret that he wrote should not be shared with Mondrian, who could not understand such "un-Dutch" things. Baljeu, *Theo van Doesburg*, pp 38-39, dates the contact with Tzara and conception of the name Bonset to circa 1918.

Therefore relationships among van Doesburg, Mondrian and Oud shift back and forth from good to bad to good again during the first two or three years of the 1920s. Despite an effort to work on each other's behalf, the presence of Oud in The Netherlands, Mondrian in Paris and van Doesburg in Germany for large segments of 1921-22, engendered difficulties and ensured that planned joint exhibitions would either fail to materialize or have only limited success. The greatest failure of all would come only in 1925 when De Stijl was not included in the Dutch contribution to the Exposition des Arts Décoratifs in Paris. Van Doesburg understandably was scandalized by this omission, but once again he was overestimating both the public support for and the group solidarity of the De Stijl movement.[30]

A further problem besetting the utopian collective dream of De Stijl to transform radically the physical environment and aesthetic sensibility of contemporary culture was the frequent lack of specialized training or technical know-how required for the realization of pet projects. One instance of this is the intensely felt wish of Mondrian to see the realization of Neoplasticism in the realm of music. Although this preoccupation has not been accorded serious study until quite recently, it was already manifest in the war years he spent in The Netherlands. In Laren, Mondrian was a regular habitué of the local dance hall and apparently was called "the dancing madonna" by fellow artists because of his spiritualized upward gaze and stylized steps. He found in both the classical "Style Etudes" of his friend Jacob van Domsalaer and in the more popular modern dance steps, an antipode to the "round lines" of the traditional waltz and an expression of the "straight lines" appropriate to the new age.[31] By June 1920 in his series "trialogue," Mondrian not only stated his preference for the "jasband" over traditional concert music, but also called for the replacement of old musical instruments, such as the violin, by machines directly controlled by the composer. These ideas were repeated in "Le Neo-plasticisme" and reached their conclusion in his 1921 article called "Italian Futurist Noisemakers and 'the' New in Music."[32] After describing the noise machines of Luigi Russolo as a limited advance, because that artist had preserved the old diatonic and chromatic scales and in his "concrete music" the sounds of nature, Mondrian called for a synthesis of jazz and new classical style in order to produce a genuinely neoplastic music. Not surprisingly this was to be based upon three tones and three non-tones in analogy with the three primary colors and the non-colors black, gray and white with all "rests" to be eliminated and the sounds to be produced by as yet undeveloped mechanical or electrical instruments. If feasible enough in today's world of the Moog synthesizer, Mondrian did not live to see his suggestions realized by a contemporary composer. Similarly his "new music hall" with its meandering audience intermittently

30. Van Doesburg's reaction to this slight by a committee of his countrymen was to publish a "Protest" in De Stijl, VI, 10/11 (1925), pp 149-150, signed by a list of 29 largely foreign artists and other art dignitaries.

31. In June 1963, the artist Kees Heynsius, then secretary of the Dutch art society, Arti et Amicitiae, recalled how Mondrian had stood out at the dance hall in Laren during World War I, not only because of his unique dancing style, but also because he wore formal dress. The late Albert van den Briel, a lifelong close friend of Mondrian, recalled how Mondrian associated the round lines of the waltz with Mozart. The artist's great respect for Bach doubtless derived in part from his association with the composer van Domselaer, who was also a Bach specialist.

32. Mondrian's extended article on "Italian Futurist Noisemakers and 'the' New in Music," appeared in De Stijl, IV, 8 and 9 (Aug., Sept. 1921) and V, 1 and 2 (Jan., Feb. 1922).

17. Theo van Doesburg
Stained-glass window, 1921
10½ x 63⅝
26.5 x 161.6
Collection Wellesley College Museum
Gift of Judith Rothschild, class of 1943,
in memory of her parents,
Herbert and Nannette Rothschild

Made for a secondary school in the small Friesian
town of Drachten, in northern Holland, this
stained-glass panel is one of several that were
installed in C.R. de Boer's traditional brick
building. The stained-glass windows are part of a
group developed by van Doesburg for the town
of Drachten. (See Troy, p 182.)

18. Piet Mondrian
Lozenge with Bright Colors, 1919
oil on canvas
30¼ x 30¼
76.8 x 76.8
Collection Rijksmuseum Kröller-Müller

33. Ironically, the Aubette redecoration by van
Doesburg and the Arps provided a setting akin to
that advocated by Mondrian.
34. Mondrian's "Realization of Neoplasticism in
the Distant Future and in Architecture Today,"
De Stijl, V, 3 and 5 (March, May 1922) may have
provoked criticism by Oud. That led eventually
to Mondrian's breaking off correspondence
between late 1922 and 2 Sept. 1923.

enjoying repeat performances of the music (here the analogy was with cinema) and its neoplastic paintings decorating the walls or approximated by projected color planes remained a forgotten project.[33]

A corresponding difficulty beset attempts to ensure a continuing cooperation between De Stijl painters and architects. Despite the already mentioned defections from De Stijl ranks, the years circa 1920-22 saw a renewed effort to resolve this problem, particularly through discussions among Oud, van Doesburg and Mondrian, who in that period clearly were the core members of the group. As early as 1920, the three were hoping to establish a relationship with Léonce Rosenberg that would allow for the regular display of architectural plans and models. In his first letter to Oud dated 23 January 1920, Mondrian assured the architect that there is ". . . the possibility of progress in architecture," suggesting that this is best served by foregoing the use of bricks. As late as spring 1922 Mondrian could credit Oud for having helped inspire his own article on Neoplasticism in architecture. Yet his insistence that the aesthetic and design principles first evolved in painting serve as the necessary guide to architecture led by summer to a conflict in points of view and termination of correspondence for a year.[34]

The record of cooperation in these years between Oud and van Doesburg takes an equally up and down course. As with Mondrian, during 1920 and early 1921, the correspondence is friendly and optimistic over the possibilty of support from Rosenberg, and by late in 1921 van Doesburg had begun to send from Weimar color designs for the Spangen architectural project by Oud. However, Oud requested changes in these, and by the end of the year van Doesburg accuses Oud of "cowardess" in the use of color and says it would have been "more honorable" if he had broken with De Stijl a year earlier. In this case, too, the correspondence was broken off for a considerable time, namely, until cooperation was again established in the collective effort to assemble an exhibition of De Stijl architecture in the fall of 1923 at Rosenberg's Galerie L'Effort Moderne. In the meantime, while at Weimar, van Doesburg had met the young Dutch architect Cornelis van Eesteren, an association that would produce the joint architectural plans and models that would finally bring De Stijl architecture the international attention that van Doesburg sought. Indeed, although subject to study from many points of view, in terms of the development of the De Stijl aesthetic, the resulting van Doesburg/van Eesteren drawings and models are the quintessential result of the varied activities and intellectual encounters undergone by van Doesburg between late 1920 and late 1923.

Previous to his 1923 Paris adventure, van Doesburg had found two German connections through the architects Bruno Taut and Walter

34

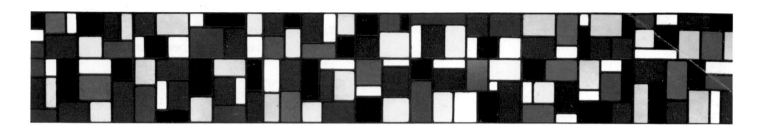

Gropius and the Dada artist Hans Richter, whose abstract film strips, made with Viking Eggeling, he published later in *De Stijl* (fig. 72).[35]

From Weimar on 21 June 1921 he wrote to Oud ". . . here tremendous things are happening." Apart from the unofficial "Style courses" that van Doesburg held near the Bauhaus, his life was passed in lecturing, the Dada tour with Schwitters, and contacts with Russian Constructivism via El Lissitzky and László Moholy-Nagy in Berlin. His openness to these contacts led to the publishing in September 1922 of both a suprematist and a Lissitzky issue of *De Stijl,* with 50 sets of loose prints by Lissitzky available as well.[36] Moholy-Nagy and his Hungarian MA group were also represented in text and picture in the Dutch journal (this being reciprocated by a special van Doesburg issue of *MA*).[37] Considering the formidable number of international contacts cemented by van Doesburg during 1922, it is not surprising that a five-year anthology of De Stijl activities was issued at year's end or that by this time the magazine cover boldly listed "Weimar, The Hague, Antwerp, Paris, Rome" as its centers of operation.

In 1922-23, van Doesburg's focus of personal creativity—apart from his literary efforts—was architecture. Following the Weimar models, executed with two students at his courses there, he began a collaboration with van Eesteren, which was to include the color orchestration for the latter's Amsterdam university hall design and to culminate in the 1923 Paris models for Léonce Rosenberg.

Although it is inappropriate here to discuss these projects in depth, two points can be made in respect to their general place in the evolution of De Stijl. First, the Weimar models and the university hall decor and, in feeling if not in fact, the second and third Rosenberg projects (a private house and a studio house) bear the imprint of the modular subdivisions of his grid paintings. It is quite possible that this aspect of van Doesburg's architectural theory (for example, in relation to Le Corbusier) should be considered one of his most important contributions. Second, as observed by Joost Baljeu, van Doesburg's approach to all these models bears a direct relationship to his influences from and reinterpretation of such movements as Cubism (the Weimar models), Russian Suprematism and Constructivism (especially the axonometric drawings for the private and studio houses), upon which a reciprocal effect may also have been exerted (fig. 54).[38] In any case, the latter two projects represented the boldest attempt to date within De Stijl to integrate fully the arts of architecture, painting and, remembering that when reproduced in September 1922 the Weimar models had been labeled ". . . studies of purely architectonic sculpture," this latter art form as well.[39] Finally, although it is the van Doesburg/van Eesteren models as exhibited

35. Having met Richter in Dec. 1920 in Kölzig near Berlin, van Doesburg first wrote about him and Viking Eggeling in "Abstract Film Image," *De Stijl*, IV, 5 (June 1921). Richter's German language "Principles of the Art of Motion," appeared in *De Stijl*, IV, 7 (July 1921), pp 109-112.
36. i.e., *De Stijl*, V, 9 and 10/11 are both imprinted Sept. 1922.
37. i.e., L. Moholy-Nagy, "Production-Reproduction," *De Stijl*, V, 7 (July 1922), pp 97-101. The first advertisement of the van Doesburg issue of *MA* had appeared the previous month in *De Stijl*.
38. See Baljeu, *Theo van Doesburg*, pp 52-53, 58-62.
39. i.e., in Theo van Doesburg, "From the Aesthetic to the Material," *Bouwkundig Weekblad*, XLIII, 38 (1922), pp 272-275.

15 October-15 November 1923 at Galerie L'Effort Moderne that have received the bulk of critical attention over the years, the invitation card to that representation of "Les Architects du Groupe De Stijl, Holland" lists as participants: van Doesburg, van Eesteren, Huszar, van Leusden, Oud, Rietveld, Wils and van der Rohe (who, of course, was German). Although including photographs of earlier designs and comprising a somewhat forced show of unity, the representation indicates a surprisingly broad coterie of architects apparently willing to be listed under the De Stijl rubric.[40] Many of the artists listed produced, both before and after this event, works of architecture or interior design as deserving of study as the van Doesburg/van Eesteren maquettes, the first of which was made on order by Rietveld. Yet in their purity of conception and despite the then probably insurmountable technical barriers to their execution, these Rosenberg private and studio house designs remain emblematic of the highest degree of consolidation the De Stijl movement ever achieved.

This is not to downplay the hallmark achievements of the realized architecture of Oud and Rietveld, following upon the De Stijl exhibition at the Rosenberg gallery. Ironically, Oud, who sometimes is thought to have viewed Rietveld as a furniture maker who was ill-advised in turning to architecture without sufficient training, nevertheless produced in his justly famous Café De Unie facade design of 1925, a work which, in this writer's opinion, is susceptible to the long-standing charge that De Stijl architecture is untrue to its medium (fig. 19). Family tradition rightly maintains that Oud consulted his small but significant personal collection of Mondrian paintings only—like a devotee of contemplation—in order to find a sense of intuited balance that would produce similarly harmonious results in his own designs. Yet, Mondrian's justly honored *Tableau I* of 1921 (fig. 20), is so close to the café in its general composition and projected color disposition that a more organic functional relationship might be presumed.[41] Whatever the break Oud intended with the "stepped pediment" tradition of Dutch building facades by his radically innovative, rectangulated composition for the Unie, it is the one executed example of De Stijl architecture which most clearly supports Mondrian's long-held belief that the aesthetic principles underlying all neoplastic art forms followed upon discoveries within Dutch painting.

While again it is not the purpose of the present essay to single out any particular development or monument as indispensible for the realization of De Stijl ideals, the Rietveld/Schröder house in Utrecht, designed in 1924 and executed the following year, stands as the archetypal example of mature De Stijl architecture from the first half of the 1920s. Not only does it follow upon and best exemplify the design principles which

40. A manuscript list of the exhibited items appears in Nancy J. Troy, "The Colored Abstract Environment: De Stijl's Collaborative Ideal" (Yale University, PhD diss., 1979), pp 343-349.
41. This painting, now at the Museum Ludwig, Cologne, could have been known to Oud either as one of two paintings listed as *Composition 1921* at the Mondrian 50-year anniversary exhibition (Holland Art Circle, Amsterdam) of 1922, or *Tableau I*, shown at the annual exhibition of the society the same year.

19. J.J.P. Oud
Café De Unie, 1925
gouache on paper
28¾ x 33
73 x 84
Private Collection

reduced
by ½

20. Piet Mondrian
Tableau I, 1921
oil on canvas
29⁹⁄₁₆ x 25⅝
75.2 x 65
Collection Museum Ludwig, Cologne
(not in exhibition)

Rietveld's participation in the Rosenberg maquettes may have required, but it defies the oft-heard accusation that De Stijl architecture is too much indebted to painting. In fact, not only does this building remain structurally intact but it deserves recognition for the lucid articulation of its three-dimensional design components. And whatever its influence on the emergence of the International Style in architecture, the affinity of asymmetrical design principles in this building to Oud's Café De Unie indicate that De Stijl architects were closer in outlook at the mid-1920s than is often supposed.

Nonetheless, disruption within the ranks of De Stijl in 1925 is a well-recorded fact, and the reasons and circumstances which caused this crisis deserve some explication. One standard view of De Stijl is that it broke up as a movement due to the introduction by van Doesburg of the principle of the diagonal, in direct opposition to Mondrian's insistence upon orthogonal (right angle) relationships. Apart from the fact that Mondrian had experimented with both orthogonal and diagonal lines in his pre- and early De Stijl production, until 1926 nowhere in the pages of *De Stijl*, least of all in van Doesburg's contributions thereto, is any systematic evaluation of this issue of the diagonal versus the right angle relationship to be found.[42] During the period 1925-26 several countercompositions by van Doesburg were illustrated that might as easily have been reproduced in an orthogonal as in a diagonal position.[43] The issue of diagonality is important enough that it should be examined here with some consideration for the implications that are entailed for the very survival of the De Stijl movement.

In terms of immediate precedents, the 1923 axonometric drawings for the Galerie L'Effort Moderne houses and the ceiling design of the university hall incorporate the principle of diagonality indirectly. Yet only in 1926 did van Doesburg reproduce a painting, *Countercomposition XV*, attributed to 1925, in which this feature is inherent.[44] Moreover, although this painting and *Countercomposition V* (fig. 21), published in 1927 but attributed to 1924, are rectangular works with internal diagonals, only in 1926 did he in "Painting: From Composition to Countercomposition" explain in writing how the diagonal represented a dynamic principle of modern life.[45] He stated that in art, the diagonal principle represented final victory over static nature as presented by the horizontal-vertical polarity. Shortly thereafter he elaborated this discussion in reference to the term "Elementarism," which among other virtues was said to involve an exploitation of the fourth dimension—the element of time.[46] However Mondrian, by 1917, felt that his painting, in its asymmetrical and rhythmic constructions, possessed a "dynamic" quality that implied the idea of time.[47] Van Doesburg's heresy thus involved not merely abandonment of the

42. In an undated letter of early 1919, Mondrian explained his introduction of the "lozenge" (or diamond) format: it enhances the sense of the vertical-horizontal polarity and de-emphasizes the sense of diagonality residing in the rectangular format.
43. e.g., *Countercomposition I* (*De Stijl*, VI, 10/11, 1925, p 156) and *Composition in White, Black and Gray* (*De Stijl*, VII, 73/74, 1926, pp 21-22).
44. This painting was illustrated in *De Stijl*, VII, 73/74 (1926), p 1. In *De Stijl*, VI, 6/7 both the university hall and Rosenberg private house are illustrated to stress the diagonal principle, and the latter is called a "counterconstruction."
45. *Countercomposition V* was illustrated in *De Stijl*, VII, 79/84, pp 19-20. The article "Painting: From Composition to Countercomposition," was published in *De Stijl*, VII, 73/74 (1926), pp 17-28.
46. i.e., in "About Countercomposition and Countersculpture: Elementarism (Manifesto Fragment)," *De Stijl*, VII, 75/76 (1926-27), pp 35-43.
47. In a letter of 12 Dec. 1917, Mondrian expressed sympathy for van Doesburg's interest in the fourth dimension.

orthogonal principle, but a transfer to the diagonal of qualities (spirit and time) that Mondrian believed were inherent in his own paintings, in the vertical movement and in the dynamism of his total compositional configurations.

Although Mondrian's official notification that he could no longer cooperate with van Doesburg came only later, on 10 March 1925 he had written Oud that he saw van Doesburg only now and then by chance in the streets or cafés of Paris, and on 22 April he reported that in a meeting requested by van Doesburg he stated his own wish that they no longer meet. This did not mean the immediate end of the Stijl group, since van Doesburg by the mid-1920s had added such new supporters as the Dutchman César Domela, the Germans Peter Roehl, Friedrich Vordemberge-Gildewart, Max Burchartz and Werner Graeff and the Austrian Frederick Kiesler among geometric abstractionists. More surprisingly, in the tenth anniversary number of *De Stijl*, he cited Jean Arp, Hugo Ball and Constantin Brancusi as further associated participants. Yet in 1928, only one other issue plus the large one devoted to the Strasbourg Aubette interior renovations were to appear, and these would be the last in van Doesburg's lifetime. Not that he wanted it this way. In the meantime the Dutch periodical *i 10* had begun publication under the editorship of Arthur Müller-Lehning and both Mondrian and Oud were contributors. By then Oud was so put out with what he considered to be the self-aggrandizement in van Doesburg's tenth year commemorative issue of *De Stijl* that on 21 January 1928 he wrote to chide the editor in failing only to take credit for the first trans-Atlantic flight and the ending of the war. This abrasion notwithstanding, on 11 November of the following year van Doesburg proposed to Oud the idea of combining *De Stijl* and *i 10* under a joint editorship with Müller-Lehning, whom he suggested was open to the idea. Van Doesburg may also have reestablished more friendly personal relationships with Mondrian by about this time, and before his death on 7 March 1931, he published one issue of *Art Concret* and had helped lay the foundation stones of the broadly based Abstraction-Creation group, which shortly after his death came into being.[48] The final issue of *De Stijl* appeared in January 1932; it was a commemorative issue devoted to van Doesburg and edited by his widow. Whether or not this issue can be considered truly to have extended the life of De Stijl beyond 1928, it did contain a selection of the latest writing and works of art by van Doesburg and a genuinely felt series of tributes from his former colleagues.

Probably the proper end-date for the life of the De Stijl movement will remain a subject for debate, and we have seen that evidence exists in support for assigning it as wide apart as 1920 and 1932. In the context of the late 1920s, the choice varies largely according to whether one

48. Baljeu, *Theo van Doesburg*, pp 101-103.

accepts van Doesburg's elementarist countercompositions as a legitimate continuation and expansion of De Stijl principles. This affects in particular any interpretation of the Aubette wall decorations by van Doesburg which, it should be noted, contain both orthogonal (the large reception room plus the decorations of Sophie Taeuber-Arp) and diagonal (the cinema-dance hall) designs (fig. 182). In any case, the color partitions of the long dance hall wall, uninterrupted by windows, seem divided according to the same modular grid system that underlies *Countercomposition XVI* of 1925, albeit in both instances, as often in other van Doesburg paintings executed throughout the 1920s, this mathematical system is intentionally camouflaged (or slightly compromised) by a shift of some of the line components from strict conformance to the grid.[49] Doubtless as much as Mondrian, van Doesburg wished to avoid slavish adherence to any sterile application of an ideal formula such as "the golden mean," and throughout the writings of both artists the word "intuition" is employed to indicate the role of creative imagination in producing works of art which each knew might be construed by others as following a formula.

In asking the question about van Doesburg's loyalty to De Stijl principles, one must also ask the same question about other participating members. Unless one is willing to accept Mondrian's 1920 assertion that no real De Stijl group any longer existed, a case could be made—as he possibly felt himself—that he remained the only true practitioner of De Stijl or of Neoplasticism, to use his own preferred term. This last point provides a convenient distinction, allowing for the inclusion in De Stijl of artists who practiced either an orthogonally or diagonally oriented variation of rectilinear abstract-geometric composition, but not necessarily all the various dadaists and other artists published in *De Stijl* who fail to qualify under either category. Certainly such artists as El Lissitzky, Moholy-Nagy and even Vordemberge-Gildewart represent the problematic borderline cases—in terms of both stylistic and organizational relationships. For the present writer, despite flirtations with Russian and related forms of Constructivism and with Suprematism, the Dutch-born De Stijl movement was different in two essential ways. First, it clung with great tenacity to a reliance upon the right angle relationship as a basic principle of composition (in both orthogonal and diagonal variations) and, with minor exceptions, upon the three primary colors and the white-gray-black triumvirate. In contrast, the Russian suprematist and constructivist traditions typically employed more varied and open types of composition, seeking a special kind of dynamism in variously scaled and positioned geometric shapes floating within a seemingly unbounded spatial continuum. In this sense, while an oversimplification, one can see De Stijl as the logical abstract form of Cubism, as Mondrian always

49. Welsh, "Theo van Doesburg," pp 90-94.

41

21. Theo van Doesburg
Countercomposition V, 1924
oil on canvas
39⅜ x 39⅜
100 x 100
Collection Stedelijk Museum, Amsterdam

50. The Düsseldorf Congress issue was *De Stijl*, V, 4 (April 1922) and includes both a reprint of the first De Stijl manifesto and a statement of opposition to the program of the Congress, signed by van Doesburg, Lissitzky and Richter. The third De Stijl manifesto appeared in *De Stijl*, IV, 8 (Aug. 1921), pp 123-126, in three languages and "Against Problem Art" in *De Stijl*, VI, 1 (April 1923), pp 17-19.

Robert P. Welsh is Chairman of the Department of Fine Art, University of Toronto, Ontario, Canada.

claimed, and the suprematist-constructivist tradition as more dependent upon futurist art and theory, with its overt sense of visual dynamics.

Second, apart from Oud's adoption of the machine ethic, De Stijl manifested only passing or tangential interest in the functional or political programs which so often accompanied the abstract art movements in Russia and Germany. If van Doesburg in April 1922 published an issue of *De Stijl* devoted to The Congress of Progressive Artists at Düsseldorf, he made clear in both the third De Stijl manifesto of 1921 and in "Anti-Engaged Art" of 1923 that the De Stijl revolution in art provides a better basis for change than international socialism, which he saw as merely another form of bourgeois materialism.[50] To the extent that he and other De Stijl artists accepted the machine aesthetic this was to serve the beautification rather than the material welfare of modern society, and the numerous photographs of modern industrial buildings and machines that appear in *De Stijl* are intended more as analogies in the world of modern technology to the aesthetic principles of De Stijl than as the propagation of a functional purpose for art.

One may finally note that withdrawal from direct participation in De Stijl activities did not always mean full rejection of its principles. Vantongerloo, for example, practiced a form of rectangular geometric abstraction throughout the 1920s, and even van der Leck retained the use of geometric planes of primary colors against a white ground, despite his reintroduction of readable figural content. Nor should the occasional employment by Oud of curved surfaces or his failure to adopt as his model the Schröder house by Rietveld blind us to the general allegiance to a De Stijl clarity of design that characterizes his buildings throughout the 1920s and beyond, a statement that holds true for van Eesteren as well. Thus, while definitions and analyses of the movement are bound to vary, De Stijl will surely be remembered for the combination of single-minded purpose and diverse realization that it embodied.

De Stijl
and the Russian Revolution

Ger Harmsen

The horrors of World War I and the expectations within certain circles excited by concurrent revolutionary disturbances made a deep impact on the intellectual and artistic life of Europe. This was particularly true in the case of the Stijl group, as it aimed to be not only an art movement, but to organize all cultural life and society in a totally new way. Many oral and written communications demonstrate the conviction held by these painters, architects and writers—that bourgeois-capitalist society was near its end.

On 7 May 1919, the architect Jan Wils wrote to painter Chris Beekman: "I am firmly convinced that communism is also bound to enter our country very soon. I should immediately add that I am a communist through and through. . . fervently and eternally. . . . We should contact communist leaders within this country and abroad without delay."[1] Within the Dutch Communist Party, opinions were divided as to which direction the arts should take. The prevalent one was that bourgeois individualism was a thing of the past and would only be able to produce decadent, doomed art. This opinion was consistent with the aspiration of the Stijl group to express the general by eliminating the particular. The group endeavored to place the community above the restricted ego, which aims to achieve individual recognition. This becomes evident when we read Theo van Doesburg's remark in a 9 September 1919 letter to Beekman: "Although we differ individually, we all live for the same cause. We should concentrate solely on that. Then attention is automatically diverted from our own personality. I completely agree with you, my friend. Personal fame or individual attention is not within the scope of our endeavors. That was good fare for the individualistic baroque culture. For us, truth is the hub of our collective attention."

With this idea of a common art production the members of De Stijl had in mind the interlinking of the visual arts and their subsequent connection to all of society. An art critic member of the Dutch Communist Party, Dr. J. Knuttel, was of the same opinion: "The

22. El Lissitzky
Proun (first version, *Proun 99*), circa 1924
ink, watercolor, collage on paper
25⁷⁄₁₆ x 19⁹⁄₁₆
64.9 x 49.5
Collection Museum of Art,
Rhode Island School of Design
Museum appropriation

"Proun" describes a composition in two or three dimensions that defines space through the arrangement of lines, planes and volumes. Lissitzky, who invented this form, describes the Proun idea in a 1922 article in *De Stijl*, V, 6. In 1923 he built a Proun Room for the Greater Berlin Art Exhibition, for which Huszar and Rietveld had also designed an environment (fig. 157) in which a number of ideas are expressed that relate to those in Lissitzky's Proun Room.

1. All correspondence is from the author's collection of documentation dealing with Dutch social history in the period 1917-22.

implementation within Western Europe in the next few years of the principles laid in Russia, will open the possibility to attain the universal view of life and unity of opinion which prevailed in the middle ages."

Naturally, the Stijl group, which considered its ideas of world-wide importance, strove to contact as many like-minded artists as possible throughout the world. Theo van Doesburg, the indefatigable apostle of the new faith, attempted to make contact with Bolshevist Russia. Though genuine communication proved difficult, van Doesburg wrote to Beekman in September 1919: "I am very happy that our first manifesto has arrived in Russia. I am eager to know how it will be received. Of course I am looking forward to communication with our Russian colleagues. Will their works still remain under the aegis of Expressionism, or will they have progressed? Russia is the only contact which we have missed." Evidently van Doesburg was not yet familiar with the Suprematism of Kazimir Malevich, even though Malevich had lived and worked in Paris before World War I.

It was not only intervention and civil war that impeded contacts with artists of the Soviet Union in 1919. The most important impediment was the refusal of The Netherlands government and those of other European countries to transmit mail to and from Russia. This refusal resulted in a campaign of protest, originated by communist artists in Holland in which Chris Beekman took the initiative. He interested several communist colleagues in it, such as painter Peter Alma, the architect Robert van 't Hoff and sculptors Hildo Krop and John Raedecker. Actor Hijman Croiset consented, after some deliberation, to having the group use his address for correspondence regarding a joint petition to the Dutch parliament. Towards the end of October 1919, the potential co-signers received the petition, which included this statement: "It is an established fact that correspondence from Netherlands artists with colleagues in Russia, even periodicals concerning art, have been returned to the sender as undeliverable, marked 'no transit.' The petition asks for abolition of all restrictions that curtail free international postal exchange between artists."

The idea was to protest simultaneously in several countries, but van Doesburg failed to send the pertinent papers to foreign countries, as had been agreed. This resulted in fervent arguments. Beekman tried on his own to interest some foreign colleagues in the campaign. Some refused to sign because they wanted to keep out of politics. Gino Severini, the Italian futurist painter who was associated with De Stijl at that time, wrote from Paris: "I am convinced that it is better for the artists residing here to keep themselves out of all political movements, for at the moment there is such confusion among the goals of the different parties that the

23. Vilmos Huszar
Hammer and Saw, 1919
oil on wood
13¾ x 18⅛
34.9 x 46
Collection Haags Gemeentemuseum

feelings, and the words in which these feelings are expressed, are completely meaningless, and we live completely as during the time of the 'Tower of Babel'. . . . That is why I abhor politics so. . . ."

Reactions differed widely in The Netherlands as well. Van der Leck did not sign because he refused to get involved in politics. Vilmos Huszar, who finally did sign, disapproved of the fact that "naturalistic" painters joined the campaign. He asked Beekman: "Whom do you ask to sign? As I see the list of names, I see all kinds of movements. This seems dangerous to me for the following reason: in case we gain influence in society and set about a reform of the arts, which will mean a clash with the old or obsolete principles, we will have associated with people who later will be our enemies. What will be the outcome?"

Poet Henriette Roland Holst, one of the most prominent leaders of Netherlands communism, did not sign because she disapproved of a campaign originated solely by artists. Moreover, she was of the opinion ". . . that revolutionaries should not address such petitions to a bourgeois government." The real reason for her refusal to sign might have been that she and her husband, who was an Art Nouveau artist, detested non-figurative art. De Stijl in their eyes was arch bourgeois. R.N. Roland Holst maintained sarcastically ". . . that an amorphous painting, the kind consisting of square blocks, must be a relief for the harassed modern businessman."

In the end, the petition was sent to parliament bearing 79 signatures. Among them were these artists and writers: Gerrit Rietveld, Antony Kok, J.F. Staal, Vilmos Huszar, H. Th. Wijdeveld, Theo van Doesburg, Peter Alma, Robert van 't Hoff and Chris Beekman. The discussions resulting from the petition are more interesting for us than its minimal effect on parliamentary activity. As a result of this petition the political differences within the Stijl group became evident. Architect J.J.P. Oud in a letter to Chris Beekman of 25 October 1919 stated: "Indeed, I was, like Kok, under the impression that it was your intent to bring 'politics' into De Stijl. . . . With your strong political convictions this could hardly be avoided, even if you would prefer otherwise." Oud's letter is based on his objection to forcing a certain life style through dictatorial means. Innovation, he felt, should grow spontaneously out of social change.

Whereas Oud reacts with calm and human wisdom, Antony Kok's reaction is more sharply articulated. He writes in the same month: ". . . as it is clear to me that van 't Hoff and Beekman apply political ideas to matters regarding De Stijl, we have to decide whether the monthly periodical *De Stijl* primarily serves the visual arts or politics. In my opinion, *De Stijl* is a periodical for the visual arts, for I feel that communism, Catholicism, and so forth, have nothing to do with the essence of the arts." Theo van Doesburg agreed with Oud and Kok. In a letter to Kok in December 1919 he sends congratulations on the occasion of the second anniversary of the October Revolution and rejoices in the failure of Western military intervention in Russia, but all the same he dissociates himself from the Dutch Communist Party, from which (according to van Doesburg) van 't Hoff and Beekman have great expectations. "But I tell them that their political stance is inconsistent with their artistic convictions. They uphold the principle that art should be subordinate to the masses and the production process. *It is inconceivable that art could be subordinate to anything whatever.* [italics, ed.] And these demands are made by the very people who rebel against every kind of subordination."

Contrary to his colleagues who wanted to separate politics from the arts, Robert van 't Hoff adhered most consistently to the idea of the bond between non-figurative art and the proletarian revolution. He wrote to Beekman in May 1919:

> I am a member of the communist party and have asked Wijnkoop [chairman of the Dutch Communist Party] to assist us in getting the first manifesto to Russia. He will try, and this proves to us that there are already ties between us. . . . Anyone who reads the manifesto in the latest issue of *De Stijl* can have no doubts about the stand of our movement regarding the new communism. . . . I myself am *convinced* that we will get a Soviet government, albeit that the transition will take a toll of some of our lives. I am trying to anticipate and to be ready for the implementation after the revolution, by designing mass-production buildings—no more private villas. Therefore, I am advocating an association of all avowed communist artists, whose work is truly communist.

When the revolution in Western Europe failed to materialize, van 't Hoff refused to surrender. Designing villas for wealthy people, instead of blocks of spacious housing for the working class, was more than a man who emphasized so emphatically the social character of De Stijl, could swallow. Van 't Hoff abandoned architecture and withdrew from "the world." Before doing so, however, he and kindred spirits tried their utmost to establish contacts with Russian artists.

In December 1920, members of De Stijl also exhibited their work in Berlin. There they became acquainted with the work of Russian painters.

In those of Kazimir Malevich, in particular, they recognized the expression of a kindred spirit. Van 't Hoff and Beekman attempted to contact him by mail. Beekman sent Malevich a letter and enclosed pictures, probably of buildings designed according to principles of De Stijl. On 12 March 1922, Malevich, who by then was a prominent artist in the Soviet Union, replied extensively. The spiritual atmosphere expressed in this letter shows a striking consonance with theosophically-tinged ideas of Mondrian, in spite of the fact that the political, cultural and social climate of The Netherlands and the Soviet Union could hardly have been more different. Malevich concludes:

> . . . a large proportion of [Russian] youngsters attends technical institutions, in order to [learn to] shape their animal, materialistic world: to be able to make a good fur coat, good houses, beds and mattresses; this [is what] they mean when they talk about great creativity in material objects. . . . The great error. . . lies in their aspirations toward a practical, effective naturalism. [Naturalism] belongs totally to the animal ideas, such as technique and mechanics. Just look how everything has been organized in animals. An animal is perfect because his whole organism is geared to devouring food as effectively as possible, and the internal generation of the substances necessary for the organism. Human culture does not emerge above this level; only the abstract elevates him to a truly higher spiritual level; only the activity of a life not geared to usefulness is directed to building a non-figurative, world architecture. Houses, forks and knives, our bodies are not essential, but the issue is a new world architecture, new fields and mountains, a new architecture of space.

Malevich's aim is to pry oneself loose from terrestrial constraints, in order to achieve a cosmic freedom:

> . . . only by developing new forms, by rising above the laws of necessity by which objects are governed, do we see man completely liberated, when he has become super-terrestrial in his actions.

This letter does appear to be super-terrestrial, especially in light of the fact that at the time of its writing a famine, in which millions of persons lost their lives, ravaged Russia. It is not surprising that the correspondence remained confined to a single pair of letters. Those who remained faithful to De Stijl turned away from politics, and those who considered politics a central part of their lives broke with De Stijl. Some returned to figurative art—in The Netherlands voluntarily, in the Soviet Union under overwhelming political and material pressures.

Ger Harmsen is a Professor of Social Philosophy and Social History at the University of Groningen, The Netherlands.

Translation by Charlotte I. Loeb

Painting and Sculpture

in the Context of De Stijl ■

Joop Joosten

A small group of painters was formed in Holland. Subject to the influence of painters such as Picasso, Cézanne and van Gogh, this group proceeded toward the destruction of natural form and to the substitution of pure flat imagery as the central principle of painting.[1]

It is clear that the impression of collectivity within De Stijl is sustained only by the activities of one man: Theo van Doesburg, founder and only editor of *De Stijl* magazine. With that in mind, one can understand the motivation behind this 1919 statement from van Doesburg's "Three Lectures," and the reasons that have led me to focus on his writings and visual works in this brief history of De Stijl painting and sculpture.

Yet, in comparison with three other painters who were also early participants in De Stijl—Mondrian, van der Leck and Huszar—van Doesburg was very slow to acknowledge in his own work the validity of the changes that had transformed the art world since the onset of Impressionism. That it took van Doesburg so long to admit the new art into his painting is more remarkable when one knows through articles he wrote in the series, *Attempt at New Art Criticism,* published in the period July 1912-December 1913 in *Eenheid,* that he was very aware of new trends in the visual arts. In these articles the Cubism of Picasso and Le Fauconnier and the Futurism and "abstract expressionism" of Kandinsky are extensively discussed in light of exhibitions of their work in Holland. The fact that he rejected those trends in his own painting does not mean that he allied himself with the more conservative art forms that he discussed in the same series of articles: he did not show much appreciation for them either. At that time, van Doesburg was convinced that art needed a thorough overhaul. It is typical of his approach to art that he did not express this need for reform through his own painting but, rather, in his theoretical-critical essays. The proposed overhaul is the central theme of all the early articles in *Eenheid* and also of a second series he wrote for the daily paper *De Avondpost,* between August 1913 and February 1914, under the collective title *Independent*

24. Piet Mondrian
Composition with Line (Pier and Ocean), 1917
oil on canvas
42⅝ x 42⅝
108.3 x 108.3
Collection Rijksmuseum Kröller-Müller

1. See footnote 12, Welsh, p 23.

Contemplations about Art. A new art could, in his opinion, only be generated when man had once again found a dominant idea, reminiscent of those residing in pre-Renaissance religions. One could say that the aim of both series of articles was to prove the correctness of this point of view, based on both historical and contemporary expressions of art. In these articles, van Doesburg adopted a tone and an approach to his subject more reminiscent of an academic researcher who aspires to objectivity than of a directly involved artist.

He never completely abandoned that tone and that approach; however, they are very deceptive. Though when writing and talking about art he persistently suggests that the subject is art in general, he actually talks, subjectively, about his own work. That is demonstrated when one reads his texts in strictly chronological order. He often shifts his position on such questions as: what is new art, who has realized it, what should new art look like? In replying to this first question, the variations in van Doesburg's position not only run parallel to the changes in his own work, but are also uniquely reflected in that work. When one looks for the answer to the second question it becomes evident that van Doesburg's point of view changes according to who is currently influencing him. New art in his point of view is consecutively realized by Kandinsky, Picasso and the cubists Huszar, van der Leck and Mondrian. But between July 1912 and March 1914 it hasn't yet come that far.

When van Doesburg writes about art, his own work is still only "réalisme vu à travers un tempérament" (realism seen through a temperament). In his criticism there is as yet no overt connection with his own work. When he talks about art he means the totality encompassed by the history of art. In van Doesburg's opinion, since the Renaissance art history reveals a continuous decline, despite a strong urge for renewal. He reproaches art critics for this decline, saying that they concern themselves only with technique—the "how" of art—and don't understand anything about the "what" of art: content. When the "what" is mentioned in art criticism it refers to subject, to the portrayal of external life around us, and does not truly discuss content in the sense of "why." Doesburg believes that the artist's task is to make visible what is still hidden, the inner life, the emotional life, that throughout history has been expressed through art. Since to him emotional life is analogous to religion and since Renaissance man has turned away from religion to search for himself, he believes that art since the Renaissance has fossilized to science, to a rather mindless concern with technique.

Van Doesburg's romantic view of art conforms totally to that of the typical Dutch artist for whom art is a matter of spontaneity, of a directly recorded discharge of emotions (Rembrandt, Hals, van Gogh are readily understood examples) and not of a search for new, unusual, contrived forms. It is logical that someone with such a point of view would reject all the avant-garde work of Paris and Berlin. For example, Futurism introduced "irrational and criminal foundation" in an article by van Doesburg in *Eenheid* of 9 November 1912; the expression of visible speed is described as ". . . in flat contradiction with the character of the art of painting which has inner life as its basis." Two weeks later, in the 23 November issue, it is the cubists—whose work was shown for the second time in the Modern Kunstkring (Modern Art Circle) in Amsterdam—who were attacked: "People like Le Fauconnier and Picasso bring us again the crude painting of savages, but without depth of feeling. We don't care if we get crude images as long as there are new feelings at the basis of it. But there is no evidence of such here. Wild sensations, brutish, frightening effects or scientific trifle. That is the basis of modern art." A year later, in the 6 December issue, Kandinsky's work and ideas are discussed in the context of a refutation of the ideas formulated in Kandinsky's essay, "Malerei als Reine Kunst" (Painting as Pure Art), which appeared in *Der Sturm* of September 1913. The increasing neglect of the object and the increasing proportion of those elements in painting which make it incomprehensible and unintelligible are represented to such a degree in Kandinsky's work—according to van Doesburg—that ". . . the greatest possible egotism in art has been reached." Abstract art was in his opinion ". . . in flat contradiction with the unbreakable law that natural forms are always necessary for the intelligibility of art."

In the last article of the *Avondpost* series which appeared on 28 February 1914, van Doesburg once more explains at length what he thinks about the problem of new art. The following two sentences are typical of his idealistic view: "The contemporary artist must express the emotions of mankind. The new art will have only one place to grow from: the world. . . . In the future there will only be one art. It will be a language that everybody will understand. This common language will carry the message of love."

In the 8 August 1914 issue of *Eenheid*, the reader is confronted with a statement by van Doesburg, written in French: "Pensées sur l'Art Moderne" (Thoughts on Modern Art), which has a totally different tone and conveys a totally different message from the earlier articles. This statement was written at the invitation of the Union Internationale des Beaux-Arts et des Lettres. The tone is now that of an engaged artist, and the message is reminiscent of Kandinsky's "Malerie als Reine Kunst:" "Throughout history, art has used nature as a crutch to convey its message to mankind. In the 20th century it threw away that crutch, it wanted to go on alone, without a crutch!" Here, van Doesburg creates

an image that seems to be a paraphrase of that used by Kandinsky who compares nature to a "prop."

With World War I came a temporary end to van Doesburg's artistic activities, as he had to enlist in the army. But his inactivity was short-lived and he managed to maintain the art world contacts he had and to make new ones as well. And in *Eenheid* of 19 June 1915, he appears again with a short review of an exhibition in which Kandinsky's artistry is seen as an enlightening example for the contemporary artist. In the 6 November 1915 issue of *Eenheid,* van Doesburg expresses his unconditional admiration and appreciation for the newest work of Mondrian: *Composition X in Black and White.* Several years later, he still recalls his reaction to it: ". . . a sensation of complete equilibrium, not only in respect to the composition of the work, but particularly in respect to the relationship between myself and the work of art." The painting was exhibited as part of a group show in the Stedelijk Museum in Amsterdam, together with other Mondrian works from 1913 and 1914. In the review, van Doesburg notes that Mondrian's work ". . . is spiritually superior to all the other exhibited works. . . and in its planned construction it is dynamic rather than static and in that there is a pure art element, for art is not a 'product' but a 'process.' The 'becoming' is expressed in black and white. . ." What struck van Doesburg as particularly remarkable about *Composition X* was ". . . that he [Mondrian] has limited himself to so little, yet creates such a pure artistic impression with nothing more than some white paint on white canvas and horizontal and vertical lines."

Some two weeks after van Doesburg had seen Mondrian's newest work he gave a lecture in Utrecht. The unabbreviated text was published in *Eenheid* in six parts between 27 May and 12 August 1916 under the title "The Development of Modern Art" and then, in 1919, it was included—with some important changes—in the volume *Three Lectures About the New Art.* In this new series of essays, van Doesburg again poses as an objective critic though the essays constitute nothing more than an explanation and justification of his own development, albeit in a larger context. Since van Doesburg continually shifts his perspective on that development, without any elucidation or explanation, it is important—as noted above—to read his writings in chronological order.

25. Georges Vantongerloo
Study, Brussels, 1918
oil on canvas
20½ x 24¼
52 x 61.5
Private collection

In his essay "The Development of Modern Art," van Doesburg presents van Gogh and Cézanne as the great innovators: van Gogh as the forerunner of Expressionism and Cézanne, with his "five mathematical forms: cubical, spherical, parallelepipedal, conical and pyramidal," as the forerunner of Cubism. Within Cubism van Doesburg distinguishes three trends: the physical or natural, the mystical and the intuitive. Through Cubism, painting became "a reflection of proportions." The big breakthrough to something completely new came with Kandinsky who found the way ". . . to express the feeling of his time and of his people on canvas through the construction of color and line, without extraneous elements, led only by the laws of emotion." To emphasize the importance he assigns to Kandinsky, van Doesburg provides a detailed biography of the Russian artist, extracted in total from Kandinsky's own *Rückblick* (Review) *1901-13*. At the end, van Doesburg notes that Holland also had a few innovators, and mentions Mondrian, Huszar, Wichman and De Winter by name. When the essay was reprinted in 1919, the part about Kandinsky had been changed and the importance of his work diminished. Furthermore, the Dutch artists mentioned by name are now Piet Mondrian, Vilmos Huszar and Bart van der Leck.

Simultaneously with the publication of the article in *Eenheid*, van Doesburg's second long essay appeared in the literary monthly *De Beweging* between May and September 1916. This essay, "The New Movement in Painting," was republished a year later as a brochure, still dated May-August 1916. "In modern painting," declares the author, ". . . plastic form is intrinsically connected to content and natural form is either externally indicated or, as with Kandinsky and Mondrian, completely abandoned." In other words, Kandinsky's abstract art is no longer seen as the terminal point, but as one of the two forms in which modern art presents itself: the bound form (Picasso), evolving from rational-compositional considerations; the unbound form (Kandinsky) proceeding from the spontaneous impulse. Throughout the essay, van Doesburg expresses a preference for bound form, for the work of the cubist ". . . who subtracts mathematical form from natural form, achieving a pure art form. This art form is the inner one, the spiritual one. The spiritual form is the image. The image is purity." Elsewhere, the author states that, through Cubism, ". . . the real matter of painting was revealed and the narrative expelled. Equilibrium and order are the two basic principles of cubistic composition:" and, ". . . when two objects have roundness in common, to the painter they are equal in respect to their form. When two objects have horizontality in common, the direction of the image is equal as well. It does not matter whether the object that serves as the aesthetic point of departure is a lamp, a tree, or a man in a boat."

26. Theo van Doesburg
Still Life, 1916
oil on canvas
26⅜ x 25⅛
67 x 63.8
Collection Rijksmuseum Kröller-Müller

2. M.I. Gaugham, "Vilmos Huszar: The Move into Radical Abstraction, 1915-1923" (Norwich: University of East-Anglia, unpublished PhD diss., 1975).

Van Doesburg distinguishes between two developmental phases of Cubism: the physical Cubism of Derain, Braque, Le Fauconnier, Picasso; the psychical Cubism of Severini, Kandinsky, Huszar, Mondrian, Wichman and again of Picasso. It is quite remarkable that now Gauguin and Matisse—along with van Gogh and Cézanne—are nominated as great innovators. Matisse, because he was the first to use "the means of the image," specifically: ". . . lines, round and square forms, vertical and horizontal planes, and colors with the intensity of white ranging to colors with the passivity of black. . ." Later, van Doesburg remarks about Matisse: "The objects of nature were useful to him only as expressions of falling, lying down, standing, floating, hanging, of horizontal or vertical."

Van Doesburg also has changed his opinion of Futurism. "Without this expression the art history of our time would be incomplete. . . . Futurism is the plastically formulated, urgent demand to revise completely the principles of traditional art." In van Doesburg's view, however, Futurism was significant primarily as a result of the contribution of Severini. When this essay was reprinted in 1917, the name Kandinsky and several less well known Dutch painters had been dropped and replaced by the name van der Leck. In March 1916, less than two months before van Doesburg started working on the second essay, he founded the artists society De Anderen (The Others), together with Erich Wichman and Louis Saalborn. Its first exhibition opened on 6 May 1916 in The Hague. There were four paintings by van Doesburg: *Heroic Movement* of 1916 and three others with *Painting* as title, numbered I, II, III and explained with the sub-title, *Motif: Still Life*. In the first painting he seems to have applied the lessons he has learned from Matisse, whose work he can only have seen in reproduction. One such reproduction of the painting *La Danse* of 1910 was included in *De Nieuwe Beweging* (The New Movement) brochure of 1917. Van Doesburg's growing interest in Cubism is clearly perceptible in two of the paintings; one is undoubtedly the 1916 *Still Life* (fig. 10), and another was probably the geometric composition, *Still Life* (fig. 26).

On the occasion of the 1916 exhibition of De Anderen, van Doesburg met Vilmos Huszar.[2] Huszar was a member of the group and had two paintings in the exhibition—*Painting (dark)* and *Painting (Yellow)*—and three *Designs for Paintings*. *Painting (Yellow)* was described in van Doesburg's volume *Three Lectures* as ". . . a fusion of Cubism and Luminism," yet ". . . in the total conception still a natural-organic entity." It is quite conceivable that van Doesburg, who was becoming increasingly interested in a more formalistic Cubism, felt immediately attracted to the work of Huszar. Formalism was quite uncommon at that time; there was much more interest in the romantic, expressionistic

27. Theo van Doesburg
Rhythm of a Russian Dance, 1918
oil on canvas
53½ x 24¼
135.9 x 61.6
Collection The Museum of Modern Art,
New York
Acquired through the Lillie P. Bliss Bequest

3. R.W.D. Oxenaar, "Bart van der Leck until
1920. A Primitive of the New Time" (Utrecht
State University, PhD diss., 1976).

Cubism of Le Fauconnier and the abstract Cubism of Kandinsky. Despite this, the contact with Huszar soon became close.

In van Doesburg's third essay, dated Haarlem 1916, and titled "The Aesthetic Principle of Modern Plastic Art," Kandinsky and Expressionism are mentioned but not elaborated. Also, the idea of the abstract, i.e. art without a representational image, is no longer a topic of discussion. The task of the painter is now, according to van Doesburg, "the visual expression of a given." The cubist was the first to understand that, for ". . . he abstracts natural form—his basic given—advances mathematical form, and thus creates a pure image—the spiritual. The spiritual is the inner. The inner is the aesthetic." The work of art best fulfills its purpose when it is ". . . composed of aesthetically assimilated forms and colors." To accomplish this, the artist must "order, multiply and measure" the forms and colors and, finally, "place them in relation to the plane of the painting." Thus, the style of that time is "the style of proportions." Van Doesburg concludes this essay by stating that the cubists and expressionists, in their innovations, went beyond painting: "The recapturing of the plane, through the destruction of perspective, created the need to paint the monumental on a flat plane—as in a fresco—painting in its deepest significance. Futhermore, technical solutions were found for traditional problems of stained-glass work, and this led to the evolution of stained-glass art. Thus, the absolute art of painting finds its perfect expression in its colorful and formal integration in the interior."

Huszar's interests became very important to van Doesburg, particularly the design of stained glass and the application of color to interior space. This is evidenced in the reproductions of Huszar's stained-glass windows van Doesburg chose to present in the *De Nieuwe Beweging* brochure of 1917, and in his own collaborations with two architects—Oud at De Vonk (fig. 148) and Wils at Alkmaar (fig. 146). The work of Bart van der Leck is also reproduced, though van Doesburg had met him only shortly before its publication. Three major van der Leck paintings of 1916 are shown: *Work at the Docks, The Storm* (fig. 9) and *Mine Triptych (Composition 4)* (fig. 38). The fact that three works of van der Leck are included is the more remarkable when one realizes that only one Mondrian painting is reproduced—the still unfinished *Composition with Line (Pier and Ocean)* (fig. 24). Van Doesburg had come into contact with van der Leck and his work through Mondrian and at the end of December 1916 van Doesburg saw van der Leck's paintings in The Hague.[3] After seeing van der Leck's work, van Doesburg had a genuine change of heart in regard to the new painting, a change that had significant repercussions in his own work.

28. Piet Mondrian
Blue Facade (Composition 9), 1913-14
oil on canvas
37½ x 26⅝
95.2 x 67.6
Collection The Museum of Modern Art,
New York
Gift of Mr. and Mrs. Armand P. Bartos

4. Robert P. Welsh, "Theo van Doesburg and Geometric Abstraction," in Nijhoff, Van Ostaijen, *De Stijl,* ed. F. Bulhof (The Hague: M. Nijhoff, 1976), pp 76-94.

When one looks at van Doesburg's paintings of the years 1917-18, and searches for the effect of the new currents, it is clear that van Doesburg oscillated between the various examples set by the paintings of contributors to *De Stijl.* Now and then, the influences seem very obvious, at other times one cannot be sure. Many more works are dated 1918 than 1917, which could indicate a long "incubation" period. It is useful to note the following statement in the essay "The Style of the Future," dated November 1917 and the third in the series of three lectures: "The modern artist does not deny nature. . . . But he does not imitate it, he does not portray it, he creates a different image of it. He uses it and reduces it to its elementary forms, colors and proportions in order to achieve a new image. This new image is the work of art." This statement by van Doesburg is clearly more along the lines of van der Leck's thinking than of Mondrian's. "Creating a different image" is the same phrase van der Leck used when he felt obliged to defend himself against the allegation that he had followed the example of Mondrian's abstract art too diligently. Yet, though a number of van Doesburg's 1917 paintings resemble those of van der Leck and several show an influence from Huszar, there are other references that lead to the conclusion that, at that time, van Doesburg remained a faithful follower of Mondrian.

In terms of style, 1918 can be seen as the beginning of a new phase in the development of van Doesburg's work. Now van Doesburg, like Mondrian, uses regular geometric, mostly 16 x 16 grids as composition diagrams (fig. 32), a method, as Robert Welsh comments,[4] that van Doesburg adopted permanently, while for Mondrian the grid was a transitory form. Though by the end of 1918 van Doesburg and Mondrian were working along the same lines, nevertheless, there existed considerable and fundamental differences in their work. Mondrian searched for a way to express a universal harmony through well-balanced proportions of purely plastic, severely limited means: vertical and horizontal lines and the three primary colors plus black, white and gray. In addition, Mondrian abandoned the use of images derived from reality before van Doesburg and van Doesburg never limited his palette to the primaries. But, the essential distinction rests, in my opinion, on Mondrian's use of lines and van Doesburg's use of planes. This difference, combined with the fact that Mondrian thought and worked in a far more abstract way than van Doesburg, was the essential cause of their later rupture.

Were van Doesburg and Mondrian conscious at this time of their essential differences? Perhaps, but if so, only of the distinctions, certainly not of their fundamental character. Mondrian returned to Paris in the summer of 1919, never to return to Holland, but in February-March 1920, van Doesburg visited him in Paris. From letters it is known that

29. Installation by Piet Mondrian in the Dutch
Art Circle exhibition 1917
Composition with Line, 1917, center;
Composition in Color A, 1917, right;
Composition in Color B, 1917, left.
Vintage photograph

(left)
30. Piet Mondrian
Composition in Color A, 1917
oil on canvas
19⅝ x 17⅜
49.9 x 44.1
Collection Rijksmuseum Kröller-Müller

31. Piet Mondrian
Composition in Color B, 1917
oil on canvas
19⅝ x 17⅜
49.9 x 44.1
Collection Rijksmuseum Kröller-Müller
on permanent loan to the
Stedelijk Van Abbemuseum

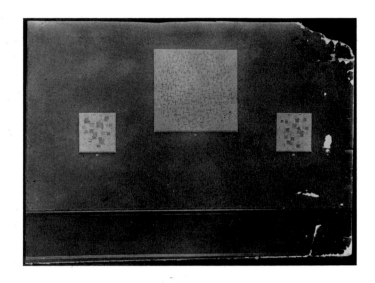

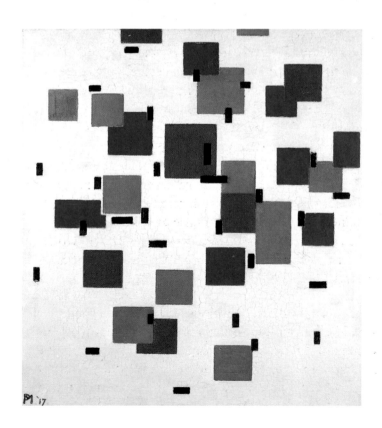

32. Theo van Doesburg
Composition XIII, 1918
oil on canvas
11⅝ x 11⅝
29.5 x 29.5
Collection Stedelijk Museum, Amsterdam

5. See Oxenaar, pp 68-79.

they maintained regular contact. In *De Stijl,* van Doesburg reported on his visit to the Salon des Indépendants, where he was attracted to the work of the cubists, and on an exhibition of exclusively cubist art organized by the Section d'Or group. Both the younger and older artists exhibiting were totally unknown to van Doesburg. In the Salon, van Doesburg had been particularly struck by the ". . . more monumental Cubism of the younger artists, who present us with pure color and *anti-modelé* (against imitation), instead of the remnants of the Picasso-Braque school. In other words, the battle for color."

Van Doesburg thought the Section d'Or exhibition so important that when plans were made to have it travel he offered to be the organizer in Holland. In the summer of 1920, when part of the exhibition did come to Rotterdam, The Hague and Amsterdam, van Doesburg added some work of De Stijl painters to it: three paintings by himself; three works by Mondrian, all of 1920; and a study by Huszar. He had also wanted to invite van der Leck, but rejected the idea so as not to face another refusal, for by that time, van der Leck had long turned his back on De Stijl.⁵ The exhibition was entitled *Section d'Or-Paris: Works by Cubists and Neo-cubists.* In his opening address, van Doesburg explained that "neo-cubists" referred to the Dutch contributions.

At this period, both Mondrian and van Doesburg composed their paintings with the help of a grid. Van Doesburg's use of green and purple adjacent to primary colors is the most striking difference between his work and Mondrian's. Less striking, but far more important, is the fact that there are no lines dividing the colors; color planes are tangent. On the other hand, another important distinction is eliminated: the need to have a realistic given, a natural form as a point of departure. Van Doesburg, in his article in the March 1921 issue of *De Stijl,* "About Modern Painting," discusses the distinction between cubists and neo-cubists. According to van Doesburg, the cubists used the object as starting point and provided a synthesis of it, whereas the neo-cubists had color as starting point and created a synthesis of that. The cubists "abstracted," the neo-cubists "realized."

Did Mondrian convince van Doesburg that it was possible to express "harmony in painting" without a realistic image as given? It seems very likely. But van Doesburg felt, typically, that harmony could only be achieved in his way: through ". . . colors far removed from each other, colors of unequal value, contrasting colors, dissonants, achieving a unity through the relationship from color to color."

After 1920, van Doesburg stopped painting for awhile. Apparently, he concentrated completely on his architectural, spatial experiments, though it is also possible that he felt he had reached a point of

33. Piet Mondrian
Composition C, 1920
oil on canvas
23¾ x 24
60.3 x 61
Collection The Museum of Modern Art,
New York
Acquired through the Lillie P. Bliss Bequest

6. See the text of the so-called "Sketchbook I" in
Two Mondrian Sketchbooks 1912-1914, eds.
Robert P. Welsh and J.M. Joosten (Amsterdam:
Meulenhoff International, 1969).

termination in his work. In this light, it is interesting to read van Doesburg's retrospective view of five years of painting within the context of De Stijl, which appeared in the *1917-22 Anthology* issue of *De Stijl* in December 1922. Only one name is mentioned in this article: Mondrian. Van Doesburg presents him as ". . . the father of the new image of plastic art," who, through his work as well as through his theoretical essays, ". . . had inspired the more consistent among the youngest generation of artists with confidence in the possibility of a new creative image."

Even in his review of the Amsterdam group show of October 1915, van Doesburg had hailed Mondrian's "pier and ocean" works (e.g., fig. 11), as the most modern expression of art. Mondrian then in the last phase of his development towards non-objective art, was ten years older than van Doesburg and had been an artist for almost 25 years. Mondrian had received a traditional 19th-century education. Despite the education, centered around academic figure painting, he always demonstrated an avowed preference for thoroughly naturalistic still-life and landscape painting. The motifs that inspired him can generally be classified as belonging to the world of pre-industrial human activity in rural surroundings. Yet there exists a fundamental distinction between his work and that of the painters of the Hague School with which it is always connected, for even Mondrian's earliest paintings have an unusually strong sense of coherence, an internal order. While the order in Hague School paintings is always extrinsically determined, created out of the need to convey external light and atmosphere, the search for internal cohesion and internal balance in Mondrian's work must have been motivated by a strong personal conviction—the conviction that these qualities were part of the essential character of art. The more familiar one becomes with Mondrian's work, the more one has the impression of a deliberate development in which nothing was left to chance. Through theosophy—which he must have discovered around 1900—he became increasingly conscious of his particular formal inclination, and from his own remarks, we know that theosophy showed him not only how to broaden and deepen his ideas about art and beauty, but also about the world around him. Theosophy helped him to arrive at a definition of beauty as the expression of the balanced relationship between the opposing elements that form the basis of life: spirit-matter, abstract-real, masculine-feminine, positive-negative, movement-rest, vertical-horizontal.[6] Theosophy also enhanced his theoretical insight into the psychic function of color.

Exposure to French Luminism and Fauvism around 1908 taught Mondrian a use of color independent of natural objects and situations. At the end of 1911, the works of Cézanne, Picasso and Braque were exhibited in Holland for the first time. Awareness of their paintings was

a turning point for Mondrian, and before the year was over he left for Paris. There he became thoroughly familiar with the changes brought about by Cubism, and the effect upon his work was so strong that one can accurately speak of a caesura—a definite interruption in the logical sequence of his development. Color was reduced to the cubistic, essentially "colorless" grays, greens and ochres. Forms were subjected to linear analysis and disintegrated into multiple facets. Despite this influence, there remains a profound difference between Mondrian's cubist work and that of the French cubists. Mondrian's faceting of forms was not primarily directed toward analyzing volumes and reassembling them into a two-dimensional plane. Mondrian had after all been brought up with and educated in the Dutch tradition, and the compelling three-dimensional character of linear perspective was of little concern to him. Like all Dutch painting, his art always inclined toward the two dimensional. Moreover, he belonged to the Art Nouveau generation. This influence is easily recognized in the flat planes and flowing lines of his early landscapes. Therefore, what fascinated him in the work of the French cubists was not so much the dissolution of volume, but its tangible result: a complex composition of lines and faceted planes.

Mondrian chose the motif of bare trees as the vehicle for the new ideas in his work. One could say that in choosing this motif, he excluded all true cubistic problems. Through a flat tangle of lines, more or less following the lines of branches and trunks, the image of a tree is expressed as an entity, without a three-dimensional character. In addition, curved lines—still somewhat naturalistic, as can be seen in the composition *Tree* (fig. 8)—are extended and then fragmented. Increasingly, the fragments are aligned either horizontally or vertically in order to express the principle of life in a progressively more abstract and minimal manner: movement versus rest, ascension versus recumbence. This process of abstraction is so extreme that eventually the original motif becomes almost unrecognizable. At that moment, a new motif is introduced in the work of Mondrian: the facade, the unadorned, free-standing side walls of Parisian buildings, with the horizontal and vertical limitations and divisions deriving from the architectural style. In the series of facade drawings and paintings, made between the end of 1913 and July 1914, one perceives how a pattern of vertical and horizontal lines gradually emerges from the construction inherent

34. Theo van Doesburg
Simultaneous Countercomposition, 1929-30
oil on canvas
19¾ x 19⅝
50.1 x 49.8
Collection The Museum of Modern Art,
New York
The Sidney and Harriet Janis Collection

in this motif. Ironically, the bond with the motif is strengthened rather than weakened by the introduction into the composition of architectonic elements which cannot be fitted into the horizontal-vertical scheme and the return of color as in *Composition 9, Blue Facade* (fig. 28), and *Oval Composition, Tableau III*, in which the significance of light is stressed by the transition from light colors in the upper half to dark colors in the lower.

When Mondrian returned to Holland in 1914, he stayed briefly in Domburg. Later, he found a permanent studio in the small town of Laren—at that time still rural but very popular with intellectuals and artists. In Domburg, nature and architecture were the sources of inspiration for his work. Two motifs were chosen: the sea and the church tower. These were incorporated into two series of studies that led to two paintings. The sea studies produced the painting *Composition X in Black and White*, 1915; the tower studies, *Composition 1916* (fig. 7). In both paintings, a horizontal-vertical system is consistently carried through.

Mondrian's 1916 meeting with Bart van der Leck and their ensuing friendship had a great impact on the work of both artists. From van der Leck he learned to paint uniform, flat color, to relinquish his still traditional, impressionistic way of painting, and to sharply separate color and line. In this same year, Mondrian crossed the boundary of figurative art and entered the still relatively unexplored area of non-objective painting. From letters to friends we know that the making of his first painting without a recognizable image, *Composition with Line (Pier and Ocean)*, 1917, was a laborious process, started in 1916 and finished in April 1917. What we don't know is whether Mondrian intended from the beginning to make this extraordinary painting. It is possible that his first intention was to combine the sea and tower motifs.

Mondrian exhibited *Composition with Line* side by side with *Composition*[s] *in Color A* and *B* (fig. 29). The paintings were hung as a triptych: in the middle the large white and black piece; at left *Composition in Color B*, with its light colors, and at right *Composition in Color A*, with its dark colors. *Composition with Line*, bracketed by the two smaller compositions in color seemed to be rising, contracting and expanding, advancing and retreating through variation in length of lines, through placement of lines and planes in relation to each other, through cutting lines off at the top and through the use of a series of gradations of gray adjacent to the black. The two works in color convey a considerably flatter effect, even though some of the color planes are overlapping, reminiscent of the way the colors in *Composition 1916* flow over each other.

Color was the point of departure for a series of works that have light and dark versions—compositions with color planes. In Mondrian's letters we read of his desire to pin down the color, to give the color planes—free-floating in the first paintings—a compositional relationship to each other. To achieve that he extended the edges of the planes to form new planes that were painted in various tones of gray. In a succeeding series, he marked the edges of the planes with gray lines, thus framing the colors. He then positioned the resulting irregular pattern on a regular 16 x 16 grid. Mondrian wanted to test this new formula by applying it to a diamond-shaped format (perhaps a development from the former use of the oval), by varying the prominence of the grid within the composition and by introducing a second grid on the basis of the diagonals (fig. 18).

Mondrian continued to develop these grid systems until his return to Paris in 1919. The work he created during the first year in Paris, *Composition C,* 1920 (fig. 33), for example, clearly demonstrates the distance he had gone from his previous, severely methodical compositions. The first Parisian paintings seem to have been composed on the basis of an irregular grid system that has wider meshes than previous grids and that is independent of the picture plane. Again, Mondrian clearly has acquired more freedom in the means of expression he developed in his previous period: the interlaced vertical and horizontal (black) lines that cross or touch to form rectangles and the flat primary and non-colors within the squares formed by those lines. This new freedom is expressed through a more lucid composition and stronger, more pronounced colors. Moreover, every painting is a solution in itself; there are no longer light and dark versions. However, from this time on, there are series based on compositional themes. In 1920, the use of the grid is completely abandoned. One is struck by the fact that the lines do not continue to the edges of the picture plane, thus stressing independence of the figuration.

Though after Mondrian's return to Paris, van Doesburg and he maintained their friendship through correspondence and an occasional meeting in the early 20s, Mondrian's active participation in De Stijl had ended by the mid-20s. Yet, as Robert Welsh points out, Mondrian may, in fact, have been the only painter to consistently maintain the neoplastic idea in his work, thus remaining the only true De Stijl artist.

While Mondrian and van der Leck were working in Laren in 1916, Vilmos Huszar, the only Hungarian-born De Stijl artist, became a member of the association De Anderen. He showed two paintings in the group's Hague exhibition that immediately attracted Doesburg. Later that year Huszar visited the Kröller-Müller collection in The Hague with van Doesburg to see the latest works by van der Leck. Looking at Huszar's painting *Composition II, Skaters* (dated Feb. 1917) (fig. 132), and comparing it to van der Leck's *Composition 1917, 5 (Donkey Riders)* (fig. 13), one can see a connection. Elements of movement that exist in the donkey riders series do not occur in van der Leck's more abstracted works, such as the *Mine Triptych* (fig. 38). But, Huszar manages to retain the element of movement in his most abstract works through variations in the posture and placement of the images. In *Hammer and Saw* (fig. 23), Huszar achieved an expression of movement within the picture plane by overlaying the red and yellow elements in varying directions. Moreover, this had the effect of equalizing background and foreground, and further strengthening the effect of motion. In a letter from Huszar to van der Leck, dated 25 September 1917, Huszar discusses the woodcut used for the cover of *De Stijl*.[7] Huszar wrote about the equality of image and ground in the black and white composition (fig. 129).

In view of Huszar's avowed interest in the expression of movement it is not surprising that he ultimately included real movement in his *Mechanical Dance Figure*, 1920, a moving silhouette that he later destroyed, and in the design for a mechanical theater, *Form Spectacle*, 1920-21 (fig. 69), never realized. In the theater, not only the puppet-like figures but the walls were to be moveable and within the walls, square planes and rectangular forms were also supposed to move. It must have been this design that inspired him to make the large gouache *Figure Composition for a Mechanical Theater*, circa 1923 (fig. 4), that is essentially an abstract work based on a figural work.

Huszar's preoccupation with film and advertising design in the late 20s seems not only to have influenced his typographical experiments, but also his painting. Ultimately these preoccupations led to semi-abstract works and around 1930 he returned completely to realism.

Exactly how and when Georges Vantongerloo came into contact with De Stijl and Doesburg is unclear, but his first contribution to *De Stijl* magazine appeared in the July 1918 issue, and in November of the same year his name was among the signatories of the first De Stijl manifesto. Vantongerloo probably took refuge in Holland after the occupation of Antwerp at the end of the summer of 1914. He had received training as a sculptor at the academies of Antwerp and Brussels and had worked for several years as an artist in Belgium before World War I. In his early Hague exhibitions, 1916 and 1917, Vantongerloo's works were essentially figurative. Through van Doesburg, Vantongerloo discovered the writings of philosopher M.H.J. Schoenmaekers whose works certainly influenced his development as they had Mondrian's.

In his *Reflexions I* and *II*, published in *De Stijl* during 1918-19, Vantongerloo wrote extensively about the thoughts behind his spherical constructions (fig. 16), about the relationship between solid and void and

7. See Broos, pp 146-163.

35. César Domela
Construction, 1929
glass, painted glass, painted metal, chrome-plated
brass, painted wood
35⅜ x 29⅝ x 1¾
89.8 x 75.2 x 4.2
Collection Hirshhorn Museum and Sculpture
Garden, Smithsonian Institution

8. See George Baines, "Georges Vantongerloo,
the Influence of the Work of Wouters and the
Creation of the First Abstract Works," in
Wonen/TA-BK, no. 9 (1981), p 6-16.

about the space in which the object exists, which in turn, reflects the
spatial effect of the volume. In his essay "L'Evolution de l'Art
Sculptural"[8] Vantongerloo explains how he had become dissatisfied with
traditional, naturalistic sculpture, particularly because of its dependence
upon matter, and had detached himself from this category of sculpture
in a search for new forms. Ultimately, this led him to abstract art, to a
strictly formal expression. According to him, sculpture was nothing
more than the expression of the relationship between volume and
emptiness and, as such, a matter between the human mind and the object.
Any references to outside elements like state of mind or features of the
model had to be eliminated to achieve pure form. In the spherical
constructions of 1917, this elimination has taken place. Vantongerloo's
starting point was the most objective delineation of space, that is to say,

36. Georges Vantongerloo
Construction of Volume Relations, 1921
mahogany
16⅛ x 4¾ x 4⅛ at base
41 x 12.1 x 10.5
Collection The Museum of Modern Art,
New York
Gift of Sylvia Pizitz
(not in exhibition)

the spherical, within which all movements, in all directions, have an equal span. The size of the sculpture was no longer important and he chose to work very small.

Van Doesburg reproduced two sculptures by Vantongerloo in the December 1919 issue of *De Stijl* and described them as being: ". . . very consistent works in which the sculptor concentrated solely on the expression of volume relations in three-dimensional balance." It is fascinating to see how the total volume is divided into vertical and horizontal thickened rectangular planes and blocks. This idea is even more clearly developed in *Construction of Volume Relations,* 1921 (fig. 36). By breaking open the closed form, through which an integration of volume and emptiness is achieved, Vantongerloo had found his style for the next ten years. In his painting of this period, Vantongerloo used the surface of the painting and not the image as the point of departure for his composition, thus recognizing the inherent two-dimensionality of the picture plane (fig. 25). Though Vantongerloo returned to Belgium in 1918, his use of a grid format with an asymmetrical overlay of black lines is closely related to the grid works of van Doesburg and Mondrian of the same period. However, Vantongerloo used a much broader palette than that of either of his Dutch colleagues. Vantongerloo was the only sculptor among the De Stijl artists and his early experiments with abstract form, with their block-like character independent of nature, amount to three-dimensional variations on the grid paintings.

An examination of De Stijl painting in the 20s supports the belief that the tentative collective nature of De Stijl was not sustained beyond its early years. Outside of van Doesburg's efforts at a group image, the only unity came through a willingness among the artists to publish works and writings in *De Stijl* magazine. Yet the early contacts between van Doesburg, Huszar, Mondrian and van der Leck laid the groundwork for the creation of the De Stijl idea that was the basis for the diversity of abstract expression to follow.

Joop Joosten is Research Curator, Stedelijk Museum, Amsterdam.

This is an abbreviated version of the original article to be published in its entirety in Dutch.

Translation by Carla van Spluntren

Van der Leck and De Stijl

Rudolf W.D. Oxenaar

37. Bart van der Leck
Poster for *Batavier-Lijn*, 1916
lithograph on paper
30¾ x 45¼
78.1 x 114.9
Collection Haags Gemeentemuseum

1. All letters to van der Leck and a number of the
handwritten answers are in the possession of the
B.A. van der Leck heirs, Blaricum. All letters to
H.P. Bremmer are in the Gemeente archive in The
Hague. The letters from van der Leck and others
to van Doesburg can be found in the van
Doesburg archive in The Hague. This article is a
revised version of the last chapter of R.W.D.
Oxenaar's "Bart van der Leck until 1920, A
Primitive of the New Time," State University of
Utrecht, unpublished PhD diss., 1976. For
complete references, see the dissertation.
2. The Kröller-Müller family collection forms the
nucleus of the Rijksmuseum Kröller-Müller
holdings in Otterlo.

The friendship between Bart van der Leck and Piet Mondrian, so important to the growth of the De Stijl idea, developed sometime after mid-April 1916, when van der Leck moved from The Hague to Laren. This relationship is confirmed by Mondrian's well-known remark in a letter to art critic H.P. Bremmer, dated 1 August 1916: "I can't tell you how pleased I was to find in van der Leck a man with similar aspirations to mine."[1]

We can be reasonably certain that Mondrian and van der Leck had seen each other's work before they met for the first time in Laren. Van der Leck had undoubtedly completed his paintings *Work at the Docks* and *The Storm* (fig. 9) before he left The Hague. He took them with him to Laren, but after July 1916 they were permanently on view in the private museum of Mrs. Kröller-Müller in The Hague.[2] It was undoubtedly in reference to these two paintings that Mondrian—15 years later, in the last issue of *De Stijl*—wrote: "Van der Leck, though still figurative, painted in flat planes and pure colors. My more or less cubistic technique—then still more or less pictorial—was influenced by his exact technique."

In Laren, Mondrian wrestled with new versions of the "plus-minus" motif (fig. 7). His pictorial use of color—pink, blue and ochre—had to yield to the solution of an essential problem of form. Van der Leck had solved the color problem, having already worked with flat primary colors, but he was open to a development of form which could satisfy his need for extreme objectification. Their talks produced important new ideas for both of them.

Following the example of Mondrian, van der Leck started to number his paintings and call them "compositions." He did this until the end of 1918 when he changed his style and returned to making the elements of his paintings more recognizable. In 1916, he painted four "compositions," the most important of these was the *Mine Triptych (Composition 4)* (fig. 38); in 1917 there were eight compositions, four sets of two, in each a

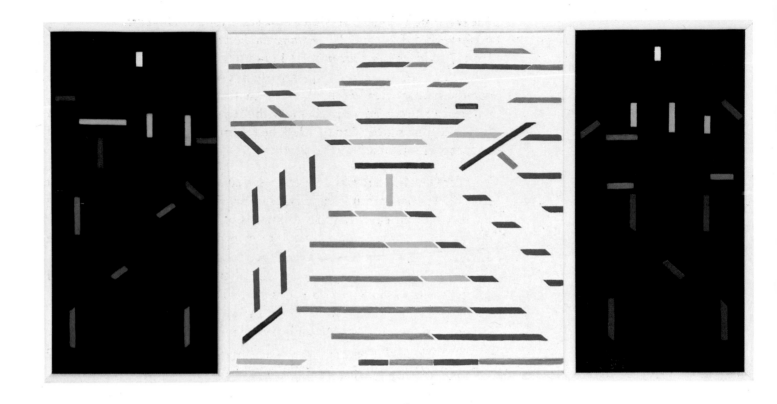

38. Bart van der Leck
Mine Triptych, 1916
oil on canvas
43⅜ x 86⅝
110 x 220
Dienst Verspreide Rijkskollekties on loan to
Haags Gemeentemuseum

"heavy" and a "light" version of the same theme: *Dogcart (Composition[s] 1 and 2); Leaving the Factory (Composition[s] 3 and 4); Donkey Riders (Composition[s] 5 and 6)* (fig. 13); *Mountainous Landscapes (Composition[s] 7 and 8);* and in 1918 at least ten compositions which he called "mathematical images" and which, on the whole, can be considered as being without a subject. With *The Horseman* (fig. 43), towards the end of 1918, he returns definitively to the principle of recognizable objects in his work.

Van der Leck has described the process that evolved in his painting at that time: "Modern painting transmutes physicality into flatness by reducing the natural to the terms and proportions of the flat plane; and through the understanding of space, painting achieves spatial relationships." The genesis of a painting was always difficult for him, but now the process of developing a theme was more intense than ever before. Before the final solution was found, an existing or new realistic sketch would often be followed by three to six subsequent stages contributing to the eventual format of the painting. Gradually, the theme was abstracted and then broken down into areas of flat color. These color segments then assumed a block form and were horizontally, vertically and diagonally arranged (figs. 39-41).

Soon the contact between Mondrian and van der Leck intensified. They saw each other almost daily and discussed mutual ideas and problems arising from their work. It is clear that it was in 1916 that van der Leck, for the first time, went beyond realism to abstraction. This new work involved the rapid development of his working method into a lucid system.

The big *Mine Triptych*, a painting which could have been a stained-glass window—the like of which had not been made at that time—was completed in the last months of 1916. The first important example of what the contact with Mondrian had brought about in van der Leck, it is nominally nonfigurative, geometrical, spatially flat imagery built up of unconnected forms in primary colors. During that same time, Mondrian was still searching for increased simplification of the plus-minus motif. He was working on the painting that later, in 1917, would become the *Composition with Line (Pier and Ocean)* (fig. 24); and he had started on the two *Composition[s] in Color, A and B* (figs. 30-31), in which this motif was combined with rectangular planes of color. Because of van der Leck's influence, these paintings showed more openness and stricter organization than had earlier plus-minus compositions. Color had returned, flat and sharply defined, but not primary. Mondrian would not reach that point until 1920. For the time being he limited himself to mixed hues in the ranges of red, blue and yellow. Van der Leck's spatially flat, unconnected elements had not yet been completely applied. From the plus-minus motif Mondrian came to connected or overlapping lines and planes, which created a spatial effect that never reappeared in his work.

None of the three paintings Mondrian was working on at the time would be completed before the end of 1916. We know of only one painting he made in 1916 and it was completed before he met van der Leck. Mondrian found himself in a transition period, partly brought about by van der Leck's influence, and getting through this period absorbed much of his time and mental energy. Thus, the best 1916 example we have of their joint aspirations is van der Leck's *Mine Triptych*.

Later in 1916, through Mondrian, van der Leck met van Doesburg. They did not get along well, although at the beginning there were no specific problems. Van Doesburg was, after all, seven years younger than van der Leck, and initially full of admiration for his work. Also, their respective principles were not yet sharply defined. Van Doesburg was enthusiastic, outgoing, active, well informed, had a quick mind and was always developing new ideas and plans. In the beginning, this no doubt impressed van der Leck, who led a much more retiring life.

In Van Doesburg's essay, "The New Movement in Painting," written between May and August 1916, Mondrian is mentioned, but not van der Leck. But in December 1916, van Doesburg asked van der Leck to send him photographs for publications and lectures. Van der Leck replied that he would like Doesburg to see his work in the Kröller-Müller collection in The Hague. Van Doesburg's response is overwhelming in its enthusiasm:

> I went to The Hague to see your last works in the collection of H. Kröller. It gave me the opportunity to study a considerable part of your artistic development. As my final conclusion I can say that I have never (not in the work of old painters, not in that of the new), seen such a complete *oeuvre*, such pure and mature application of the principles of plastic art as in your work—the rhythmic translation of the universal life. I was particularly impressed by the *Mine Triptych*, the way the universal qualities of life were dealt with in relation to the pure means of the art of painting.

Van Doesburg's letter confirms that the *Triptych* was considered to be the most important "new" painting of that time. The degree to which van Doesburg was impressed by this painting is also revealed in his own work. His first paintings in the new style were two compositions with rectangular planes of primary color on a black ground. Both were clearly inspired by the *Triptych*. He never used black as background again.[3] But

3. For a later example of primary color on a black ground by a De Stijl artist see Vilmos Huszar's collage, *Figure Composition for a Mechanical Theater*, 1923 (fig. 4).

van der Leck's use of black was not based on artistic principle but on fact: the miners and the mine.

In the first months of 1917, preparations were made for the publication of the magazine *De Stijl*. Previously, van Doesburg had talked with Mondrian about his idea for a magazine that would be devoted to the new art. He was the one to take the initiative and to contact possible contributors, but van Doesburg, Mondrian and van der Leck together determined the character of the magazine during their many talks in Laren. In the beginning of 1917 van der Leck received a more or less official invitation from van Doesburg to become a contributor:

> Because it is really necessary to clear up the hopeless confusion that exists in the minds of the public and the 'quasi' modern artists, I have decided to start an unpretentious magazine in the near future: *De Stijl*. Everything has been arranged. You would do me a great honor by writing a little article for it. The magazine will only concern itself with the modern style (the rectangular versus the baroque). I will be the editor and C. Harms in Delft will publish it. Typographically and aesthetically it will be austere, without any trappings.

Van der Leck's answer was positive and even enthusiastic: "I wish you a lot of success with your new enterprise and thank you for the invitation to contribute. There is a lot to do and I hope to find time and energy—amidst the problems in my work—to help with the spreading of the new."

A few days later, Mondrian wrote van Doesburg about eventual contributors to the magazine: "Of the people you mentioned, Picasso and van der Leck are *the* people. . . . Write we must, you and I and van der Leck, but he won't come up with something that quickly, he hasn't even begun yet and just like me, he will want to spend a lot of time on it." And a little bit further: ". . . in this way, Schoenmaekers could be of use, if only he wasn't such a rotten sort of a guy—also I don't believe that with him it's real." Then, as a postscript: "Tonight I again talked it over with van der Leck; we think it best if you alone are mentioned as editor (on the title page, etcetera). You work pretty fast and are also known as a 'writer;' they might laugh at us."

The first issue of *De Stijl* was published in October 1917; van Doesburg was officially the only editor. Van der Leck's article, "The Place of Modern Painting in Architecture," appeared in it and he was the only painter whose work was represented in the appendix. In the article he briefly and succinctly summed up the ideas that he had been expressing, in various ways, for years. Painting is the destruction of the natural; and space, and its equilibrium is in the imagery. Architecture is construction of the natural. It is enclosing, confining, colorless, flat, and its

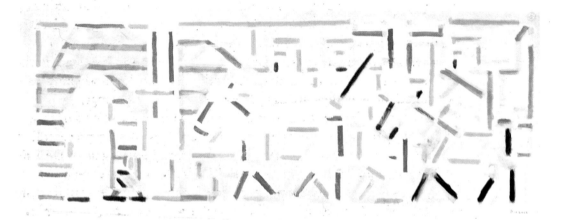

39. Bart van der Leck
Study for Composition 1917 no. 2
(Donkey Riders)
gouache on paper
25½ x 60
64.8 x 152.4
Courtesy J.P. Smid, Kunsthandel Monet

40. Bart van der Leck
Study for Composition 1917 no. 3
(Donkey Riders)
gouache on paper
25½ x 60
64.8 x 152.4
Courtesy J.P. Smid, Kunsthandel Monet

41. Bart van der Leck
Study for Composition 1917 no. 5
(Donkey Riders)
gouache on paper
24⅝ x 47⅝
62.5 x 121
Courtesy J.P. Smid, Kunsthandel Monet

equilibrium is in the construction. Functionalism, austerity and reticence are pre-supposed in the architect. The giving of color and space imagery are reserved for the painter. The destruction of the natural as a continuation of a slowly accomplished reduction is the only new element in this theory. Van der Leck had Mondrian to thank for this idea, but in the last paragraph of his article it becomes clear that he accepts it only for stylistic reasons and that otherwise he sticks to his position as a realist: "And this is the positive result of the destructive character of modern painting. It carries through the portrayal of visual reality. . . to the cosmic values of space, light and proportion, in which the art of representation is included and remains pre-supposed."

However cosmic the values, representation was not abandoned. Painting continued to "represent visual life." Van der Leck's struggle in these years is concerned with the boundaries of recognition that must be observed. This article was his manifesto; he never endorsed anything else. In the paintings of 1917 the theme is not directly recognizable. It is not without reason that they have been known for so long as "mathematical compositions," but there remained an ambivalence in the way the forms were organized; exactly why the "blocks" and "lines" are positioned the way they are in the plane was not convincingly demonstrated. Van der Leck was certainly aware of the effects of this, but he had, after all, no theory; he did not want a system, representation had to remain pre-supposed. As illustration for the first issue of *De Stijl* he chose the block version of *Donkey Riders* (fig. 13)—the most recognizable of the six paintings completed at that time. Mondrian wrote van Doesburg about this: "I told van der Leck that I thought this thing he reproduced was still too abstracted (you can still see the donkeys). He agreed, but felt it had to be like that for this thing (and I think so too) and that it went well with his article."

Van der Leck persisted and achieved good results: he created a varied series of works based on spatial flatness using unconnected color planes and primary colors. These paintings were striking and compelling because of the way they were executed and their use of primary color. Mondrian tried using fixed planes, but he did not like the suggestion of space they created. Later he followed van der Leck's example, and in 1917 he made a series of compositions with color planes in which the rectangles of color are either completely free against a white ground or linked in groups against the background. But this was not the solution for him. In the beginning of 1918, he wrote Bremmer: "Those eight pieces are again part of a phase of development in which I found a better solution for color planes and background. While working I discovered that the color planes against a plane of solid color do not create a unity for my work. In van der Leck's work it seems to be possible, but he works in a totally different way."

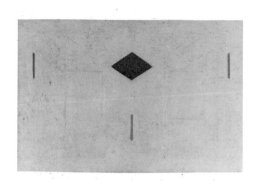

42. Bart van der Leck
Composition, 1919
oil on canvas
13¾ x 20½
34.9 x 52
Private collection

Mondrian was searching for a solution which would be more two-dimensional than the one van der Leck wished to achieve with his spatial flatness. Van der Leck creates an indeterminant space that nevertheless is suggestive and is determined by the edges of the image or by the format of the wall, because his work is always dominated by a concern with architecture. It is exactly this effect that Mondrian does not want. For Mondrian, the painting is the painting is the painting—without suggestions, without directions, but with an all-pervasive definition of order.

In 1917 van der Leck's work was the clearest and most principled painting De Stijl had to offer. Mondrian, van Doesburg and Huszar, each in his own way, were looking for similar solutions, but were at that time not able to come to such a monumental and cohesive statement. The recognizable images of the *Donkey Riders* did point to the fact that van der Leck worked in a unique way, but van Doesburg also made several paintings in 1917 that were directly derived from reality and in which a certain naturalism was maintained (his *Composition IX, The Cardplayers* (fig. 131), for example). Reality as the source of fundamental ideas still meant so much to Mondrian at that time that he could accept the *Donkey Riders*. But his search for the absolute, the elementary, the universal, subsequently led him to banish every possible reference to reality by using a grid as a basic structure. This meant that he made everything "fixed" again; for van der Leck this was an unthinkable step—representation can no longer be presumed and the spatial flatness is lost.

During that time a great deal of attention was given to problems such as the static versus the dynamic, the oblique versus the straight, the rectangular versus the rectilinear. About the latter, Mondrian wrote to van Doesburg: "I read my essay to van der Leck; he is against rectangular closing of color and wanted it changed to rectilinear. But my convictions don't allow that and therefore I wanted to leave it the way I had written it." For Mondrian, the rectangular position of lines and planes was the only possible equilibrium for imagery. Van der Leck, on the other hand, obeyed no rules but took the position that he would be directed by what he learned from reality. Rectilinear was a sufficient directive for him. Oblique lines were introduced into compositions by van der Leck as a way to activate spatial flatness, to introduce an element of movement. For him, this had nothing to do with perspective, but with spatial tension or, as van Doesburg put it—architectonically—with support and load. Mondrian discussed the subject in a letter to van Doesburg: "I also agree with you about the oblique line, as soon as it appears in combination with the straight I disapprove of it." Nevertheless, Mondrian himself had started to make diamond-shaped paintings, but he explained that this was a way to show the rectangular shape more organically and to its full advantage. Late in 1918, the first manifesto of De Stijl was published. Without giving a reason, van der Leck had refused to sign it.

Increasingly, points of view within De Stijl began to diverge and it was felt that van der Leck did not really belong. In spite of this, van der Leck thought it important to maintain a good relationship with Mondrian to whom he was devoted as artist and as friend. He also had become friendly with Robert van 't Hoff, the only architect of De Stijl with whom he felt any affinity. Van der Leck had little contact with Oud, Rietveld and Wils in this period. He was not in favor of collaboration with architects in the context of De Stijl and he disapproved of the fact that the architects wanted to apply color to their architecture. Huszar was too much a follower of van Doesburg to be able to gain van der Leck's confidence. In van der Leck's eyes, van Doesburg became more and more the intellectual opportunist who took over ideas from others. Van der Leck saw van Doesburg as a propagandist who assailed him with theories, with requests for articles and photographs and with invitations for exhibitions. Van der Leck had very strict ideas about exhibiting his work. He was willing to show, but only if it was his own one-man exhibition, or a group exhibition where only new art was shown. Consequently, van der Leck declined almost all invitations to exhibit his work and after a while people stopped asking. Van Doesburg, on the other hand, took every opportunity—whatever the context—to show new art.

Against the background of what happened to and around van der Leck in the first half of 1917, his refusal to sign the first manifesto of De Stijl becomes more understandable. He had said what he had to say; in the manifesto there was little that affected him personally, little of real importance to him, and by this time he wasn't eager to belong to the group. Sometime after the publication of the manifesto, he wrote van Doesburg a note:

> There is, as far as I am concerned, no question of estrangement from De Stijl and I wish you would consider my not signing the manifesto as an isolated event. As far as exhibitions are concerned, which you talk about in your last letter, I have to—regretfully—tell you I cannot participate. First of all because I already have a better idea about what to do with my new work and secondly because my convictions do not allow me to exhibit in the way you describe in your letter.

It can be deduced from a letter Mondrian wrote to van Doesburg that this attitude cost van der Leck his close relationship with Mondrian:

> I don't talk to van der Leck about this business; after his refusal without explanation to sign the manifesto I don't want to mention

43. Bart van der Leck
Horseman, 1918
oil on canvas
37 x 15¾
94 x 40
Collection Rijksmuseum Kröller-Müller

it anymore. He seems to find that a bit strange—during my last visit I talked about general matters but did not bring up this subject and when I left he mentioned he had received a letter from van Doesburg. My answer was that he should answer it if he wanted to but that I did not want to discuss it until he was ready to supply his explanations and ideas on the new art. He said very kindly that he would do that one day and since then I haven't heard a thing about it—we see each other as friends once in a while.

Of course, the explanation never came. Van der Leck did not wish to explain himself. After a long, lonely struggle that went on for years, van der Leck made contact with like-minded artists and his ideas were appreciated. Mondrian had done a great deal for him, as had he for Mondrian. To van Doesburg and Huszar, van der Leck's work was, in the beginning, a pure example of the principles of new art. Van der Leck had welcomed enthusiastically the idea to collectively agitate for the new art, but his growing dislike of van Doesburg, the adroit initiator and organizer, impeded his active participation.

During 1916-17, van der Leck's part in the development of De Stijl was clear and fundamental, to himself as well as to the others. He was the painter who first used primary color in spatial flatness; he developed the neoplastic idea and incorporated it in a consistent way in his own style. For him, geometry was the logical conclusion to his search for elementary design. However, he did not want to go any further. Through everything, despite the theories with which he was assailed, he remained a realist. He did not wish to engage in speculative mathematical systems, or to limit himself to rectangular form. He did not want to be limited to the horizontal and vertical, but to include the diagonal. He wanted to paint spatial flatness but did not choose to describe exclusively two-dimensional space. Movement into space, the fourth dimension, was important to his painting. Basically, he was not interested in theories; he clung tenaciously to his own naïveté and remained a realist. Nevertheless, in 1918, under the pressure of circumstances, he attempted to reconcile his views with a strictly non-figurative approach to painting. For the first time, he made a series of works that were not based in reality. In these images the composition is always centered, with a strong emphasis on diagonals and accents in the four corners. Within that context, there is a search for free arrangement, in which diamond shapes play a striking role (fig. 42). Sometimes stripes appear next to blocks. The few studies for these paintings that have survived show how order and equilibrium are achieved through shifting formal elements around in the space without the use of any kind of grid structure. Though these paintings are non-figurative, they do not conform in any way to the principles defined by Mondrian and van Doesburg. Even while making this gesture to his fellow artists, van der Leck retained his individuality;

he provided a personal solution with its own validity. It seems that van der Leck used these paintings as study material for his architectural ideas. Notably, the diamond shape appears from that time on in his interior designs. Also, variations on these compositions were later used as patterns for carpets and tapestries.

In the last months of 1918, he returned to realism. There was no searching for a subject to be hidden by extreme abstraction; reality is right there, in simple, ordinary, human themes. He painted *The Horseman* as a manifesto, as a celebration of his convictions. What he had gained from his non-figurative explorations was a greater freedom of imagery. The rigid geometry of 1917 was mitigated and modified, and mathematics and reality were fused into a unity. He had found his style and he would maintain it for 40 years.

The mathematical image and realism had become interchangeable aspects of his work. At the point where his painting merged with reality, reality could slip from his painting. This was the essence of his conception and it is where he differed from Mondrian, van Doesburg and Huszar. They saw the interior as an environment to be "plasticized" in the absolute sense, or as Hans Jaffé put it: "It is a conception, which, after all, is typical of De Stijl; to give a definite shape to an interior without leaving anything to chance or to individual temperament."

In June of 1918, van der Leck moved from Laren to Blaricum, where he had designed and built a house in collaboration with his brother Willem—a contractor and architect. On the exterior, this small brick house with thatched roof looks almost like a Blaricum farmhouse. Inside, there are a number of very small, intimate spaces, quite a large studio with beautiful proportions and many restful unbroken white walls. Its simple, but ingenious details of construction are reminiscent of the architect P.J.C. Klaarhamer. There is no reflection of De Stijl in this house; it reflects only the personal way in which van der Leck used light, color and space. He lived there until his death in 1958.

Visiting van der Leck's house in Blaricum today—where the interior is practically unchanged—one sees a white volume with a few accents of primary color. One studio wall is empty; *The Horseman* lithograph hangs on another wall. Van der Leck remained true to himself. He had retained his openness and maintained his contact with life, which in his work perished and then rose again in a binding way. He remained a primitive of the new time.

Rudolf W.D. Oxenaar is Director of the Rijksmuseum Kröller-Müller, Otterlo, The Netherlands.

Translation by Carla van Spluntren

Mondrian's Paris Atelier

44. Entrance to Mondrian's atelier, Rue du Depart, 1926. According to Mondrian's biographer, Michel Seuphor, the round vase on the hall table always held a single artificial tulip, its leaves painted white to remove the color green he had banished from the studio.
Vintage photograph by André Kertész

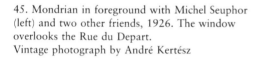

45. Mondrian in foreground with Michel Seuphor (left) and two other friends, 1926. The window overlooks the Rue du Depart.
Vintage photograph by André Kertész

Although Mondrian remained committed to easel painting, insisting to van Doesburg that his paintings were independent of their surroundings, and "not a part of a building," he also believed that Neoplasticism heralded the end of painting as an independent art: "The abstract-real (or neoplastic) picture will disappear as soon as we transfer its plastic beauty to the space around us through the organization of the room into color areas." Thus, sometime in the early 1920s, Mondrian began to transform his studio into a neoplastic work of art by attaching to the walls movable planes of primary colors, along with others that were white, gray and black. Color planes were also occasionally applied to the furniture, which was carefully arranged

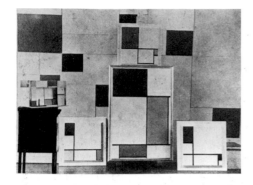

46. This picture includes: Mondrian's model for the Seuphor play, *L'Ephémère est Eternel* (on table, left); *Composition with Red and Blue*, 1929 (Stedelijk Museum, Amsterdam); *Composition with Yellow and Blue*, 1929 (Museum Boymans-van Beuningen); *Composition with Red, Blue and Yellow*, 1929 (Sidney Janis Gallery); *Composition*, 1929 (Kunstmuseum Basel).
Vintage photograph

47. Piet Mondrian, circa 1930
Vintage photograph

so as not to compromise the overall composition.

In part, Mondrian's motivation for treating his studio as a neoplastic environment was a desire to create a "sanctuary," in which the surroundings would reflect the principles of order and harmony he sought to realize in all aspects of his life. But the studio also served a more practical function: it was used as an area where Mondrian received visitors who wished to see his paintings. Conceived as an exhibition space, the studio provided an environment whose organization manifested—and consequently reinforced—the intent of his paintings.

> As my painting is an abstract surrogate of the whole, so the abstract-plastic wall takes part in the profound content that is implicit in the whole room. Instead of being superficially decorative, the entire wall gives the impression of the objective, universal, spiritual condition that comes to the fore in the most severe style forms.

Another aspect of the interplay between painting and environment is evident in the notion of "extension" that many critics attribute to Mondrian's work. According to this idea, the black bands that divide Mondrian's canvases not only define the area of the rectangular color planes, but also imply infinite extension beyond the borders of the canvas. The neoplastic picture, then—though autonomous by virtue of the harmonic combination of all its parts—is understood as representing a greater reality, a materialization of the invisible principles that underlie the essential order of the universe. This idea of extension would seem to be supported by photographs showing several paintings on display that virtually disappear into the surroundings, subsumed into the overall abstract environment.

Reflecting on a 1930 visit he made to Mondrian's Paris studio, Alexander Calder remembered:

> It was a very exciting room. Light came in from the left and from the right,

82

48. Here Mondrian's easel is placed against a wall of variously colored and sized rectangles in such a way that the painting on the easel becomes an integral part of the wall pattern. The artist's indispensable companion—his record player—is close at hand.
Vintage photograph, circa 1931

49, 50. Two views of the atelier in 1926. Among the paintings in the lower photograph: *Composition in Gray, Red, Yellow and Blue*, 1920 (Tate Gallery) hangs over the doorway; and above the stove, *Pier and Ocean*, 1914 (fig. 11). Vintage photographs

and on the solid wall between the windows there were experimental stunts, with colored rectangles of cardboard tacked on. Even the victrola, which had been some muddy color, was painted red.

I suggested to Mondrian that perhaps it would be fun to make these rectangles oscillate. And he, with a very serious countenance, said:

'No, it is not necessary, my painting is already very fast.' This visit gave me a shock.... This one visit gave me a shock that started things.

Mondrian's treatment of his studio as a work of art in itself underscores the depth of his commitment to the neoplastic ideal. There, removed from the demands of everyday life, he could retreat into his private world and dream of the utopian future, of the day when the whole environment would be transformed according to neoplastic principles.

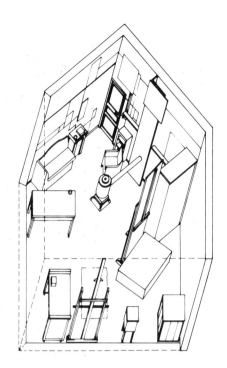

51. All existing evidence suggests that Mondrian's Rue du Depart atelier was irregularly shaped. (The room is drawn after a diagram by Nancy J. Troy.) This bird's-eye view indicates the probable placement of the furnishings based on analysis of the photographs included here. Two easels were used to display paintings against a changing background of colored rectangles. From the door (top, right) moving clockwise: wicker chair, stove, clothes closet and easel, placed to obscure bed and crate for storage (a high window, not drawn, overlooked the courtyard); continuing around the room, the work table on which Mondrian made his paintings (a large window above this table looked out on the Rue du Depart); and finally a couch and another small table.

52. Mondrian's glasses and pipe.
Vintage photograph by André Kertész, 1926

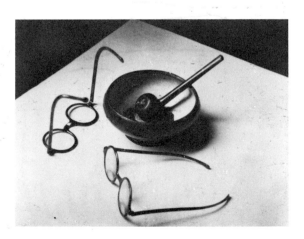

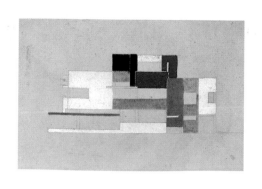

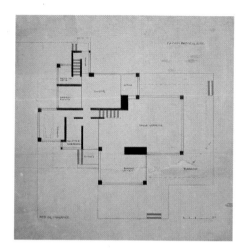

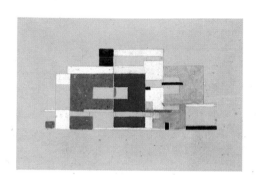

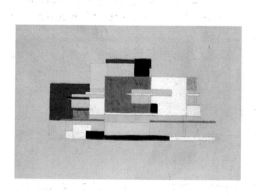

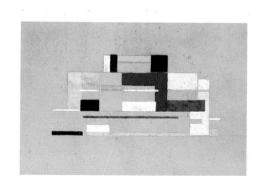

86

De Stijl/Architecture = Nieuwe Beelding

Sergio Polano to mbC

The complex ideology of De Stijl encompasses a series of insoluble tensions: the movement attempts to reconcile chaos and order, destruction and construction, abstraction (from the particular of nature to the universal of the inner self) and transformation (from abstract language into collective behavior). The tragic, which has held sway over nature and life itself since the loss of an original golden equilibrium between the individual and the universal, must, in fact, resolve its painful conflict in the death of art. Art will achieve its destiny in the aestheticization of the environment and the transformation of metropolitan life into art.

The artist's task, within De Stijl, is to produce metaphorical images that foreshadow the dissolution of art into the new harmony. Therefore, the artist will limit his language to the creation of a balanced composition of pure geometrical *signs:* this will enable him to represent the opposing tensions that generate tragedy. Consequently, in all of the movement's mature pictorial production, one finds surfaces that are not concluded within a painting, lines cut off at the margins, a hint of the unfinished within the perfectly defined. Thus painting projects itself into space (and time), pointing beyond its own two-dimensional confines. Here ambiguity arises. The work of art contains a fragment of the invisible—but real, since it can be represented—order of the world; at the same time, it seeks to impose order on a world that is perceived as fragmentary. De Stijl exists in an uncertain space, in a space that extends from the metropolis of its origins to the metropolis of its destination. It is no coincidence that the ideology of De Stijl betrays its ineffectuality in an "architecture" that is the catalyst for the sublimation of art into a higher unity, into a resolution of the *tragic.* Architecture for De Stijl turns out to be a tantalic objective: the greater the efforts to achieve it, the more elusive it becomes.

Therefore, a De Stijl architecture does *not exist.*

53. Cornelis van Eesteren/Theo van Doesburg
Ground floor plan (rez de chausée) and four elevations, Maison Particulière, 1922
ink, watercolor on tracing paper
Collection Nederlands Documentatiecentrum voor de Bouwkunst, Stichting Architectuurmuseum
(not in exhibition)

54. Cornelis van Eesteren/Theo van Doesburg
Axonometric drawing, Maison Particulière, 1923
pencil, watercolor on tracing paper
Collection Nederlands Documentatiecentrum voor de Bouwkunst, Stichting Architectuurmuseum
(not in exhibition)

87

This statement may not seem paradoxical in view of what we have already said. But it must be carefully qualified if we are to avoid the generality of an absolute—and thus perfectly symmetrical—negation.

First of all, a De Stijl architecture does not exist just as, for example, an expressionist or a functionalist or a modernist architecture does not exist; the examples could obviously be multiplied. Historical analysis shows that such threadbare labels do not adequately reflect the facts in all their complexity. If they are to be applied, the facts must be compressed and unified and essential distinctions must be suppressed. Labels reflect constellations of events, like warped mirrors: ideology speaks through the distortions and visions are produced that express historical constructs that all attempts at interpretation must take into account.

In the second place, as we have already seen, De Stijl is inexorably attracted to architecture, to the metropolis. This is apparent in a series of writings that we can interpret *a posteriori* as a kind of *theory* of architecture, developed gradually, by fits and starts. We would be contradicting our own premises were we to attempt to reconstruct from these writings a *true* architectural theory of De Stijl; it is not our intention to establish an orthodoxy of Neoplasticism by justifying the spurious elements and the lacunae that we encounter in De Stijl texts. On the other hand, to single out the gaps in what we have called a De Stijl "theory of architecture" would be a facile undertaking and would serve no historical purpose. Interpretative hypotheses such as ours must be judged according to their historical productiveness.

In the third place—and this is the most obvious and, at the same time, the most important point—our analysis becomes clearer and simpler if instead of "architecture" we speak of "architects" in the largest sense of the word: that is, of "operators." In other words, we shall turn our attention from a term whose meaning, for De Stijl, is indefinite and changeable, and concentrate on works by members of the group. Only by so doing can we assess the translatability into projects of what we hold to be an architectural theory, albeit an incomplete, ephemeral, and retrospectively reconstructed one. And, by so doing, we can also verify the historical utility of our hypothesis.

Let us examine in greater depth the theory and work of the architects themselves. The architectural theory of De Stijl was formed through the accumulation, over a ten-year period, of diversified contributions to the journal *De Stijl*, a publication that remained inextricably tied to the personality of Theo van Doesburg throughout its existence. One fundamental fact must be clear from the beginning: the essentially pictorial ideas of Neoplasticism were at the very core of De Stijl. With painting as their starting point, the theorists of De Stijl assaulted, by extrapolation, the other areas of art—such as architecture—with a logic that aped the scientific process. This led van Doesburg onto the marshy terrain of four-dimensionality. The centrality of van Doesburg's role in the movement is another fundamental fact. The dynamic element that he brought to the journal in 1917 was the confrontation that he had originated and maintained, as part of his militancy as a critic, with Mondrian, van der Leck, Huszar, Oud, Wils and the other early members of the group between 1915 and 1917. The discussion centered around the definition of monumental art: art as *gesamtkunstwerk*, an idea that in itself was not new at that time and in that place. In 1916, van Doesburg wrote:

> When everything has been expressed on the present level of painting, new aesthetic potential will emerge therefrom for extending the scope of expressive possibilities. In this way the human spirit will be elevated to a new level. Not applied art, but a monumental cooperative art is what the future holds. In this new form, various spiritual means of expression (architecture, sculpture, painting, music and literature) will be universally realized—i.e., each will be enhanced by collaboration with the others.[1]

In other words, as van Doesburg announced in a lecture in 1916, anticipating the space/time theme:

> The visual artist *orders, multiplies, measures* and *determines* congruences and proportions of forms and colors and their relations to space. For the artist, every object has a particular relationship to space; it is an image of space. The artist derives his repertoire of color and form from a certain number of objects. With a constantly changing spatial scheme, with a moving object, a space-time framework is generated. It is the visual artist's function to amalgamate these into a harmonious, melodious unity. I believe that the same holds for architecture and that the modern painter, sculptor and architect find each other in this visual consciousness, with only this difference: architecture has to cater not only to spiritual, but also to material needs.[2]

In fact, all of the architectural theorizing that can be culled from the texts published in *De Stijl* revolves around this concept of *architecture as the synthesis of the arts*.

In the first phase of the group's activity, from 1917 to 1920, the discussion did not go beyond the clarification of van Doesburg's notion of monumentalism, though one must not underestimate the contributions of single members of the group or their analyses of the thematic relationship between painting and architecture, between the "spiritual" and the "material" exigencies of architecture, and between architecture and the metropolis. Nevertheless, the principal task that the journal undertook, the dissemination of the monumentalist concept,

1. Theo van Doesburg, *De Nieuwe Beweging in de Schilderkunst* (Delft: Technische Boekhandel en Drukkerij, J. Waltman, Jr., 1917), pp 43-44. The essay, dated May-August 1916, was originally published under the same title as a series of articles in the journal *De Beweging* in 1916.
2. Theo van Doesburg, "Het Aestetisch Beginsel der Moderne Beeldende Kunst," in *Drie Voordrachten over de Nieuwe Beeldende Kunst* (Amsterdam: Maatschappij voor Goede en Goedkoope Lectuur, 1919), pp 45-46. The lecture, the second of the three that make up the volume, was delivered in Haarlem in 1916.

55. Theo van Doesburg
Countercomposition in Primary Colors for the
Maison d'Artiste, 1923
pencil, gouache, crayon on tracing paper
14⅛ x 15
35.9 x 38
Dienst Verspreide Rijkskollekties

3. [For a further discussion of collaboration
among De Stijl painters and architects, see Troy,
pp 165-189.]
4. Theo van Doesburg and Cornelis van Eesteren,
" −□+ =R₄," *De Stijl*, VI, 6/7, 1924, p 91.

finally ended in an impasse. Between 1917 and 1920, the attempt to translate this theoretical process, the monumental integration of the arts, into a *style*, to be achieved through collaboration with the architects in the group—an attempt that had its most fervent supporter in van Doesburg—led, in fact, to a breakdown in the relationship between the members and to thoroughly inconclusive results.[3]

By 1920, the original De Stijl group had almost completely disintegrated; not surprisingly, we find van Doesburg alone with *his* journal, ready to seek out greener pastures: Germany (or, to be exact, the Bauhaus) first, and later France. Thus begins the second phase of De Stijl, lasting from 1921 until 1928 and reaching its apex in 1923-24; after this apex comes a long decline, and not only with regard to architecture. Van Doesburg is, more plainly than ever, the only source of continuity, both for the journal and for the development of an architectural theory. During his years in Weimar, 1921-22, he succeeded in enlisting a number of the newer members of De Stijl for a "skirmish" with the Bauhaus, and in strengthening the group's international ties at the meetings of the International Congress of Progressive Artists in 1922. But his theory of architecture developed no further, and the results of courses he organized at Weimar in 1922, in open opposition to the Bauhaus, must have been meager. All that van Doesburg published were his students' models with a symptomatic caption: "Studies in pure plastic architecture."

Not until the "collective effort" on the famous architectural models for the exhibition at Léonce Rosenberg's Galerie L'Effort Moderne in Paris in 1923, did architecture again acquire a real importance in the pages of *De Stijl*. "Towards a Plastic Architecture" and " −□+ =R₄," the two manifestoes that van Doesburg published in 1924, constitute the high point of the theoretical elaboration of De Stijl's architecture. "Towards a Plastic Architecture," in particular, establishes a program based on precise linguistic references. It was the fruit of a collaborative effort on the part of van Doesburg and Cornelis van Eesteren, an architect, at last, open to "a collective construction." The text sets forth 16 axioms, announcing an architecture that is anti-cubic, anti-symmetrical, anti-gravitational and anti-decorative. In other words, it is a purely theoretical construct, incorporating the tensions implicit in Neoplasticism's unrealizable concept of architecture. Architecture is conceived as a synthesis of Neoplasticism. "In a collective enterprise," wrote van Doesburg and van Eesteren, ". . . we have examined *architecture as the plastic unity of all the arts . . .* and we have discovered that the result will constitute a new Style."[4]

The circle is closed. The name of the style of De Stijl, architecture, has been uttered. There is no going beyond.

90

Theo van Doesburg is the protagonist who maintains continuity in De Stijl. He is the animating force in both the journal and the movement; he demonstrates a constant and profound interest in architecture on both the theoretical and the practical levels. He writes about architecture a great deal, especially in periodicals. His judgments are often contradictory, but they are always consistent with his fundamental idea: architecture is a synthesis of all the arts. He assigns a primary role to color. He is not only the most prolific writer of the group where architecture is concerned; his ideas are also the most interesting.

Apart from theory, van Doesburg was active as a painter, as a designer, and, towards the end of his life, as an architect. From 1917-20, he worked out "color solutions" for buildings by Oud, Wils and C. R. de Boer (fig. 162). With little help from colleagues and with disappointing results, he attempted to integrate the arts, radicalizing the ideas of the painter Bart van der Leck, who had himself for some time been interested in the use of color in architecture. After his German period (1921-22), van Doesburg moved definitively to Paris in 1923: this marked the beginning of the critical phase of De Stijl architecture. In 1923 he worked with van Eesteren, developing architectural "models" to be shown in an exhibition (fig. 56). These models, on the one hand, constituted a *summa* of the architectural theory of De Stijl, coinciding with the 16 points of the manifesto published in the following year; on the other hand, they were the natural outgrowth of his experience as a painter. Thus they represent an "aesthetic transfiguration." With his counterconstructions (fig. 55), van Doesburg attempts to analyze and interpret these models, to evoke an architectural image. The counterconstructions are, in fact, pictorial reconstructions of van Eesteren's axonometric designs for their joint works, suggestions of space created by potential encounters of colored planes. These images, however, are so visually appealing in themselves that they could never be translated into the concrete dimensions of architecture. The introduction of the diagonal, which sums up the new definition of Neoplasticism that van Doesburg devised in 1924, in other words the Elementarism of his countercompositions, is the direct consequence of his collaboration with van Eesteren.

But van Doesburg's and van Eesteren's paths were soon to diverge. El Lissitzky declared in 1926 that van Doesburg had already betrayed architecture: "He says that it is a utility, not an art; he wants to be a *painter*."[5]

Paradoxically, it was in the same year, 1926, that van Doesburg was given the chance to execute a monumental work—the reconstruction of the interior of the Café Aubette in Strasbourg (figs. 169-182). He completed it in 1928, in collaboration with Sophie Taeuber-Arp and Jean

5. Letter from El Lissitzky to his wife, 30 January 1926, in *El Lissitzky* (Dresden: VEB Verlag der Kunst, 1967).

56. Cornelis van Eesteren and Theo van Doesburg (right) working on the model for the Maison Particulière, 1923.
Vintage photograph

57. Galerie L'Effort Moderne, Paris, 1923
Exhibition of De Stijl architecture
Vintage photograph

Represented in this landmark exhibition were: Theo van Doesburg, Cornelis van Eesteren, Vilmos Huszar, W. van Leusden, J.J.P. Oud, Gerrit Rietveld, Mies van der Rohe, Jan Wils and Piet Zwart. Many projects shown in the exhibition in drawings and model form were never realized, yet they have become icons of Modernism.

Seen in Salle I (clockwise from rear wall): floor plans and model for the Hotel Particulière by van Eesteren and van Doesburg (model executed by Rietveld); Oud's drawing for the Purmerend Factory and an unidentified model; model for Maison d'Artiste by van Eesteren and van Doesburg. Through the doorway at left: model and drawings for the Maison Particulière by van Eesteren and van Doesburg; and through the doorway at right: two drawings by Huszar and Zwart for the interiors of a women's residence in The Hague by Jan Wils; the model for Rietveld's G. & Z. C. jewelry shop, Amsterdam.

6. Theo van Doesburg, "Notices sur l'Aubette à Strasbourg," *De Stijl*, VIII, 87/89, 1928, p 8.
7. Theo van Doesburg, "Farben im Raum und Zeit," *De Stijl*, VIII, 87/89, 1928, p 36.
8. "Uit de Dagboeknotities van Theo van Doesburg," *De Stijl*, dernier numéro, 1932, p 20.

Arp. In reality, however, van Doesburg here disguised his inability to come to grips with space in practical terms by blowing up his countercompositions into gigantic murals. He turned the project into an exercise in environmental calligraphy, chromatically exalting in itself, and expressive of van Doesburg's true artistic nature. As he put it, he ". . . opposed an oblique, supra-material, and pictorial space" to the "material, three-dimensional room."[6] In other words:

> Architectural space must be considered a blind, absolute *void* until color turns it into something concrete. The spatio-temporal painting of the 20th century, with its plastic, structural possibilities, allows the artist to fulfill his dream: to place man, not *before* painting, but *inside* painting itself.[7]

The Aubette is therefore painting—or, more precisely, "being in a painting."

Other designs and projects executed between 1925 and 1930 are of little interest from our point of view, except as proof that the actual elaboration of the Parisian models should be attributed almost entirely to van Eesteren.

However, immediately after the Aubette (which was inaugurated simultaneously with the publication of van Doesburg's last issue of *De Stijl*), he arrived at a radical negation of the principles that had inspired his architectural theories. He noted in his diary on 1 May 1928, that ". . . architecture must be *neutral,* not *figurative;* in any case, it must do without pictorial means."[8]

In the last years of his life, van Doesburg finally did succeed in executing an architectural project: his own house at Meudon (fig. 58). But he died in 1931 without achieving the goal implicit in his multiform endeavors—architecture.

Piet Mondrian's relationship with van Doesburg between 1915 and 1924 was crucial for De Stijl and also for architecture, for Mondrian was the most rigorous, incorruptible theorist of the movement. His essays, in which the themes of architecture and the city are constantly present, are of extreme importance: in them, the ideals of Neoplasticism are completely realized. In 1922, expressing ideas he had already formulated during the previous decade, he wrote:

> Dominance of life's tragedy has come to an end. The 'artist' is immersed in an existence as a complete human being. The 'non-artist' is his equal: he is equally imbued with beauty. Talent will cause one person to occupy himself with aesthetics, another with science, a third with something else—as a 'profession;' each is an equivalent part of the total. Construction, sculpture, painting and crafts will then be merged

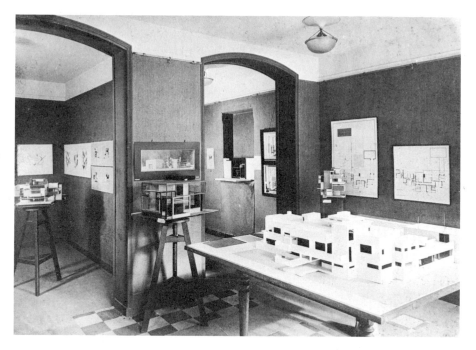

into architecture, i.e., into our environment. The arts of a less 'material' kind are realized in 'life.' Music (as art) then is finished: the beauty of the sounds around us—purified, categorized, brought to (a new) harmony—will then be enough. Literature as 'art' has also no reason for existence. It evolves into usefulness and beauty per se, without lyrical attire. Theatrical arts and dance can be dropped, along with the dominant embodiment of tragedy and harmony: life-movements are then harmonious in themselves.[9]

From the beginning, however, Mondrian was consistently cautious with regard to van Doesburg's theoretical impetuosity. In 1917 he wrote, in a letter to van Doesburg, "Please don't forget that my artistic productions are meant to be paintings—that is, autonomous figurative representations, not constituent parts of architecture."[10] His caution led him to avoid becoming directly involved, as for example in the case of the "fourth dimension." Again he wrote to van Doesburg:

> I'm extremely interested in your experiments with four-dimensionality, but I doubt if we can go very far towards representing it. We would have to develop another (new) sense, as I *think* occultism would have it.[11]

One conclusion may be drawn from the coloristic designs of van Doesburg, Mondrian, van der Leck and Huszar: the abstract colored environmental design of De Stijl is not, in itself, architecture. But there were several architects who made significant contributions to De Stijl's history.

9. Piet Mondrian, "De Realiseering van het Neoplasticisme in Verre Toekomst en in de Huidige Architectuur," *De Stijl*, V, 3, 1922, p 43, and 5, 1922, p 66.
10. Letter from Piet Mondrian to Theo van Doesburg, 13 February 1917, in *De Stijl* (Amsterdam: exh. cat. no. 81, Stedelijk Museum, 1951), p 72.
11. Letter from Piet Mondrian to Theo van Doesburg, 13 June 1918, quoted by Joost Baljeu in "De Vierde Dimensie," in *Theo van Doesburg 1883-1931* (Eindhoven: exh. cat., Stedelijk Van Abbemuseum, 1968), p 11.

J.J.P. Oud, an aloof master of contemporary architecture, worked in the De Stijl milieu in the years 1915-20. In 1918 he was made chief architect of Rotterdam and from that time on he kept his distance from the painters of the group. Like van der Leck, he did not sign De Stijl's first manifesto. The connection between Oud's work and De Stijl theories has been re-examined in recent years; on the whole, it seems limited to a debate over monumentalism, together with attempts at linguistic experiment (tempered by the fact that the group had not yet formulated precise views about architecture). Those of his projects that were published in De Stijl show that he was familiar with what he called "cubist decomposition" and with the architecture of Frank Lloyd Wright; the latter, which he sought to reconcile with European tradition, was one of the few points of reference common to all the early De Stijl architects. If these unexecuted projects strike us as uninteresting pastiches, the buildings that he constructed in Rotterdam during the same years are not much better in their excessive simplicity.

Oud's projects after his defection from De Stijl are highly personal in character, worked out in minute detail and executed with great care. They draw upon De Stijl's vocabulary, particularly in their refined (though parsimonious) use of primary colors; often the results are of very high quality. In a sense, Oud comes closest to De Stijl in his Café De Unie of 1925 (fig. 19). But here too, elements originating with De Stijl are combined with simplified, decorative elements that have their roots in the Amsterdam School. (What the two movements have in common has not, in fact, been examined sufficiently.)[12]

One of Oud's reasons for abandoning De Stijl was the impossibility of reconciling the uniqueness of the new style with the exigencies of mass housing. As he wrote to van Doesburg: "In the modern city we can be pure only in an isolated building. The facts impose an impure, but necessary solution."[13]

The central problem for Oud in his De Stijl years was the search for the "image of the monumental city." This, in fact, was the title of his first article in the journal, where he writes, in a manner reminiscent of Camillo Sitte, "Architecture is a plastic art, an art that models space; it finds its most general expression in the image of the city: in the individual building and in the conjunction and reciprocal opposition of many buildings."[14]

Oud's architectural projects from his De Stijl period are of limited interest, representing as they do an attempt to fuse extrapolations from Cubism with motifs borrowed from Wright's architecture and reminiscences of Berlage. But his written contributions are of considerable importance. Together with the recurrent theme of the

12. [The Amsterdam School of architecture whose primary practitioners were H.P. Berlage, J.M. van der Meij, Piet Kramer and Michel De Klerk, was an expressionist episode (1910-25) in Holland between Art Nouveau and Modernism.]
13. Letter from J.J.P. Oud to Theo van Doesburg, probably of 1920, in De Stijl, op. cit., p 80.
14. J.J.P. Oud, "Het Monumentale Stadsbeeld," De Stijl, I, 1, 1917, p 10.

"monumental style," he explores the "machine aesthetic," seeking to come to terms with the pressing issues of mass housing, and offering an original interpretation of Wright and of the artistic avant-gardes.

Despite the group's devotion to collective experimentation, Oud never permitted van Doesburg to contribute more to his projects than designs for details and "color solutions." He certainly never took up the challenge to "resolve architecture in color."

During the years in which he collaborated with Oud, van Doesburg also worked with Jan Wils. Here too he was given little opportunity to experiment with color in architecture. Wils's work during these years was professionally correct, dignified, and often interesting. As with Oud, his regard for Wright's architecture is evident, though it had little effect on the theorizing of De Stijl. His photographer's studio of 1921, however, was one of the first applications of the De Stijl vocabulary to interior decoration, though it was carried out rather mechanically. From 1919 on, Wils kept his distance from the group; he collaborated occasionally with the painter Vilmos Huszar. His contribution to the journal was negligible, and it cannot be said that he was one of the key figures in De Stijl.

Gerrit Rietveld was a cabinetmaker, like his father. This ingenious artisan of Dutch architecture attended an evening course given by the architect Pieter J. C. Klaarhamer where he became acquainted with van der Leck, through whom he later met some of the other De Stijl artists. Van Doesburg admired Rietveld's work as a designer (though he was more reticent about the Schröder house) and wrote a lyrical article about him in which he compared the red/blue chair of 1918 to a "slender spatial animal." Rietveld wrote next to nothing for *De Stijl*; we mention him here among the protagonists because his justly famous designs caused him to be considered, by many, the quintessential exponent of De Stijl. But here once again we must make the necessary distinctions. Rietveld produced his celebrated red/blue chair, which became the symbol of De Stijl design, *before* he entered the group. His case is thus similar to that of Robert van 't Hoff. Van 't Hoff's presence in the group was indubitably the result of two buildings that he constructed at Huis-ter-Heide in 1915-16 (again, before De Stijl existed), which are obvious paraphrases of Wright. He was made a member of De Stijl because van Doesburg wanted him there. Van Doesburg, in fact, published van 't Hoff's buildings—which really were novelties on the Dutch scene—as "architectural exemplars" for the studies that the group intended to carry out.

Rietveld's equally famous Schröder house in Utrecht, built in 1924, seemed to demonstrate that De Stijl's contemporaneous manifesto on

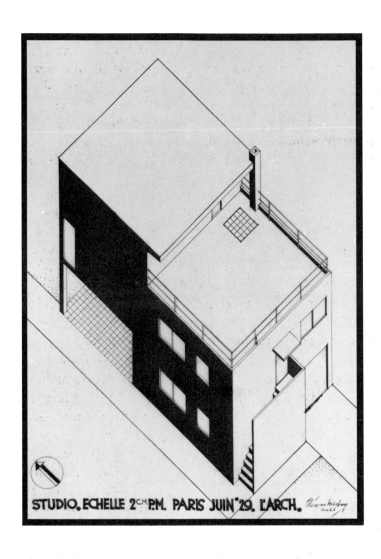

STUDIO. ECHELLE 2^{CM} P.M. PARIS JUIN °29. L'ARCH.

58. Theo van Doesburg
Axonometric drawing, Meudon house, 1929
ink on paper
22⅞ x 16⅛
58.1 x 41
Dienst Verspreide Rijkskollekties, on loan to the
Stedelijk Museum, Amsterdam

59, 60. Rear facade and interior views of Meudon
house, 1931.
Vintage photographs

This exterior view shows the steel studio windows
and the second floor raised on columns at the
building's edge. Clearly more Corbusian than De
Stijl in its final resolution, this simple house was
van Doesburg's only realized building.

Countercomposition VIII (fig. 6) is seen above a
built-in concrete table and the leather and
chrome-plated steel armchair, designed by van
Doesburg in 1929.

architecture could in fact be translated into actual buildings. But on closer scrutiny the Schröder house too turns out to be a fascinating but necessarily unique experiment; it justifies Oud's prophetic statement that ". . . we can be pure only in isolated buildings." It is, implicitly, the negation of the premises for the possible application of this *image* of architecture on an urban scale. This conclusion is confirmed by the ambiguous impression that it is not a building, but a model blown up for experimental purposes.

Cornelis van Eesteren is an extraordinary, insufficiently known figure who must be credited with at least two important achievements. First of all, it was van Eesteren who made possible De Stijl's most significant venture into architectural theory by providing the designs that van Doesburg used in drafting the manifestoes of 1924. It is probable that the conception and execution of the architectural models of 1923 should be attributed to van Eesteren, though they would hardly have had the same importance and influence without van Doesburg, who had the ability to formulate their theoretical implications. Van Eesteren wrote to van Doesburg, "You're more of a writer than I am, so it's logical that you should put together an article like this. But it's the other way round when we come to architecture: I'm more of an architect than you are, so it's logical that I should take care of the architecture."[15] It should be recognized especially that it was van Eesteren who, during this period, made axonometry the classical instrument of modern representation of architecture. Second, it was van Eesteren who soon came to understand that De Stijl had set out on a one-way street, and who then set out himself in the opposite direction.

Van Eesteren was to draft the Expansion Plan of Amsterdam in 1934 and was to play a major role in the C.I.A.M.[16] In brief, he is a major figure in contemporary architecture and town planning.

15. Letter from Cornelis van Eesteren to Theo van Doesburg, 15 August 1924, quoted by Jan Leering in "De Architectuur en van Doesburg," in *Theo van Doesburg 1883-1931, op. cit.,* p 23.
16. The C.I.A.M. (International Congress of Modern Architecture) was an organization that included 24 European architects at its founding in 1928.

Sergio Polano is on the faculty of the Institute of Critical and Historical Analysis, Venice, Italy.

Translation by John Daley

Architecture :

Neoplasticism and

Formation and Transformation

Kenneth Frampton

We tend to underestimate the seminal role played by American culture in European avant-garde art during the first quarter of the 20th century. This influence was never more intense than in the case of Frank Lloyd Wright whose formative impact after the Wasmuth publication of his work in 1910 was both immediate and extensive. Wright's catalytic import at the turn of the century is evident from H.P. Berlage's address, *New American Architecture,* given in 1912, soon after his return from a trip to the United States. That Wright's concept of spatial continuity was to make a deep impression on Berlage's sensibility is clear from the latter's account of the Martin house in Buffalo (fig. 62):

> The ground floor lends itself to an organization in extended horizontal sequence since all the rooms open into each other and are also connected by long corridors. The Americans do not like to separate living areas with doors. . . . As a result, the interior affords beautiful views, not only from room to room, but also from rooms into the halls, toward the staircase and so on. These effects are heightened because the Americans are adept at decorating their houses with objects of art. Americans are fond of books as well, and often have shoulder high bookshelves along the walls. . . . I had the impression of an extraordinary intimacy, and only with great effort could I tear myself away from these rooms. The originality of the rooms can be best described by the word 'plastic'—in contrast to European interiors which are flat and two dimensional.[1]

It is curious that Berlage's use of the term "plastic" should coincide with a similar coinage made by Dr. M.H.J. Schoenmaekers in *The New Image of the World,* a text that was published in 1915 and was later the source of Piet Mondrian's Neoplasticism in his essay "Neoplasticism in Painting," which appeared in the first issue of *De Stijl.*[2] It is equally significant that the other name for Neoplasticism—De Stijl— had its origin in Berlage's essay "Thoughts on Style in Architecture" of 1905.

The Dutch origins of De Stijl and Neoplasticism—(the first as a polemic and the second as a cultural concept) do not detract from Wright's

61. Jan Wils
Perspective drawing of Daal en Berg housing estate at Papaverhof, The Hague, 1920
ink on paper
8½ x 11⅝
21.6 x 29.5
Collection Nederlands Documentatiecentrum voor de Bouwkunst, Stichting Architectuurmuseum

62. Frank Lloyd Wright
Darwin D. Martin house, Buffalo, New York, 1904
Living room
Vintage photograph

1. H.P. Berlage, "Neurere Amerikanische Architektur," *Schweizerische Bauzeitung,* Zurich, vol LX, nos. 11 and 12, 14-21 Sept. 1912. For English trans. see D. Gifford, ed. *The Literature of Architecture* (New York: E.P. Dutton, 1966, pp 611, 612).
2. *De Stijl,* I, 1 (1917), pp 2-6.

decisive influence in determining the spatial and tectonic essence of neoplastic architecture and it is one of the characteristics of the early years of De Stijl that those architects who were closely associated with the movement remained for the most part neo-Wrightian, rather than neoplastic. This phenomenon manifests itself most clearly perhaps in the work of Robert van 't Hoff and Jan Wils, who while they were signatories of the first De Stijl manifesto of 1918, continued nonetheless to practice in a manner that was close to Wright. This Wrightian propensity is comprehensible in the case of van 't Hoff who had worked for Wright in the States in 1913 and who on returning to Holland immediately built a Wrightian summer house in Huis-ter-Heide, near Utrecht. This work was followed in 1916 by van 't Hoff's flat-roofed, concrete villa, also erected at Huis-ter-Heide (fig. 64); an exemplary proto-neoplastic work, this house served as the context for Rietveld's earliest attempts at the red/blue chair which he finally produced in 1918. This rather abstract house, finished in white stucco, shows the extent to which van 't Hoff was willing to depart from the Wrightian syntax.

The same cannot be said for Jan Wils whose neo-Wrightian manner is fully in place by the time his brick-clad, pitched-roofed De Dubbele Sleutel restaurant is built at Woerden in 1918 and his style is only marginally more abstract two years later, when he designs the Daal en Berg housing estate, built at Papaverhof in The Hague (fig. 61). It is clear that these counterpointed relief compositions in brick were far removed from the centrifugal spatiality that was to become the touchstone of De Stijl, and while one has to acknowledge the neoplastic influence on Wils, only the more superficial aspects of the style were finally accepted by the neo-Berlagian school that included such architects as Willem M. Dudok and Johannes Duiker.

Among the professional architects who were associated with De Stijl, J.J.P. Oud was surely the most enigmatic. Steeped in the Dutch brick tradition as this had been developed by Berlage, Oud, while aware that a stylistic break was imminent, not only resisted the influence of the Prairie Style in its pure form but also refused to enter into its neoplastic abstraction. This is evident in his 1917 apartment complex for Strandboulevard published in the very first issue of De Stijl. It is surely this traditionalism that imparts to Oud's ostensibly neoplastic work such an unconvincing air, for all that his theoretical position was influenced by the thought and work of Wright. This much is clear from his statement about Wright's Hull House lecture, The Art and Craft of the Machine of 1901, published as "Art and Machine" in 1918.[3] And something similar is apparent from his enthusiastic appraisal of Wright's Robie house published in the next issue:

3. De Stijl, I, 3 (1918), pp 25-27.

Wright has laid the basis of a new plasticism in architecture. The masses shoot about in all directions, forwards, backwards, to right, to left. In the interpenetration of planes the way has been cleared for the new plasticism and a pure and constructive foundation prepared for new aesthetic possibilities in architecture. This is a good deal greater and more modern than anything that our own modern architecture, the so called Amsterdam school, has achieved with its methods of detailing.[4]

The most decisive evidence of Oud's caution with regard to avant-gardism is the "De Vonk" vacation house (fig. 66), built at Noordwijkerhout in 1917, from designs elaborated in collaboration with van Doesburg whom Oud had met in the previous year. The absolutely symmetrical pitched-roofed *parti* of De Vonk is surely derived from the work of Granpré Molière, whose Tuindorp Vreewijk garden city in Rotterdam was already under construction by 1916. And it was the traditionalist Granpré Molière who was to be the primary influence on all of Oud's built work until he converted to the *Neue Sachlichkeit* ethic in his Hook of Holland housing estate built in Rotterdam in 1924. The insistently tripartite symmetrical rhythms displayed in the various housing schemes built by Oud, as city architect to Rotterdam between 1918 and 1922—the extensive Spangen and Tuschendyken layouts of those years and the Oud-Mathenesee estate of 1922—are all erected under the sign of Granpré Molière's traditionalism. The singular exception to this was the interior of De Vonk, particularly the main stair which was obviously elaborated by van Doesburg (fig. 68). Occasionally Oud flirted with cryptic motifs drawn from the theosophical works of J.L.M. Lauweriks and Adolf Meyer, as in the temporary builder's hut, erected at Oud-Mathenesee in 1923 or parts of the facade that he created for the Café De Unie built in Rotterdam in 1925, but in the main he seems to have remained unconvinced by any kind of avant-gardist discourse. It appears that he regarded it as a form more suitable for what Vantongerloo called the destructive aims of painting rather than for the constructive necessities of architecture. This distinction had first been advanced by the painter Bart van der Leck in the inaugural issue of *De Stijl*, wherein he declared: "Modern painting is destruction of naturalistic plastic expression in contrast to the plastic naturalistic constructional character of architecture" and ". . . modern painting is plastic expression in spatial flatness: extension, in contrast to the space-restricting flatness of architecture."[5]

The important role played by the Hungarian emigré Vilmos Huszar has never been adequately accounted for and yet it is clear that he was prominent in the early days of the movement, for not only did he design the logo used for the cover of *De Stijl* during the first three years of its publication, but he also featured prominently in its initial polemic, both as painter and theorist. Thus we find his *Hammer and Saw* (fig. 23)

4. *De Stijl*, I, 4 (1918), pp 63-65.
5. *De Stijl*, I, 1 (1917), pp 6-7.

composition appearing in color in the third issue of the journal, while his long serial essay entitled "Aesthetical Exposition" was published intermittently throughout this period. The cause of his withdrawal from the journal in the following year is unclear as is his reemergence in the fourth volume of *De Stijl*, edited out of Weimar by van Doesburg in 1921. That he was still avant-gardist is apparent from the electro-mechanical, kinetic theatrical piece that he depicted as being played by neoplastic robots before a mobile neoplastic set—his so-called *Form Spectacle* of 1920-21 (fig. 69). This work was in advance of its time, and it seems to have influenced El Lissitzky's *Victory Over the Sun* designs published in Hannover in 1923. Lissitzky's electro-mechanical spectacle was intended to be a reworking of Kazimir Malevich's designs for Alexi Kruchenykh's cubo-futurist play, *Victory Over the Sun,* first performed in 1913. While Lissitzky's figures of 1923 were hardly neoplastic, the same cannot be said for Kurt Schmidt's *Mechanical Ballet* first performed in the Bauhaus in the same year, or for the figures employed in Schmidt's *Man and Machine* and *The Adventures of the Little Hunchback* (fig. 70), both of which were staged in 1924. The mechanical marionettes featured in this last piece were uncannily close to Huszar's *Form and Spectacle* automatons of three years before. Apart from its influence, *Form and Spectacle* demonstrated Huszar's preoccupation with the use of large-scale neoplastic devices in the restructuring of interior space—an approach which he had first attempted in the decoration of the Bruynzeel apartment built in The Hague in 1917. He carried this approach a stage further in an interior that he realized in collaboration with Jan Wils in 1921 and in a dining room color study projected in the same year (fig. 71).

That the Dutch furniture maker Gerrit Rietveld was moving in a similar direction is clear from the neoplastic interior that he designed for Dr. A.M. Hartog in Maarssen in 1920 and by the G. & Z. C. jewelry shop front and interior that he realized in Amsterdam in 1922. A fruitful collaboration between these seminal artists came with their exhibition room designed for the Greater Berlin Art Exhibition of 1923, a neoplastic set piece for which Rietveld designed his famous "gray on gray" asymmetrical Berlin chair (fig. 89).

Rietveld's importance to the evolution of Neoplasticism is by now well known although it is important to note how he enters only reluctantly into the polemic—first with a short note accompanying the publication of his Mackintosh-like child's chair and in the later publication of the 1917 version of his canonical red/blue chair, accompanied by a brief caption written by van Doesburg.[6]

The red/blue chair, designed in 1917 but painted somewhat later is, in its final form, the first attempt at a dematerialized, neoplastic

6. *De Stijl*, II, 9 (1919), pp 102-103; *De Stijl*, II, 11 (1919), pp 134-135.

architecture. Through their apparent translucence, the lightly stained wooden surfaces of the orthogonal spars serve to suggest the literal suspension of the primary colored planes that lie cradled within its matrix: that is to say, the seat, the back and the ends of the spars which are rendered throughout in glossy enamel (fig. 84). It is pertinent to note that this use of primary color was probably in advance of the appearance of saturated primaries in the painting of Mondrian and van Doesburg.

At the end of 1923 Rietveld began to collaborate with Madame Truus Schröder-Schräder on the design of the Schröder house, completed in Utrecht in 1924 (fig. 94). This house was in many respects an exemplary demonstration of Theo van Doesburg's "Towards a Plastic Architecture," published in *De Stijl* at the time of its completion. Rietveld and Madame Schröder thus fulfilled van Doesburg's demand that neoplastic architecture should be *elementary, economic, functional, formless* and *unmonumental,* that is, points two to six of his 16 points first published in 1924.[7] Where point seven argued that the new architecture was *dynamic* and knew no passive moment, point eight went on to demonstrate how Neoplasticism intended the exfoliation of Wright's pinwheeling plan. To this end van Doesburg wrote:

> The new architecture has broken through *the wall* and in so doing has completely eliminated the *divorce* of *inside* and *out. The walls are non-load bearing;* they are reduced to points of support. And as a result there is generated a new open plan, totally different from the classic because inside and outside space interpenetrate.

The transformable plan of the second floor of the Rietveld/Schröder house with its sliding-folding walls was celebrated in points nine and ten of the manifesto while point eleven reads:

> The new architecture is *anti-cubic,* that is to say, it does not try to freeze the different functional space cells in one closed cube. Rather, *it throws the functional space cells* (as well as overhanging planes, balcony volumes, etc.) centrifugally from the *core of the cube*. And through this means height, width, depth and time approach a totally new plastic expansion in open spaces. In this way architecture gets (insofar as is possible from a constructional point of view—the task of the engineers!) a more or less floating aspect that, so to speak, works against the gravitational forces of nature.

This last point, followed by further riders insisting on *asymmetry, afrontality* and the *anti-decorative* integration of color as an instrument of spatial displacement, was to condense in absolute terms the essence of a de-materialized neoplastic architecture. Nothing now remained but to realize this architecture in actual space, as in the Rietveld/Schröder house, or otherwise to project its realization in more audacious terms as in the van Eesteren/van Doesburg "counterconstructions," dating from

7. *De Stijl*, VI, 6/7 (1924), pp 78-83.

103

63, 64. Robert van 't Hoff
Henny house at Huis-ter-Heide, 1916
Exterior and interior views
1981 photographs

(facing page)
65. Robert van 't Hoff
Interior grilles for Henny house, 1916
1981 photograph

Originally used to screen radiators, these metal
grilles are now used as decorative cabinet doors.
Raised, circular metal studs join metal linear
elements, much as round-head screws are used
decoratively on the ceiling and soffit linear wood
pattern (right).

their earliest collaboration in 1922. 1923 seems to have been the *annus mirabilis* of Dutch neoplastic architecture in as much as the Rietveld/Schröder house entered construction and van Doesburg and van Eesteren exhibited the fruits of their labors in Léonce Rosenberg's Galerie L'Effort Moderne, Paris. That exhibition included their didactic neoplastic house projects displayed as "anti-gravitational structures" and the large villa that they designed for Rosenberg himself (fig. 57).

The intensity with which van Doesburg strove to liberate neoplastic architecture from the influence of Wright (following his move to Weimar in 1921), was to be complemented by his encounter with a parallel school of elementarist-construction originating in the East, whose prime practitioner, the Russian El Lissitzky, van Doesburg first met on a visit to Berlin early in 1921.

The crystallization of the neoplastic architectural aesthetic (from which all subsequent variations on three-dimensional Neoplasticism appear to derive) came into being in an international climate that was permeated by the ethos of *elementary constructivism*. Everywhere at this time there was the incipient notion that the world could be literally rebuilt in both spiritual and concrete terms. There was the prevalent concept that constructive universal culture, acting alone, could transcend the tragic antipathy between the extremes of capitalism and socialism. It was this notion that gave rise to De Stijl's third manifesto obviously written by van Doesburg alone, since it was simply signed, "De Stijl." This text, entitled "Towards a New Formation of the World," radically and arrogantly dismisses both capitalist and socialist hegemonies as materialistic manipulations and goes on to assert a world order based upon a new spirit, a spirit that for van Doesburg and Mondrian alike, subsumed the programmatic implications lying beneath the surface of neoplastic form. Thus, van Doesburg wrote in the third manifesto:

> Europe is lost. Concentration and property, spiritual and material individualism were the basis of old Europe. It has imprisoned itself in that. It cannot free itself anymore. It is going to rack and ruin. We look on calmly. Even if we were to help, we would not want to help. We do not wish to prolong the life of this old prostitute. A new Europe has already begun to grow within us. The ridiculous, socialist 1-2-3 internationals were only external; they existed in words. The international of the spirit is internal, unspoken. It does not exist in words, but in visual deeds and inner strength. With that the new world scheme is being formed.[8]

The Congress of International Progressive Artists staged in Düsseldorf in May 1922, was to elaborate the terms in which future international debates were to be conducted, and the minority report, prepared by the so-called International Faction of Constructivists (I F de K) and

8. *De Stijl*, IV, 8 (1921), pp 123-126.

submitted at the end of the Congress, was to represent a radicalization of van Doesburg's previous position. This is obvious from the second point of the platform, which states, in implied opposition to the mystical cosmology embedded in the ideology of De Stijl that:

> We insist that today art is no longer a dream set apart and in contrast to the realities of the world. Art must stop being just a way of dreaming cosmic secrets. Art is a universal and real expression of creative energy, which can be used to organize the progress of mankind, it is a tool of universal progress.[9]

It is significant that this declaration was jointly signed by Theo van Doesburg, El Lissitzky and Hans Richter. The degree to which van Doesburg was to be committed to the international-constructivist position is reflected in the next few issues of *De Stijl*, beginning with *De Stijl*, V, 4 of 1922 which reported the entire Congress proceedings, including the I F de K declaration. This was followed by *De Stijl*, V, 10/11 published in October 1922, which reproduced El Lissitzky's suprematist-elementarist pamphlet of 1920, "Of 2 Squares" (fig. 143). That this was a transition point for *De Stijl* is confirmed by the fact that from June to September the magazine became increasingly devoted to international and Russian constructivist art—a trajectory which culminated in an anthology ostensibly covering the first five years of De Stijl activity. From this date onwards the Stijl movement is increasingly influenced by Suprematism, Futurism and Dadaism as is clear from the subsequent content of the magazine, including a surprising article by Mondrian on Italian futurist music.[10]

The most symbolically significant contribution to *De Stijl* during the early 1920s is surely the joint work of Hans Richter, Viking Eggeling and Werner Graeff. This editorial line is initiated by van Doesburg's critical appraisal of Richter's constructivist cinema, written out of Weimar in May 1921. From 1921, abstract frames or conceptual sketches drawn from the films of Richter and Eggeling are frequently featured in *De Stijl*, a process which culminates with Richter's *Filmmoments* published in 1923. These seem to synthesize the two rival "elementarist" visions of abstract space; Neoplasticism on the one hand and Suprematism on the other.[11] It is through international contacts such as these that van Doesburg drew progressively closer to the Berlin G group, which in 1921 had still to be constituted.

Following the direct influence of van Doesburg during his stay in Weimar in 1921 and the impact of the Düsseldorf Congress, held in the following year, Neoplasticism spread into Germany through two basic channels. The first of these was the Weimar Bauhaus where Neoplasticism was to have an immediate effect on the work of young students such as Farkas

9. *De Stijl*, V, 4 (1922), pp 61-64. For English trans. see "Statement by the International Faction of Constructivists" in *The Tradition of Constructivism*, Stephen Bann, ed. (New York: Viking, 1974, pp 68-69).
10. *De Stijl*, VI, 2 (1923), pp 19-25.
11. *De Stijl*, VI, 5 (1923), pp 65-66.

Molnar, Herbert Bayer and Marcel Breuer. Breuer's development as a furniture designer initially takes place under the influence of De Stijl as he moves away from the hand-crafted primitivism of his early student work under Johannes Itten towards an explicitly neoplastic assembly which is already evident in his cherry wood and canvas easy chair of 1922. It is ironic, given Gropius's apparent ambivalence towards van Doesburg, that the Bauhaus faculty is quick to respond to the Dutch influence; witness Gropius's adaptation of the neoplastic light fitting designed by Rietveld for his 1920 Hartog interior (fig. 76) and witness also the Gropius and Adolf Meyer entry for the Chicago Tribune Tower competition of 1922 and their related designs for the Erlangen Philosophical Academy of 1924 and finally the Dessau Bauhaus complex of the following year. And yet in all these buildings the influence was on a superficial level. Only the asymmetrical suspended tubular glass lighting unit across the ceiling of Gropius's Weimar office (fig. 77) really testifies to any acceptance of neoplastic spatial principles and much the same can be said of the later public interiors of the Dessau Bauhaus, such as the lighting fittings designed by Breuer for the main lecture hall. And while in 1923, this resistance to neoplastic space stemmed to a large degree from an evident preference for monumental cubic form, two years later the orientation of the school had shifted toward an incipient *Neue Sachlichkeit* expression, that is to say, towards a materialist and ostensibly economic assembly of light weight steel and canvas pieces—to the *Produktform* as this manifested itself in the tubular steel furniture that Breuer designed for Standard Möbel between 1926 and 1928. Breuer's Wassily chair, first produced in 1926, exemplifies the productive approach which was to eclipse the influence of Neoplasticism in the Bauhaus. While the interpenetration of the canvas planes was related to the system posited by Rietveld in his 1917 chair, the rendering of this matrix in light-weight material undermined the initial neoplastic intent of revealing, through the suspension of primary colors in orthogonal space, the ineffable presence of a transcendent and redeeming principle.[12]

The second channel for De Stijl influence was the Berlin G group centered about the charismatic figure of El Lissitzky and comprising the dadaist-constructivists Hans Richter and Viking Eggeling who together with Lissitzky and Werner Graeff founded the magazine *G*, standing for *Gestaltung* (Form) in 1922. However, none of these men was to be specifically influenced by Neoplasticism, except possibly for their general predisposition towards orthogonal abstract space which they may have acquired from van Doesburg prior to 1922. In fact, the sole member of the G group to prove susceptible to the influence of Neoplasticism was Mies van der Rohe, despite his attack on aesthetic speculation which appeared in the first issue of the magazine *G*. This debt was publicly

12. See the cosmology of Schoenmaeker's *The New Image of the World*, 1915.

66, 67. J.J.P. Oud/Theo van Doesburg
"De Vonk" holiday residence, Noordwijkerhout,
1917
1981 photographs

This traditional brick building was Oud's earliest
collaboration with Theo van Doesburg, who
designed the exterior glazed-brick mosaics, the
interior color scheme and the patterned tile floor
(see fig. 148).

68. J.J.P. Oud/Theo van Doesburg
"De Vonk" central stairway, 1917
as illustrated in *De Stijl*, II, 1, 1918

It may be assumed that van Doesburg was
involved in the design of the central stair, repeated
in a slightly different form in the Café Aubette
(fig. 145).

acknowledged in his project for a brick country house that was published in *G* in 1923 and from this point on, Mies's work is patently influenced by De Stijl. Although Mies never really abandons his *Baukunst* predilection for the precise assembly of load-bearing brickwork, he eventually renders the neoplastic canon as an ineffable vision of limitless centrifugal space and it is this intention that will inform his work throughout the next decade.

While Mies and his close collaborator Lilly Reich categorically rejected the primary colors of Neoplasticism they nonetheless introduced into the orthogonal concept the idea of a layered and varied transparency, most notably in their glass industry pavilion erected in Stuttgart in 1927, on the occasion of the *Weissenhofsiedlung*. This "monochromatic" neoplastic concept—antipathetic to van Doesburg—consisted of solid planes, limited to the floor and the ceiling, which were combined with full height translucent and transparent sub-dividing walls. This combination postulated for the first time the spatial matrix that Mies was to pursue in his next works: his canonical Barcelona Pavilion of 1929, his Tugendhat house of 1930 and finally the exhibition house erected for the Berlin Building Exhibition in 1931—a work which as far as its plan was concerned was the most neoplastic of all.

Aside from its play with transparency, the Miesian reworking of Neoplasticism introduced an illusory dimension that would have been an anathema to its founders, for the limitless space involved was presented as much in terms of mirror images as in any palpable extension of the physical domain. This is never more evident than in the famous Berlin *Bild-Bericht* photo of the inner court of the Barcelona Pavilion depicting Georg Kolbe's dancer reflected in the depth of the pool (fig. 79). A planar analysis of this image reveals first the frontal plane bounding the patio and then four planes which perspectively converge in real space: the roof, the podium and the curtain wall together with the flanking wall of the patio. In addition to this there are, of course, a series of parallel virtual planes that exist only in terms of reflection.

The Barcelona Pavilion was a fundamental departure from the neoplastic mass composition employed by Mies in the Wolf house erected at Gubben in 1926, and from this point on he seems to be obsessed with the idea of centrifugal space, articulated not in terms of primary planes and colors, but in terms of tactile, material boundaries, reflections, translucence and transparency. Thus Mies's court house projects of 1931 to 1935 effectively work out the architectural implications of Richter's *Filmmoments* of 1923 and in so doing exhaust the dematerialization latent in the neoplastic concept. His somewhat contradictory disclaimer, made in later life, to the effect that he was not influenced by the Russians, not even by Malevich, testifies to the proximity of his vision to

69. Vilmos Huszar
Form Spectacle, 1920-21
as illustrated in *De Stijl*, IV, 8, 1921

70. Kurt Schmidt
Puppets from *The Adventures of the Little Hunchback*, 1924
Vintage photograph by Moholy-Nagy

A marionette play that was part of a series of productions for a stage at the Bauhaus.

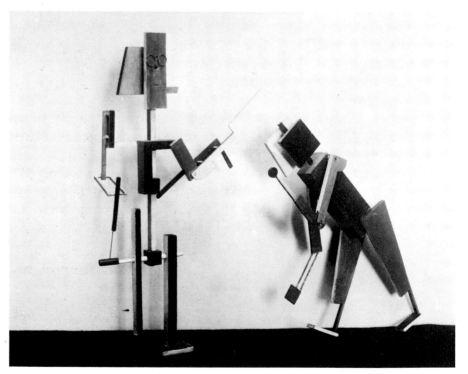

Suprematism—at least in the early 1930s. It is important to note, however, that Mies's elementarist-suprematist vision was always mediated by a vestigial *Schinkelschuler* concern for architecture and for precisely modulated inter-columnar space, and it is this that progressively comes to the fore after the symmetrical monumentality of his entry for the Reichsbank competition of 1933. Thus Mies's designs for the IIT campus made soon after his emigration to the United States in 1937, together with the preliminary studies that he projected for the same campus on an imaginary site, seem to disavow progressively the plastic presence of his previous career, for where the earlier maquettes still implied rotational space, the penultimate project of 1939 had already become crystallized into the bi-axial symmetry that was to characterize his post-war architecture.

The vicissitudes suffered by Neoplasticism from the end of 1923 were to arise out of van Doesburg's brief and intense exchange with Lissitzky. Without doubt Lissitzky's *Prouenraum*, created for the Greater Berlin Art Exhibition of 1923, had a decisive impact on van Doesburg, for the components of this elaborate relief were basically orthogonal. Van Doesburg realized that Lissitzky's overriding intent had been to disrupt the orthogonality of the given volume and from this point onwards he was possessed by a similar aim, evident for the first time in the flower room that he designed for the Comte de Noailles's villa at Hyères in 1924 (fig. 154). The article, "Towards a Collective Construction," written with van Eesteren and published in the same year, already betrays an ambivalent, not to say negative, attitude toward abstract painting.

> We have established the true place of color in architecture and so declare that painting without architectural construction (that is easel painting) has no further reason for existence.[13]

This statement together with van Doesburg's essay "The End of Art," challenged the canonical orthogonality of Neoplasticism by arguing that its *abstract* nature still lies within the rubric of Renaissance culture.[14] This open critique of Neoplasticism made the 1925 split with Mondrian inevitable and thereafter van Doesburg openly contested the neoplastic dualism which, since Schoenmaekers, had assigned the physical to the horizontal and the spiritual to the vertical. Instead, van Doesburg posited the diagonal as the reified dynamism of the spirit that would be made manifest through its contrast with the orthogonal as it appears in both nature and art.

His militant advocacy of the diagonal did not prevent van Doesburg from identifying with Frederick Kiesler's *Cité dans L'Espace* that was exhibited in the Austrian pavilion of the 1925 Paris Exposition des Arts

13. *De Stijl*, VI, 6/7 (1924), pp 89-91.
14. *De Stijl*, VI, 9 (1925), pp 135-136.

Décoratifs (fig. 78). This *architecture élémentarisée,* to coin Kiesler's own terminology, was to dematerialize neoplastic form, not through translucence and transparency as in the case of Mies, but through a gargantuan extension of its coordinates, so that incidental planar elements were minimalized and the work became little more than an orthogonal vortex of Cartesian coordinates sailing endlessly through space. Kiesler's exaggerated attenuation of the orthogonal, defections from the movement by Mondrian, Rietveld and van Eesteren and the adaptation of Neoplasticism by architects such as Mallet-Stevens, who while stimulated by the aesthetic had little regard or understanding for its philosophical base—all of this tended to confirm van Doesburg's commitment to the diagonal as the sole remaining principle of an elementarist, progressive culture. Van Doesburg's break with the intuitive orthogonality of Neoplasticism was consummated in the refurbishing of the Café Aubette, executed in Strasbourg after 1926 in collaboration with Jean Arp and Sophie Taeuber-Arp. This work was sufficiently complete as to permit its presentation in a special issue of *De Stijl* published in the autumn of 1928. In retrospect, the Aubette may be seen as a summation of the conflicting interwoven strands that made up the spectrum of van Doesburg's artistic position in the late 1920s. Within this rambling building three different but complementary plastic conceptions were combined into a hierarchical sequence, where the principle of diagonal countercomposition was reserved for the most important volume, the cinema-dance hall, while the ancillary spaces were articulated by concrete orthogonal systems. These orthogonal compositions were *concrete* in the sense that they were arithmetically mediated by the use of modular components. The vestigial pinwheeling effect, where it was still in evidence, was induced solely through color displacement and shallow relief. What van Doesburg meant by concrete as opposed to abstract seems to have been best expressed in his manifesto on concrete painting published in *Art Concrete* in January 1930, wherein he wrote: "Most painters work like pastry cooks and milliners. In contrast, we use mathematical data (whether Euclidean or not) and science, that is to say, intellectual means." This theme was taken up again in the same year, in a short manifesto, not published until 1947—a posthumous text making explicit the critical role to be played by arithmetic in the formation of concrete art. As Joost Baljeu has revealed, van Doesburg already used such means in the remodeling of the Aubette (figs. 169-182).

> . . . in one case he mounted thirty-centimeter-wide and three-centimeter-thick strips on the wall surface, which produced planes separated by low relief; in the other he raised the planar surfaces four centimeters above the wall surface with thirty-five centimeter-wide strips lying in between, which produced high relief. Thus van Doesburg came very close to that phase of spatial

development which would evolve from Neoplasticism and Constructivism, in which painting evolved into relief. . . . His earlier experience with architectural models notwithstanding, actual working in the architectural space of the Aubette doubtless provided the necessary opportunity suited to such an approach. The neoplastic design of the festivity hall and the elementarist oblique composition of the cinema-dance hall showed respectively how static Neoplasticism was presented in (passive) low relief, whereas 'dynamic' Elementarism employed (active) high relief.[15]

Having finally demonstrated that relief structure alone could suffice to articulate architectural space, van Doesburg unexpectedly reconciled himself to admitting to a division of labor between architecture and art, particularly as this concerned the house that he designed for his own occupation in Meudon, in 1929 (fig. 59). Despite the concrete Elementarism present in the early sketches, the final design abandons the transcending plastic principles of De Stijl and instead embraces the precepts of functionalism, particularly as these had appeared in the purist works of Le Corbusier—above all in the prototypical Citrohan houses which had been exhibited in the *Salon d'Automne* in 1920 and 1922. This astonishing about-face is surely the definitive end of the avant-gardist phase of Neoplasticism; one which preceded by barely two years van Doesburg's own untimely death.

Irrespective of how totally modified it became, neoplastic space eventually returned to its fundamental point of origin; namely, to the United States and above all, to Wright himself, first somewhat tentatively, in Wright's House on the Mesa project, exhibited in The Museum of Modern Art in 1932, and then more decisively in the Malcolm Willey house, projected in the same year and realized in Minneapolis in 1934. The Willey house was essentially the first in an extended series of so-called Usonian houses built by Wright almost without a pause between 1934 and 1950, including the extravagant 1936 masterpiece, the Kaufmann house, known as Falling Water, which in terms of centrifugal spatial composition was both typically Usonian and neoplastic. While Wright never accepted the neoplastic palette, he nonetheless took the spatial conception of the Dutch avant-garde and reintegrated this paradigm within the fundamental emphasis he had always placed on the hearth, the chimney and the staircase, as the core of any free-standing domesticity. In so doing of course, he categorically stripped the ideological (or should one say cosmological) heart out of van Doesburg's space conception and given Wright's poetic empiricism, this could have been nothing less than intentional. At the same time neoplastic rationalism was to leave its mark on Wright. This much is obvious from the way in which Wright brought his conception of domestic space closer to the pinwheel, spatial structure of the Dutch.

15. Joost Baljeu, *Theo van Doesburg* (New York: Macmillan, 1974, p 85).

113

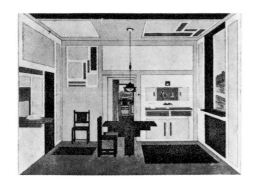

From 1934 on, Wright organized his houses in terms of flat roof planes or slabs of varying height, to be bounded by outriding walls and clerestories. Indeed, it could be claimed that Wright's genius was able to exfoliate and modulate the neoplastic space concept in a way that had always eluded van Doesburg.

Wright's 1934 transformation of the neoplastic space-form into the Usonian house plan found its parallel in the field of painting, initially through the influence of Piet Mondrian. Broad examples of Mondrian's mature work had already been exhibited in New York by the mid-30s and from this point onwards an American school of Neoplasticism can be distinguished, most notably in the works of Burgoyne Diller, Harry Holtzman, Ilya Bolotowsky, Leon Polk Smith, Charmion von Wiegand and the Swiss émigré, Fritz Glarner.

All of Mondrian's American paintings are strongly suggestive of spatial relief, not only in terms of their illusory depth, but also with respect to the way in which they were actually conceived and constructed, namely, through the use of colored adhesive tapes. And while these tapes may have been initially nothing more than an expedient method, they clearly affected the "collaged and overlaid" conception of the works themselves, thereby inaugurating a final series of canvases that were virtual three-dimensional reliefs: *New York City I* of 1942, *Broadway Boogie-Woogie* of 1943 and *Victory Boogie-Woogie* of 1944. Aside from these illusions of relief, Mondrian entered wholeheartedly into three-dimensional relief construction in the furnishing of his New York studio (as he had previously done in Paris), applying a series of rectangular colored planes to the walls of the room and allowing similar planes to advance from the wall and float in the improvised bookshelf and the adjacent fireplace surround. As Nancy Troy has written:

> The collage elements of *Victory Boogie-Woogie* had an unmistakable affinity with the way Mondrian treated the white walls of his apartment by pinning up rectangular planes of red, yellow and blue cardboard in temporary compositional clusters. Cognizant of its importance, Harry Holtzman arranged to keep the studio intact for several months after Mondrian's death on 1 February 1944. At that time, he invited anyone interested, including Burgoyne Diller and Katherine Dreier, to see the environment Mondrian had created as an extension of his other work. While the studio was open, *Victory Boogie-Woogie* was placed on an easel which 'stood like an altar, alone at one end of the barren room.' The effect was much like a temple of pure art to which the visitors were making their final pilgrimage.[16]

Van Doesburg's abandonment of the elementarist project in his Meudon house of 1929 was to establish the cultural frame of concrete art for the

71. Vilmos Huszar
Design for a dining room, 1921
as illustrated in *De Stijl*, V, 1, 1922

16. Nancy J. Troy, "De Stijl's Collaborative Ideal: The Colored Abstract Environment, 1916-1926" Yale University, PhD diss., 1979, p 221.

114

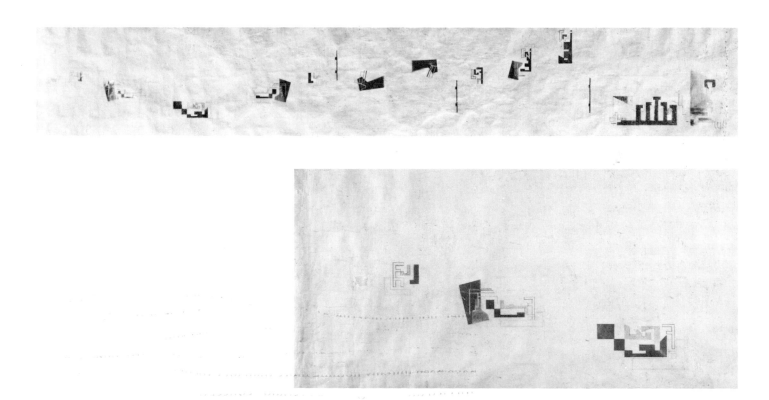

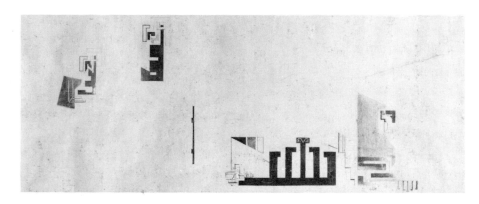

72-75. Hans Richter
Fugue (project for a film), 1920
pencil on paper scroll
18½ x 110
47 x 279.4
Collection The Museum of Modern Art,
New York
Gift of Mr. and Mrs. Irvin Shapiro

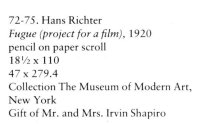

115

76. Gerrit Rietveld
Study for the office of Dr. A.M. Hartog, Maarsen,
1922
Vintage photograph

77. Walter Gropius
Director's office, Weimar Bauhaus, 1923
Vintage photograph

next 25 years. From now on most constructivist artists were to regard the realms of art and architecture as complementary, yet separate. A number of non-figurative factions continued to proliferate in Europe and the Americas both before and after World War II. Such diverse figures as César Domela, Friedrich Vordemberge-Gildewart, Max Burchartz, Michel Seuphor, Auguste Herbin, Jean Gorin, Joaquin Torres Garcia, Max Bill, Richard Lohse, Tomás Maldonado, Charles Biederman, Victor Pasmore, Anthony Hill, John Ernest and Gillian Wise all developed rival strains of elementarist-constructionist art and theory. They are arranged above roughly according to national lines of influence, with Domela heading the Dutch and German development, Seuphor initiating the Parisian-based Abstraction-Creation movement, Torres Garcia and Bill helping to propagate concrete art in South America and Charles Biederman being largely responsible for the post-war Anglo-Saxon school of "structuralist-constructivism." Biederman's *Art as the Evolution of Visual Knowledge,* 1948, was seminal in this regard, particularly for his formulation of structural art as an analog for structural order in nature; a position that was contested by Hill in his 1959 essay, "On Construction, Nature and Structure," in which he argued for an art predicated on the introspective beauty of mathematics.[17]

Jean Gorin in his reliefs and constructions was to follow the orthogonal, neoplastic paradigm almost throughout his career; including in the early 50s a number of neoplastic architectural projects which were published in the Dutch magazine *Structure,* edited by Joost Baljeu. In the late 1950s and early 1960s, Baljeu attempted, in a number of houses designed in collaboration with architect Dick van Woerkom, to reassume the "total work of art" position abandoned by van Doesburg after 1923.

In a house projected in 1960, Baljeu and van Woerkom took the pinwheeling spatial principle, underlying the van Doesburg/van Eesteren Maison d'Artiste of 1923, and elevated this format to a much higher level of syntactic coherence and density (fig. 80). Baljeu did not regard the emergence of relief construction as an indication that plastic art should withdraw into the maturity of its own domain. On the contrary, he seems to have seen the arrival of planar construction as an occasion on which to repostulate the Wagnerian aim of achieving a total work of art. Thus we find him writing of his collaboration with van Woerkom:

> When the architect abandons the use of three-dimensional mass and visualizes each architectural space as consisting of six planes, and when the painter has developed from painting on a flat canvas surface toward colored planes in actual space, the two can come together and begin to think about architecture. The plane as a means is the first agreement their meeting is based upon. Secondly, if they both agree on how to use it, the method—an architecture

17. Anthony Hill, "On Construction, Nature and Structure," *Structure,* 2nd Series, no. 1, 1959.

of space-time expressed by colored rectangles in orthogonal relationship—then the way to architecture as synthesist art lies open. Intrinsically, this method represents an architecture of idea, not to be confounded with the presentation of ideas in architecture. The latter approach produces 'solutions' by the hundred, the first searches for a new grammar.[18]

Meanwhile, van Woerkom accounted for his own role in the following terms:

It is not identification with De Stijl we are after, but the orientation of our own mind to the purpose of achieving more. . . . Since I believe with Mondrian that easel painting has come to an end, it is in the shape of constructionist artist that the painter reappears. Maybe some day one man alone can handle the job; however, in my view, we have far to go to arrive at that stage. Thus, when, in their collaboration, architect and painter each abandon part of their atmosphere, they can together arrive at a polychronic 'sculpture' functioning in life, . . .[19]

18. Joost Baljeu, "Report on the Work," *Structure*, 4th Series, no. 1, 1961, p 8.
19. Dick van Woerkom, "Architecture as an Art," *Structure*, 4th Series, no. 1, 1961, p 14.

The attempt of Baljeu and van Woerkom to surpass the level of plastic-space composition attained in the Léonce Rosenberg De Stijl exhibition of 1923 was to make itself manifest at three interrelated levels: first, in the remarkable ingenuity with which they were able to reduce all the main architectural elements to pure rectangular planes suspended in space; second, in the mathematical progression according to which the spatial centrifuge evenly distributed itself in all directions from the center of the composition; and last, but not least, in the rupture with the neoplastic canonical colors, not only in terms of employing colors other than primaries, but also with regard to exploiting color as a notational indicator. In Baljeu's houses color is not only supposed to reinforce axial movement, but also to arouse certain sets of behavioral responses.

> Color is the final means of experiencing the size of space, the individualized function of architectural space, its interrelated location as well as its orientation towards environmental space. When going from sleeping to living or vice-versa a similar spatial color-scheme makes one experience their orientation along the main N-S axis in environmental space. In contradistinction a similar spatial color-scheme in kitchen and office (E-W axis). . . adds meaning to the 90-degrees change in spatial location. The living being oriented toward the sun and representing restful space, [while] active modal colors [are] used to stress kitchen and office as spaces in which to work.[20]

However disproportionate its functional distribution may have been, the brilliance of this polychromatic, plastic house can hardly be denied, but the real dilemma, remarked on even by Baljeu himself, (and that which had caused van Doesburg to retreat into the domain of pure art) was how should this method and syntax be extended to structures other than the free-standing house? This dilemma is generally evident in Dutch avant-gardist architectural circles of relatively recent date—above all, in the school of Aldo van Eyck which includes such architects as Jan van Stigt, Piet Blom and Herman Hertzberger. This perennial Dutch obsession with the spiritual totality of Neoplasticism may well indicate the "idealistic" impasse which has always lain at the heart of the conception: namely, that while intending the deconstruction of Humanist culture, Neoplasticism has always remained fundamentally centroidal in its formation, thereby making linear and serial compositions extremely difficult to attain.

This intrinsic limit may explain van Doesburg's late preoccupation with the diagonal and with the countercomposition as a strategy for transcending the conceptual and physical boundaries of a centralized perspectival space. It was of no importance to him whether this constraint presented itself in terms of a rectangular canvas or an orthogonal room. The diamond canvases, intermittently resorted to by

20. Joost Baljeu, "Report on the Work," *op. cit.,* p 8.

118

78. Frederick Kiesler
Cité dans L'Espace (City in Space), 1925
A daring structure, designed and built for the
Austrian pavilion of the Paris Exposition
des Arts Décoratifs.
Vintage photograph

79. Mies van der Rohe
German pavilion, International Exposition,
Barcelona, Spain, 1929
Vintage photograph

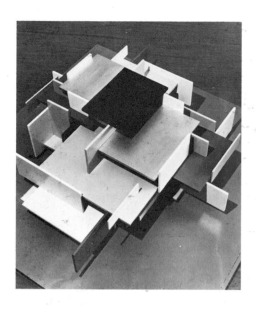

80. Joost Baljeu/Dick van Woerkom
Model of a single family house, 1961

81. Robert Slutzky
Diamond paintings installed in an exhibition
at the Architectural League, New York, 1967.

Mondrian throughout his career, also suggest a similar intuitive concern for decentering the unavoidable rectangularity of Western art, as do certain of his idiosyncratically condensed compositions of the early 1920s, wherein for the first time, all the black lines, save one or two, stop short of the picture's perimeter.

Many of these concerns were to return in a paradoxical way in the work of certain young American artists in the early 1960s; above all, in a series of diamond canvases produced by the painter Robert Slutzky over a decade, and a set of apparently parallel diamond houses projected between 1962 and 1966 by the architect John Hejduk. These works were publicly assembled as a kind of complementary didactic display in the diamond exhibition staged by the Architectural League of New York, in 1967 (fig. 81), when the two men demonstrated the poetic potential and limit of setting an orthogonal grid against its diagonal counter thesis. Where Slutzky attempted to extend the discourse of Mondrian's diamond canvases so as to imply a universal planar layering in depth, rather than Mondrian's linear articulation of a virtual void, Hejduk reversed the strategy of van Doesburg's diagonal wall relief in the Aubette, by exploiting the oblique corners of a rotated cubic volume. He was to render this volume as a cubic diamond, thereby amputating the potentially limitless linear extension of the orthogonal composition within. It is paradoxical, to say the least, that what interested Hejduk on this occasion was not the potential reality of the projected space, but, rather, the axonometric reduction of his three-dimensional propositions as two-dimensional graphic realities (fig. 83). At this juncture, the legacy of De Stijl appears to implode upon itself, as though to deny the original neoplastic vision of forms infinitely exfoliating in space. In the last analysis, despite his preference for primary colors, simple geometries and pinwheeling arrangements, Hejduk was never to project works which were truly De Stijl in spatial terms. On the contrary, his poetic virtuosity was always contaminated by synthetic cubist concerns foreign to the neoplastic vision.

Peter Eisenman is the one other American architect of stature who participated in this paradoxical, late avant-garde of the 1960s, wherein the original utopian impulse of 40 years before was reread and reenacted in terms of a late modernist, realist sensibility, while the artists removed themselves from the early avant-garde desire to transform the world. Eisenman looked to the pre-war avant-garde solely for the substance of a rigorous modern grammar, for a syntax with which to sustain an invincibly modern poetic; one which would be capable of resisting, to an equal degree, the deliquescence of a vulgar modernity and the recurrent, naive nostalgia for utopia.

82. Peter Eisenman
House III, Connecticut, 1970

83. John Hejduk
Project A: House, 1967
Axonometric of ground floor
ink on paper
24¼ x 19⅞
66.7 x 50.5
Collection the architect

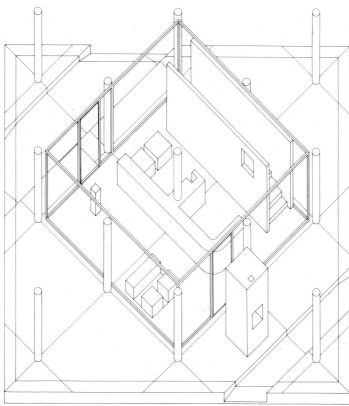

Throughout his career, Eisenman has suspended his work between two antithetical hypotheses. The first of these derives directly from the pre-war Italian rationalist movement, which, while decidedly abstract, remained, nonetheless, pro-classical, in as much as its general grammar was predicated upon orthogonal post and beam elements that retained a propensity for a frontal assembly. The second premise stems from van Doesburg's Elementarism of the early 1920s; that is to say, from a movement that was anti-classical to the degree that its syntax was compounded out of a proliferation of "floating" orthogonal elements centrifugally arranged about a vortex, elements which were ill-disposed to any kind of frontal resolution.

Eisenman's work has oscillated between these poles; between the fragmented frontality of the Barenholtz Pavilion, Princeton, of 1966 and the latent idea of rotational collision, explicitly realized in his Miller house (House III), built in Connecticut in 1970 (fig. 82). It is interesting to note how House III was originally conceived as a diamond composition, something along the lines of Hejduk's diamond houses of the early 1960s, and that this initial image was then destructively transposed into a 45-degree collision between two separate orthogonal grids. What the Miller house and Hejduk's diamond projects have in common is the aesthetic strategy of interference. However, that which remains hermetic if not passive in Hejduk's conception, is all too violently activated in the work of Eisenman.

Italian Rationalism and Dutch Neoplasticism were both predicated on a linking together of congruent elements, even though the generic components and unifying principle varied from frontality and perspectival recession in the first instance, to rotation and peripheral dispersal in the second. This essential difference, however, indicates how Eisenman's ultimate point of departure is neoplastic rather than rationalist, for all that, he uses the strategies of the second in order to deconstruct the first, through the intervention of specific architectural elements such as columns, beams and stairs that were almost always repressed in the work of van Doesburg. It seems as though the generic architectonic differences between these elements preclude their closure within a total abstraction. In this way, Eisenman's post-neoplastic *order/disorder* is always shot through with absences, interferences and inversions: columns that support nothing; transparent floors; or elements whose simultaneous conjunction and disjunction preclude a singular reading. The motive behind this negative exacerbation of the avant-garde has, perhaps, been best accounted for by Eisenman himself. In writing about his penultimate work, House XIa, Eisenman brings the long trajectory of Neoplasticism to an unpredictable close.

122

We live today in an age of partial objects. The fragments we are surrounded by are the pieces or approximation of absent wholes. This is so, however, not in the sense of evolving any original totality—one that has been lost, waiting to be turned up and glued back together like the pieces of an antique statue. . .—but, rather, in the sense of approximating a subsequent condition. And, far from being a unity, that subsequent condition may be one where the only relationships between the parts may be their difference: the whole is full of holes.[21]

It is disquieting to look back over the trajectory of history and to recognize not only that avant-gardism is at an end but that it had already ceased to exist as a primary motivating force some 50 years ago. Already then, around the time of van Doesburg's death, avant-gardism had been replaced by Modernism as a generic position from which to continue with the pursuit of Western culture.[22] In retrospect it is possible to see that after 1931 Neoplasticism continued only as a simulation of itself and that with each successive generation, the apocalyptic vitality of its initial vision was reduced to a genre—to just one wavelength within the modernist spectrum. Clement Greenberg was the first to acknowledge this situation when he saw that Modernism—close to traditionalism in its emphasis on structural autonomy—would have to be maintained as a holding pattern, until such time as a transformed society would release an unspecified cultural energy of an entirely different kind. Looking back at Neoplasticism today, what we experience is largely an afterglow; on the one hand a curatorial nostalgia momentarily recuperating the essence of a lost vitality; on the other, in the case of those intellectual artists who remain close to the line, a perennial de-construction of the myth of modernity made in the name of a disenchanted Modernism; a kind of perpetual "emancipation of dissonance" executed within the fissures of history.

21. Peter Eisenman, "Sandboxes: House XIa," *A + U Architecture and Urbanism,* January 1980, p 223.
22. I am indebted to Andreas Huyssen's essay, "The Search for Tradition: Avant-Garde and Post Modernism in the 1970s," for pointing to the distinction between avant-garde and Modernism. *New German Critique,* no. 22, winter 1981, p 26.

Kenneth Frampton is an architect and an architectural historian/critic who teaches at Columbia University and is a fellow of the Institute for Architecture and Urban Studies.

Manifestoes for a New Revolution

The Furniture of Gerrit Rietveld

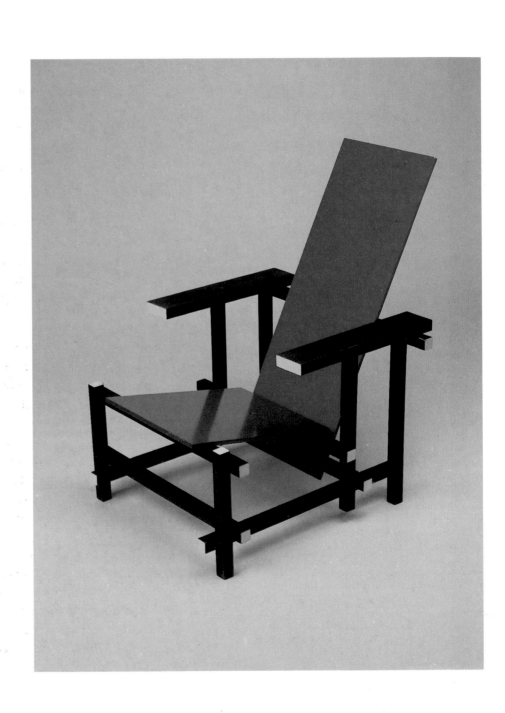

Martin Filler

When Sigfried Giedion observed that the furniture designs of Gerrit Rietveld dating from the years just after 1917 were "manifestoes. . . [that] guide the direction of an entire development"[1] he acknowledged the central fact of that furniture's uniqueness: never before (or since) has furniture design been at the very forefront of an artistic revolution. Customarily considered one of the so-called "minor arts," furniture in fact has often anticipated stylistic developments that only later have been realized fully in the more costly, more slowly moving, and therefore more conservative and more permanent medium of architecture. Yet invariably, as soon as a translation of formal concerns can successfully be made from decorative objects to objects on an environmental scale—from teapots to temples, as it were—it is architecture and not furniture design that receives the lion's share of attention.

This disparity has not always depended solely on the inherent merit of furniture design within a given period, but rather has had more to do with the relative equilibrium of quality between furniture design and architectural design (as well as the general level of artistic innovation). Epochs rich in decorative invention but thin in authentic architectural inspiration—such as the essentially superficial Empire, Gothic Revival, and Art Nouveau styles—tend to be remembered as much for their furniture designs as for their architecture. In contrast, the gigantic architectural achievements of the modern movement have put the impressive furniture designs of that period into a somewhat subsidiary position. Perhaps that tendency to consign interior design to a secondary role helps to explain why the history of furniture has not enjoyed the kind of intellectual status standardly accorded architectural history. But there can be no question that in the De Stijl movement there existed a remarkably high parity of design quality among architecture, furniture, painting and typography to an extent comparable in modern art only to the contemporary work of the Russian constructivists and the artists of the Bauhaus.

84. Gerrit Rietveld
Red/blue chair, 1918
painted wood
33⅞ x 25⅛ x 26¾
86 x 63.8 x 67.9
Collection Stedelijk Museum, Amsterdam

"With this chair an attempt has been made to have every part simple and in its most elementary form in accordance with function and material—the form, thus, which is most capable of being harmonized with the whole. The construction is attuned to the parts to insure that no part dominates or is subordinate to the others. In this way, the whole stands freely and clearly in space, and the form stands out from the material."
Gerrit Rietveld, 1919

1. Sigfried Giedion, *Mechanization Takes Command: A Contribution to Anonymous History* (Cambridge: The Harvard University Press, 1947), p 487.

85. Rietveld's cabinet shop in Utrecht, 1917, with Rietveld seated in a prototype for the red/blue chair; G.A. van der Groenekan, long-time fabricator of Rietveld's furniture, stands behind the chair.

2. Gerrit Rietveld, "Mondriaan en het nieuwe bouwen" (Mondrian and the new construction), *Bouwkundig Weekblad,* 73, 11, 15 March 1955, pp 127-128.

The furniture designs of Gerrit Rietveld—no fewer than 75 objects, most of them produced between 1917 and 1934—yielded three pieces that undoubtedly rank among the most original and most important art of this century. What makes Rietveld's *rood/blauwe stoel* (red/blue chair) of circa 1918, *Berlijnse stoel* (Berlin chair) of 1923, and *divantafeltje* (end table) of 1923 so particularly significant is not only their complete and succinct summary in physical form of the philosophical tenets of the De Stijl movement; more significant is that the first and most famous of that great trio of designs served as a major stimulus for the coalescence of the conceptual formulations of the two primary theorists of the De Stijl group, Piet Mondrian (whom, amazingly, Rietveld never met[2]) and Theo van Doesburg. The red/blue chair proved to them that a satisfying artifact could be created in accord with the emergent neoplasticist belief in formal reductivism motivated by a rigorous objectivity. Using the simplest repertoire of shapes and colors, the red/blue chair had an anonymous, modular quality that effectively effaced the supposedly subjective hand of the artist. This remarkable design can rightly be called the central artifact of De Stijl, and one would be hard pressed to cite a comparable example in the whole history of design of theory induced by a "minor art" object.

This seems all the more impressive an accomplishment because of the very character of Gerrit Rietveld himself: simple and unpretentious, taciturn but kindly, principled but undogmatic, thoughtful but not bookish, inventive but essentially pragmatic, this cabinetmaker son of a cabinetmaker was one of those apparently intuitive artists who, like Paul Cézanne or Jackson Pollock, seemed to rise up unheralded from the mysterious sources of spontaneous genius. The emergence of Rietveld reminds us of the changing roles of artist and craftsman during the 19th century. Born in Utrecht in 1888, Gerrit Thomas Rietveld was apprenticed in his father's shop at the age of 11 (fig. 85), in the last year of the century and at the very apogee of the Arts and Crafts movement. It is safe to say that Rietveld's father had little use for (or even knowledge of) the self-conscious attempt of high-style furniture designers of the day to reintegrate the traditional pre-industrial unity of art and handcraft. Most small cabinetmakers in Holland at the turn of the century still worked at a pre-industrial level, and they were mostly unaware of the rift that the Arts and Crafts movement sought to heal.

But there is no denying that Gerrit Rietveld from the first was greatly influenced by the forms and types of Arts and Crafts furniture. He remained very much a craftsman throughout his creative life, in contrast to the role of artist-as-intellectual that was later devised and assumed by his colleagues in the De Stijl movement. Rietveld's earliest documented pieces from the first years of this century have a pronounced Arts and

86. Gerrit Rietveld
Armchair, 1919
painted, stained wood
36⅝ x 25⅛ x 23⅝
93 x 63.8 x 60
Collection Stedelijk Museum, Amsterdam

"Through its new form, this furniture gives a new
answer to the question of what place sculpture
will have in the new interior. Our chairs, tables,
cabinets and other objects of use are the (abstract-
real) images in our future interior."
Theo van Doesburg, 1918

3. Giedion, *op. cit.,* p 485.

Crafts flavor. And no wonder, for that movement was widely
transmitted, primarily through periodicals that were circulated more
easily and more cheaply than the pattern books that served as the
primary disseminators of furniture design ideas during the 18th and early
19th centuries. The basic characteristics of Arts and Crafts furniture at
its least complicated—strong orthogonal lines, clear emphasis of edges,
simply expressed construction, and modest (though substantial)
materials—stayed with Rietveld long after the Arts and Crafts movement
was seen by some as little more than a quaint precursor of Modernism.

At the age of 20, Rietveld began to take courses in architecture at night
school, and later continued his studies full-time under a practicing
architect. Rietveld set up shop as an independent cabinetmaker in
Utrecht in 1911, but continued his architectural training in advanced
courses under the architect P.J.C. Klaarhamer (an associate of H. P.
Berlage, leader of the dominant Amsterdam School) until 1915. In that
year Rietveld executed three pieces of furniture to designs by
Klaarhamer—two chairs and a buffet. While unexceptional in light of
what Rietveld was to create on his own shortly thereafter, his
Klaarhamer pieces nonetheless typify the kind of solid, well-rounded
professional grounding in architecture, furniture and interior design that
a talented, aspiring young cabinetmaker could obtain in The
Netherlands during the years just before World War I.

But there is little in Rietveld's development up until 1917—or in the
course of design in general for that matter—to directly account for his
staggeringly original red/blue chair, which marked the turning point of
his career. The catastrophe of the great war acted as the catalyst that
independently led each of the future members of the Stijl group to believe
that a totally new kind of art and design had to be devised to raise
mankind from the morass of tragedy and degradation that the war had
created. Extreme times called for extreme measures, they felt, and the
safe haven of neutral Holland allowed these revolutionary new attitudes
to take concrete form several years before conditions in Germany and
Russia permitted the parallel efforts of Constructivism and the Bauhaus
to get underway. In Sigfried Giedion's momentous words, "As in
painting and architecture, it was necessary temporarily to forget
everything and begin afresh, as if no chair had ever before been built."[3]

Essentially, the red/blue chair is a treatise on the nature of space. Perhaps
Rietveld's clearest statement about his conception of the object in space
(and, by inference, his intentions in designing the red/blue chair) was
contained in a lecture he gave in 1957:

87. Gerrit Rietveld
Prototype for the red/blue chair, 1917-18
unpainted wood
34¼ x 23⅝ x 23⅝
87 x 60 x 60
Collection Mr. and Mrs. J. Dibbets

88. Gerrit Rietveld
Sideboard, 1951 reproduction (original 1919)
paint-stained wood
41 x 78¾ x 17¾
104.1 x 200 x 45.1
Collection Stedelijk Museum, Amsterdam

89. Gerrit Rietveld
Berlin chair, 1923
painted wood
41¾ x 27½ x 21⅝
106 x 69.9 x 54.9
Collection Stedelijk Museum, Amsterdam

90. Gerrit Rietveld
End table, 1923
painted wood
24¼ x 19¼ x 19¼
61.6 x 48.9 x 48.9
Collection Stedelijk Museum, Amsterdam

91. Gerrit Rietveld
Piano chair, 1923
painted wood, leather
29½ x 14 x 13⅝
74.9 x 35.6 x 34.6
Collection Stedelijk Museum, Amsterdam

4. Gerrit Rietveld, "Levenshouding als achtergrond van mijn werk" (View of life as a background for my work), lecture delivered at the Stedelijk Museum, Amsterdam, 27 June 1957, trans. in Theodore M. Brown, *The Work of G. Rietveld, Architect* (Utrecht: A.W. Bruna & Zoon, 1958), p 162.
5. Giedion, *op. cit.*, p 364.

If, for a particular purpose, we separate, limit, and bring into a human scale a part of unlimited space, it is (if all goes well) a piece of space brought to life as reality. In this way, a special segment of space has been absorbed into our human system.[4]

That is precisely what the red/blue chair does, and its simultaneous appropriation and definition of space is what makes it such an intriguing design (fig. 84). The chair is composed of 13 wooden listels, equilateral in cross-section: they interrelate like Cartesian coordinates that touch but do not intersect. The basic module of the chair is 10 cm; the listels are 3.3 cm in section, or one-third that dimension (2.5 x 2.6 cm in the first version). There are also two armrests, plus the two major departures from the orthogonality of the framework: the two broad planks set diagonally within the supporting members that form the seat and the backrest. In its first incarnation, the red/blue chair also had two pentagonal side panels set below the armrests, but they were removed at some point after the chair was published in *De Stijl*, II, 11, in 1919. One can imagine the unrecorded great moment in design history when Rietveld, after prolonged contemplation of the red/blue chair, shook his head and said something to the effect of: "Nee, laten wij het proberen zonder de zijkanten" ("No, let's try it without sides").

In addition to the presence of the side panels, the first rendition of the red/blue chair differed from the ultimate version in that it was actually not red and blue at all (fig. 87): it was left unpainted until some time after 1919. Early in that year it was seen by the architect Robert van 't Hoff, who suggested that Rietveld get in touch with the other members of the then two-year-old De Stijl group. Rietveld did so, and was asked to join them. Theo van Doesburg may have been the source of the suggestion that his new colleague Rietveld paint the chair as we now know it—backrest red, seat blue, listels lacquered black with their terminal edges in yellow. The addition of color does indeed further explicate Rietveld's conception of the chair as the nexus of an almost infinitely extendable spatial continuum. Though a seemingly small detail, the yellow ends emphasize our reading of the listels as having been "severed" from longer "pieces"—a skillful demonstration of Gestalt perception, which is known to have interested several of the artists of De Stijl.

The other major impression most commonly derived from the red/blue chair (and accepted unquestioningly by many observers) is the notion that it is so uncomfortable as to be unusable. This is patently untrue. It should be remembered that today our conception of "comfort" derives rather disproportionately from the period of 19th-century furniture manufacture that Giedion aptly termed "the reign of the upholsterer."[5] Comfort, as any office worker possessed of a good back-support chair will testify, is not necessarily synonymous with softness, and is correctly

92. Gerrit Rietveld
Hanging lamp, 1920
3 tubular glass lamps, glass tubes, wood
55⅛ x 15¾ x 15¾
140 x 40 x 40
Collection Haags Gemeentemuseum

93. Gerrit Rietveld
Child's chair, 1920-21
painted wood, leather
35½ x 17½ x 15¾
90.2 x 44.5 x 40
Collection Haags Gemeentemuseum

gauged only in terms of a specific activity. It was Rietveld's express intention that his chairs not lull their occupants into a stuporous state of relaxation. The red/blue chair was meant above all to keep the sitter firmly supported and thereby alert, and that it does admirably well. Admittedly, Rietveld himself complained that he often bumped his shins on this chair.[6] But far from the fakir's seat that some presume it to be, it is quite functional according to its designer's primary purpose.

Yet it is as a piece of sculpture that the red/blue chair chiefly interests us today, and that it is sculpture as well as seating is obvious. The intimations of space, both contained and contiguous, that are a basic element of Rietveld's furniture designs were evoked in a poetic appreciation written by Theo van Doesburg for *De Stijl* in 1920. This excerpt from van Doesburg's text, which compares Rietveld's *armstoel* (armchair) (fig. 86) of 1919 to a painting of imaginary urban spaces by Giorgio de Chirico, shows how keenly the writer apprehended the similarly suggestive spatial allusions of each:

> Difference and correspondence.
> Difference in intention, in expression, in means.
> Correspondence in metaphysical feeling and mathematical indication of spaces.
> In both: spaces bounded by spaces.
> Penetration by space.
> Mystique of space.[7]

Rietveld's next major furniture design, his *beukenhouten dressoirtje* (beechwood sideboard) of 1919 (fig. 88) is rather a letdown after the red/blue chair for several reasons. First, as a furniture type the sideboard has the kind of dated, petit bourgeois associations that more universal and less specialized pieces such as chairs and tables do not. Secondly, in contrast to the linear economy of the red/blue chair, Rietveld's sideboard seems finicky and overworked, to say nothing of impractical, with its numerous hard-to-reach, dust-collecting interstices. Thirdly, neither formally nor functionally is it really innovative, and its elaborate application of motifs previously given striking compositional validity through structural simplicity in the red/blue chair impresses one here as unfortunately *retardataire*. Several critics have cited the English architect and furniture designer Edward William Godwin's 1867 sideboard in the Victoria and Albert Museum in London as a probable influence, but one need not look further back than the innumerable buffet designs that appeared in crafts movement magazines at the turn of the century. The particular importance designers of the Arts and Crafts movement attached to formalized family dining—Frank Lloyd Wright during that period was fairly obsessed with its ritualistic aspects—only confirms that this was a design that looked backward to the Victorian era in its social application more than it looked ahead to the modern age.

6. Brown, *op. cit.*, p 20.
7. Theo van Doesburg, "Schilderkunst van Giorgio de Chirico en een stoel van Rietveld" (Painting by Giorgio de Chirico and a chair by Rietveld), *De Stijl*, III, 5, March 1920, p 46. Symonds trans.

8. I am indebted to Prof. Dr. Pieter Singelenberg of the University of Utrecht for generously providing the elusive initials of Dr. Hartog, which do not appear in the standard literature on Rietveld.

9. *Constructivism and Futurism: Russian and Other*, Ex Libris 6 (sales catalogue), New York, 1977, item 612. The catalogue's claim that "The cradle was realized and is still in use by the grandchildren of Oud" was corrected in a letter to Ex Libris from Oud's son, Hans Oud, Hemelum, 22 April 1981: ". . . not only is it not 'still in use'. . . but it was never made. The most dreadful thing for me is my father found it too expensive and did not order Rietveld to make it." Rietveld's drawing is dated 13 August 1919.

10. Rietveld's children are Elizabeth, born 1913; Egbert, born 1915; Vrouwgien, born 1918; Johannes Cornelis, born 1919; Gerrit, born 1920, died 1961; and Willem (Wim), born 1924. Their names and dates were graciously supplied by Elizabeth Eskes-Rietveld and transmitted by Prof. Dr. Pieter Singelenberg.

In 1920 Rietveld was commissioned to design a new consulting room the clinic of Dr. A.M. Hartog[8] at Maarssen (fig. 76), an interior that was one of the most important early environmental works of De Stijl. Though regrettably it has since been destroyed, the survival of a single photograph of it and artifacts from it attest to its quality. The doctor's desk chair was a variant of Rietveld's 1919 armchair, and the Hartog version differed from the first version as did the first and second editions of the red/blue chair: side panels in the first model were removed in the second. The armchair was not lacquered completely as was the red/blue chair, but rather was rubbed with white pigment that heightened the grain and let the natural color of the oak show through. Only the terminal edges of the listels and some of the edges of the seat, back and side panels were lacquered, in this case a deep violet, thus performing the same visual function as the yellow terminal edges of the red/blue chair. One of Rietveld's most evocative sculptural compositions was his *hanglamp* (hanging lamp) (fig. 92) for Dr. Hartog's office, a simple but dazzlingly inventive fixture put together from four (a later variant uses only three) standard Philips tubular incandescent bulbs and suspended from the ceiling by stock electrical wiring. This is one of the most beguiling ready-mades from a period that offered some excellent competition. It relates closely to Rietveld's approximately contemporary sculpture (now in the Centraal Museum, Utrecht) representing the Cartesian node. Both that construction and the light fixture capture the spirit of Rietveld's design at its most essential. Walter Gropius designed a quite similar fixture for his office at the Bauhaus in Weimar in 1923 (fig. 77) and it represents one of the clearest influences of De Stijl on the artists of the Bauhaus. But Rietveld's lamp is by far the more imaginative design. He set the horizontal and vertical bulbs at parallels and perpendiculars that do not touch, thereby creating a lively spatial volume. Gropius, however, placed the bulbs of his lamp end to end at right angles, a more obvious, more static and less sculptural conception.

Also dating from the years between 1918 and 1923 are several designs for children's furniture, which include four high chairs, a baby buggy, a toy wheelbarrow, and a never-executed crib (a working drawing[9] for the latter was a gift from Rietveld to his colleague J.J.P. Oud on the birth of a child). Rietveld's *kinderstoel* (baby chair) of 1920 (fig. 93) is perhaps the most characteristically Rietveldian of his high chair designs: its attenuated legs, high back, and rigid orthogonal emphasis were given a somewhat less forbidding appearance by its red lacquer finish and white terminals. But its numerous squared-off protuberances—much like those of a related design of 1919—strike one as eminently unsuitable seating for a flailing child. Rietveld's interest in children's furniture was no doubt stimulated by his own six children, three of whom were born within three successive years.[10]

The high-water mark of Rietveld's career as furniture designer came in 1923. His *pianostoetje* (piano chair) (fig. 91), done in that year, is memorable primarily as his first departure from quadrangular listels, and makes use instead of rounded mahogany dowels, forms which point to his experiments with bent metal tubing from 1926 to 1933. But of much greater interest is one of Rietveld's most important and impressive efforts: his Berlin chair (fig. 89), made for the model room he and the painter Vilmos Huszar designed together for the Greater Berlin Art Exhibition of 1923 (fig. 157). This chair is certainly Rietveld's most abstract composition. The legs, arms, seat and back are dematerialized to an astonishing degree through Rietveld's highly sophisticated plays of orthogonal form and neutral color. The Berlin chair is one of Rietveld's most architectonic pieces. Its strong planar elements—the large black panel that serves both as back and as rear "leg," the broad black horizontal armrest supported by a slightly narrower white leg panel, and the high, light gray, vertical side panel—are strongly evocative of the rectangular planes of Rietveld's Schröder house in Utrecht, completed in the following year, and for which this chair served virtually as the conceptual sketch. Relying little on conventional chair morphology—its asymmetrical form being its most striking departure—the Berlin chair complemented the volumetric quality of the Berlin room design perfectly, making the painted wall, ceiling and floor treatment (Huszar's contribution) read much more convincingly as three-dimensional space than, for example, Mondrian's 1926 design for the *Salon de Madame B. . . ., à Dresden* (fig. 161).

Rietveld's other great 1923 furniture design is the small end table (fig. 90) he designed for use in the Schröder house. The table is made from just five members, as opposed to 17 for the red/blue chair and eight for the Berlin chair. What Rietveld was able to do with five pieces of pine board and five colors of lacquer is nothing short of breathtaking. The sculptor and critic Scott Burton has written one of the best appreciations of the end table:

> . . . it is so satisfying formally, with its slight but sharp displacements, and coloristically. Notice its subtle concentricity of square and circle, its splitting of the vertical support into two not quite equal-size parts, its confinement of primary colors to top and bottom, its simultaneous expression and concealment of structure in the blue rectangle painted over the dovetail joining top and support. . . The listel, by being painted a bright yellow and being shifted a cube's worth out from under the top, acts to lead the eye underneath, to a hitherto neglected zone of furniture. Here is a maximally considered object. . .[11]

11. Scott Burton, "Furniture Journal: Rietveld," *Art in America*, November 1980, p 106.

(See Friedman, pp 212-216, for Scott Burton's views of the De Stijl movement in general, and Rietveld in particular.)

Furthermore, the attention Rietveld paid even to the edges of the end table is no less superbly thought out, and adds greatly to its compositional success. The edge of the circular base is white, emphasizing the planar horizontality of the base's red top, as the white edges of the table's square black top likewise do. The narrow edges of the vertical black rectangle above the base are white, while those of the white rectangle joined at a right angle above it are black, giving a subtle continuity of color and visual line to those two perpendicular upright pieces. In position in the living room on the upper floor of the Schröder house, the end table, together with its setting, represented one of the most brilliant conjunctions of furniture and architecture ever to come from the hand of the same designer.

Rietveld's ensuing designs for bent tubular metal furniture (a dozen pieces in all) were not nearly so important either as his own earlier work or as the superior bent-tube designs of several of his contemporaries, such as Mart Stam, Marcel Breuer and Ludwig Mies van der Rohe. In fact, it might be said that Rietveld had but one truly great furniture design left in him: his zig-zag chair of 1934 (fig 96). But as an object the zig-zag chair is of more conceptual than sculptural interest, and as fine a design as it is, it nonetheless signifies a retreat from the free abstractions of the Berlin chair—as indeed all of Rietveld's other furniture after 1923 did as well.

What, then, is Rietveld's place in the history of furniture design? In the first rank, certainly, a consignment confirmed by the interest his designs still command today, not least of all in the marketplace. Several of Rietveld's best known designs—the red/blue chair, the beechwood sideboard, the zig-zag chair and several pieces from his *krat* (crate) series of the mid-1930s—have been available in reproductions made by the Italian firm Cassina since 1971. Though public acceptance of Rietveld's furniture designs never has supported van Doesburg's optimistic claim that these pieces "will become the abstract-real artifacts of future interiors,"[12] it can now be seen that Rietveld's masterful sculpture-that-is-furniture and furniture-that-is-sculpture occupies a rightful place among the most extraordinary works of art created in our times.

12. Theo van Doesburg, "Aanteekeningen bij een leunstoel van Rietveld" (Notes on an armchair by Rietveld), *De Stijl,* II, 11, September 1919, p 135. Giedion trans.

Martin Filler is an architectural critic and editor of *House and Garden*.

The 1981 photographs of the Rietveld/Schröder house by Frank den Oudsten were commissioned for this publication.

94, 95

"Without bothering to adapt the house to some extent to the traditional houses on the Prins Hendriklaan, we simply attached it to the adjacent house. It was the best thing we could do—to make it stand out in contrast as much as possible. Understandably, it was very hard to square this with the local building code. That's why, on the ground floor, the house presents a rather traditional layout, i.e., with fixed walls; but the level upstairs we simply dubbed an attic, and there we realized the house we intended to make."
Gerrit Rietveld, 1963

136

Toward the end of 1923, Rietveld was commissioned to design and build a house on the outskirts of Utrecht by Mrs. Truus Schröder-Schräder, with whom he had collaborated since 1921. The project was Rietveld's first major architectural enterprise and was a collaborative effort from the beginning; Rietveld was responsible for the overall design and colors, Schröder-Schräder conceived the innovative, open plan of the upper floor.

Rietveld's biographer Theodore Brown has pointed out that the most conspicuous aspect of the Schröder house's design is the visual independence of its parts. This independence is achieved in various ways: through the use of overlapping components, the use of color to accentuate the identity of different elements, and the physical separation of planes. The overall effect is one of openness and weightlessness; one perceives the Schröder house not as a monolithic, cubic mass, but as a group of freely related planes and lines that appear to hover in space.

The interior exhibits the same flexibility of design as the exterior. The only fixed volumes on the upper floor are the bathroom and the stairwell. The rest of the space is one large area that can be subdivided into smaller volumes by sliding panels. The "rooms" created when the panels are moved into place are adaptable to a variety of functions, ensuring that the space can be modified according to the changing needs of the inhabitants. One always experiences a richly articulated space, even when the panels are fully drawn back. The built-in furniture is so successfully integrated into

96. Truus Schröder-Schräder, 1980, seated on a Rietveld zig-zag chair (1934), in the north-east corner of the Schröder house first floor, overlooking the garden.

97. Rietveld (center) with Dutch designer Mart Stam (left) and Russian constructivist El Lissitzky, circa 1926.
Vintage photograph

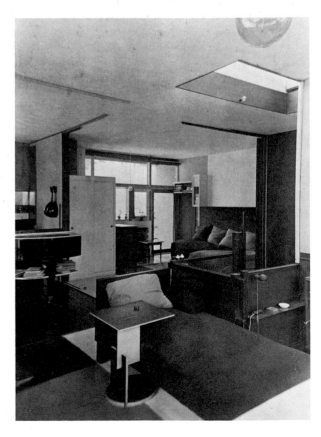

98. This exterior view of the Rietveld/Schröder house from the south-east, circa 1925, vividly demonstrates the startling contrast between it and the 19th-century terrace housing for which it became the corner block.
Vintage photograph

99. Interior view, looking south, showing stairwell without its transparent glass enclosure, circa 1928.
Vintage photograph

the surroundings that it seems a part of the architecture. As on the exterior, primary colors and the neutrals white, gray and black are used to emphasize the integrity of individual planes and linear components. Indeed, drawings show that Rietveld intended to use color much more extensively than on the exterior, giving the interior a pictorial quality previously known only in painting.

After seeing the house in 1926, El Lissitzky wrote:

...the fine and unique specimen of work, the Schröder house in Utrecht. The external view of it already gives the feeling that the inside of these walls should be the fresh work of Rietveld—a foremost leader of the contemporary art of housing. He is not an architectural student, he is a carpenter, and he was not able routinely to draw out a plan. He does all with models, feeling things with his hands; and therefore his product is not abstract. Hence one cannot judge such works by photographs, since by photographs we see only a view and not the life of the form.... The entire upper floor presents itself as one huge room in which furniture, with the exception of the chairs, is closely arranged [i.e., built-in]: cupboards, sofa-beds and tables are arranged like houses in a town, in such a way that there are areas for movement and use as if they were streets and squares.

100. View from the north, circa 1926, with first floor corner windows open. In this configuration, the distinction between interior and exterior disappears through the elimination of the building's corner.
Vintage photograph

101. Dining area looking east with the Berlin chair and the original dining table, circa 1926.
Vintage photograph

139

102-109. 1981 exterior views of the Rietveld/
Schröder house as restored in 1974.

Rietveld's vivid details—black, white and
brightly-colored linear elements—activate the
white and gray stucco planes of the building's
exterior.

141

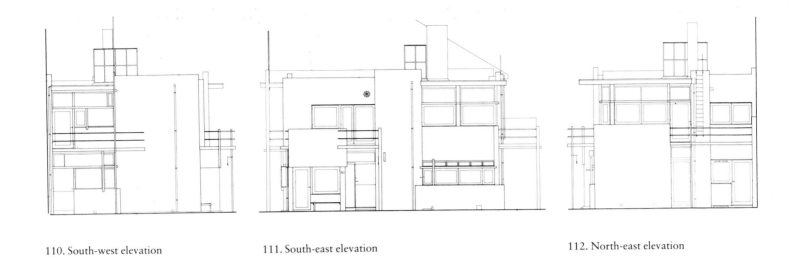

110. South-west elevation   111. South-east elevation   112. North-east elevation

113. Early Rietveld sketch, circa 1924.

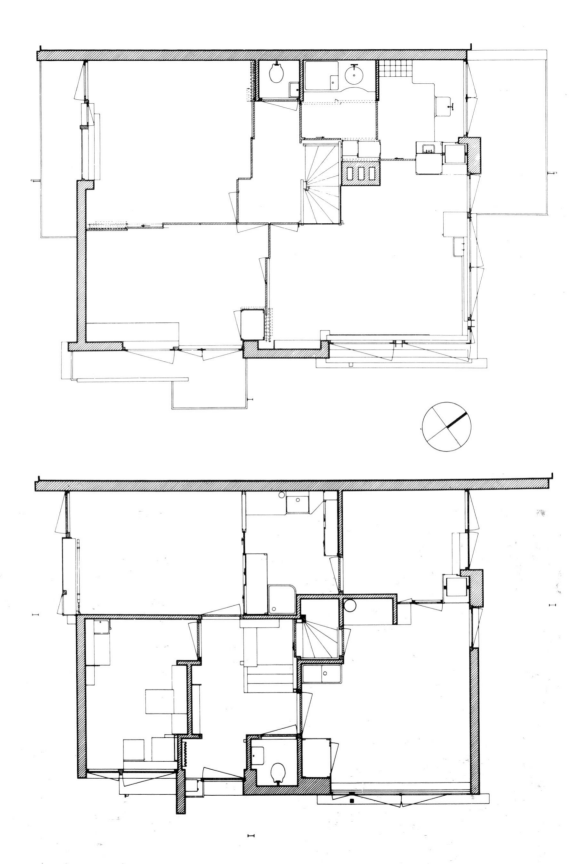

(facing page, top left)
117. An important aspect of the new architecture
is the striking similarity between inside and
outside form, color and detail, that is particularly
noticeable in the Rietveld/Schröder house. One
sees a repetition of the neutral gray planes with
linear detailing emphasized by the use of black,
white and bright color. The wood floors on the
first floor are covered with red, black and gray
felt in order to express horizontally, the ideas that
occur in the vertical plane.
View toward first floor kitchen.

(facing page, top right)
118. Looking north past the central stairway with
the glass enclosure in place. The rectangular
elements of the white chair (1963) are a variation
on the 1923 Berlin chair.

124, 125. In the lower view, looking south, the
movable panels of the first floor are seen in their
open position. Rietveld's hanging lamp is installed
in front of the free-standing blue chimney column.

It is evident that Rietveld's major concern in the
design of the house was the opening up of interior
space and the ambiguity between interior and
exterior achieved through translucency. Details
such as hardware and heating elements are the
inexpensive traditional systems of the 1920s.
Only the radiators were custom-made for the
house. It is essentially a very simple, rational
analysis of spatial needs that inspired this rather
humble, but historic structure. Rietveld's
experience with De Stijl architecture in the 1923
Paris exhibition, combined with the
sophistication of Truus Schröder's attitudes,
produced genuine invention.

126. El Lissitzky
Single page from "Of 2 Squares," 1922
(one of 12 pages from *De Stijl*, V, 10/11)
letterpress on paper
8½ x 11
21.6 x 27.9
Collection Haags Gemeentemuseum

From De Stijl to a New Typography

Kees Broos

Let us define the word "typography" here as the deliberate use of letters, in the broadest sense of the word. The user can be printer, typographer, architect, poet or painter. The materials are not restricted to those of the typechest or typesetting machine, but encompass every suitable medium from linoleum to electronic news marquees and from a tile tableau to television. It is important that the user be aware of the shape and function of each letter and consequently of the expressive potential in the design and arrangement of letters and text opened up to the reader and the viewer.

Roughly speaking, the use of letters can have two entirely different purposes. The first one is summarized in Beatrice Warde's adage: "Printing Should Be Invisible."[1] Here, typographic arrangement is subservient to content; its principal requirements are clarity and optimum legibility. The autonomous material presence of the letter and its substance—printer's ink on paper, paint on wood—should be as discrete as possible in relation to the substance of the text. The typographer is definitely in the service of the writer. The second purpose is practically opposed to the first. Here, typography has an autonomous function. Such typography emphasizes the visual potential of letter shape and the arrangement of text; symbolic, associative and expressive possibilities of typography affirm the content of the text or weaken it.

Some of the artists of the Stijl group have practiced typography in this latter sense. *De Stijl* magazine also kept track of similar typographical experiments by non-members. For those outsiders who experimented with typography, such as Paul van Ostaijen, H.N. Werkman and Piet Zwart, De Stijl ideas were a challenge and touchstone. Beatrice Warde disapprovingly called them "stunt typographers;" Herbert Spencer classified them as *Pioneers of Modern Typography*.[2] One of those pioneers was Theo van Doesburg himself, whose artistic and literary versatility and eclecticism were evident in his use of typography. As

1. Beatrice Warde, "Printing Should Be Invisible," in Paul A. Bennett (ed.) *Books and Printing* (Cleveland and New York: World Publishing Co., 1951); and a recent advocate for classical typography: John Ryder, *The Case for Legibility* (London, Sydney, Toronto: Moretus Press, 1979).
2. Herbert Spencer, *Pioneers of Modern Typography* (London: Lund Humphries, 1969).

127. Theo van Doesburg
Design for poster, *La Section d'Or*, 1920
pencil, ink on tracing paper mounted on
cardboard
25½ x 24⅝
65 x 62.5
Dienst Verspreide Rijkskollekties

128. Theo van Doesburg
Mécano magazine, Red, 1922
letterpress on paper
6½ x 5
16.5 x 12.7
Collection Mr. and Mrs. Arthur A. Cohen

3. L. Leering-van Moorsel, "Annotations on Theo van Doesburg's Typography," in *Theo van Doesburg 1883-1931* (Eindhoven: exh. cat. Stedelijk Van Abbemuseum, 1968).

4. It is a bit odd that the abstract composition on the cover was characterized as "typographical." This would imply that it had been put together from separate typographical constituents, such as copper lines. The original print does not indicate anything of the kind. I suspect that the word "typographical" here means that the composition was not printed directly from a woodcut, but from a line plate after a drawing. Judging from the typography of the inside of *De Stijl*, five volumes of the periodical seem to have been printed by the same printing house with the exception of IV, 5, which was set in a different letter type and probably was produced in Weimar. The first four issues of the 1923 volume do not seem to have been printed in The Netherlands either. Particularly in the sixth and seventh volumes, different types of letters are used for the text; van Doesburg was apparently very constrained by the printer's limitations: "Roman" (VI, 6/7, 8; VII, 79/84, 87/89); "light Bodoni" (VI, 9); "Cheltenham, old style" (VI, 10/11, 12; VII, 73/74-78, 87/89); "Baskerville" (dernier numéro).

5. Spencer and Leering-van Moorsel both cite van Doesburg as the designer of *De Stijl*'s title lettering.

6. R.W.D. Oxenaar, "Bart van der Leck until 1920—A Primitive of the New Time" (Utrecht State University, PhD diss., 1976), p 126.

7. Vilmos Huszar summarized both aspects in a painting dated 1916, which shows a variant of the cover picture in color, including the title. The simpler composition of the color surfaces and the extension of the lower horizontal beam of the letter Y to the full width of the letter image—a correction which was applied to *De Stijl*'s title page in the issue of August 1919—suggest that this painting has been dated at least three years too early.

editor-in-chief of *De Stijl* he used at first a rather symmetrical, plane-filling typography, and later an asymmetric one, tending towards the principles of the functional "new typography" (fig. 127). He used a less conventional typography in his dadaistic pamphlet *Mécano*, (fig. 128), and in his collaborations with El Lissitzky and Kurt Schwitters. In van Doesburg's typographic works we encounter both his dadaist and constructivist sides.[3]

Typographically, the first three volumes of the monthly periodical *De Stijl* are not very remarkable. Its design is solid and seems to have been delegated by van Doesburg to the small printing house in Leiden where the monthly was produced. Only in the cover and in a few advertisements do we perceive some deviations from the classic typographical image. In the first issue the cover design is specially annotated: "The typographical ornament on the cover, between title and text, is by the Hungarian artist Vilmos Huszar. It is taken from a woodcut, which was intended to be pure visual art, but has been applied here in order to create an aesthetic harmony and unity with the printing."[4] Letters and image have been deliberately balanced with each other.

The design for the title "De Stijl," over the abstract composition, has sometimes been attributed to van Doesburg, but since the dimensions of the letters correspond exactly to those of the composition, we appear to be entirely justified in assuming that Huszar designed both.[5] Moreover, the fragmentation of the letter images fit perfectly well into the context of Huszar's paintings of that particular period. In a letter to Bart van der Leck, some months later, he explained his point of view regarding the figure-ground problem in a painting. According to him, these should be "equivalent:" "This is the same process I have used on the cover of *De Stijl*, namely: to give white and black equal value, without ground. You may agree or disagree with this method, but the point is to understand it from the perspective of a solely aesthetic solution."[6] This cover design shows, as much as his paintings from 1917, to what extent Huszar was wavering between van Doesburg's and van der Leck's ideas (fig. 129). The abstract representation shows an affinity to van Doesburg's *Composition IX*, 1917 (fig. 131), while the letters of the title are more closely related to Huszar's own painting *Composition II*, 1917 (fig. 132), in which he reduces tiny skating figures to small horizontal and vertical rectangles with white interspaces.[7] The problems in a painting, as experienced by Huszar in 1917, are reflected in the shape of the letters in the title DE STIJL. The meaning of the words "De Stijl," as well as their shape embodied a program. When van Doesburg modified his ideas about visual art, these letters disappeared from the title and were replaced, starting in the fourth volume, by a more dynamic use of typographical resources (fig. 130).

129. Vilmos Huszar
De Stijl cover, I, 1, 1917
letterpress on paper
10¼ x 7½
26 x 19
Collection Haags Gemeentemuseum

130. Theo van Doesburg
De Stijl cover, as reproduced in VIII,
85/86, 1928

131. Theo van Doesburg
Composition IX, Card Players, 1917
oil on canvas
45¾ x 41¾
115.9 x 106.1
Collection Haags Gemeentemuseum

132. Vilmos Huszar
Composition II, Skaters, 1917
oil on canvas
29⅛ x 31⅞
74 x 81
Collection Haags Gemeentemuseum
(not in exhibition)

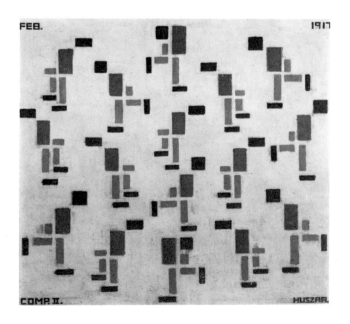

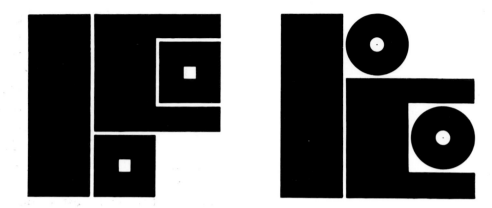

133. Piet Zwart
Designs for logo, IOCO, 1922-24
ink on paper
3½ x 12⅜
8.8 x 31.4
Collection Haags Gemeentemuseum

8. Hans Oldewarris, "Wijdeveld's Typography,"
in *Forum*, XXV, 1, 1975, p 3.
9. Spencer, *op. cit.*
10. Fridolin Müller, Peter F. Althaus, *Piet Zwart*
(Teufen: Verlag Niggili Arthur, 1966), pp 15, 17.
They incorrectly attribute Jan Wils's seal to Piet
Zwart.
11. This portfolio was published on the occasion
of an exhibition dedicated to low-income housing
in the Haagse Kunstkring, September 1919. The
plates—after works by Granpré Molière, Dudok,
Vorkink and Wormser, and others—were drawn
by Jan Wils; H.P. Berlage wrote the
introduction.

Geometrical experiments with letter shapes and letter combinations were rather popular in the post-World War I years. The most prominent representative of this deliberately anti-classical typography was the architect H. Th. Wijdeveld who, in his luxuriously laid out periodical *Wendingen*, founded in January 1918, devised extremely complicated typographical constructions with typographical materials. This made the design of *Wendingen* compatible with its contents and consequently the antipode of van Doesburg's austere *De Stijl*. In spite of this antithesis, both show a certain tendency toward systematizing and plane filling, which can be traced back to the work of the important but somewhat forgotten architect J.L.M. Lauweriks.[8] His "systematic design" of his periodical *Ring* (from 1908 on) considerably influenced such outsiders as architects, interior designers and other letter designers, with ". . . scant regard to the traditions of the printing industry."[9]

Theo van Doesburg designed monograms for his friends Antony Kok and J.J.P. Oud. These monograms were executed on graph paper. Gerrit Rietveld designed a monogram for the front of an Amsterdam jewelry shop, consisting of the capital letters G, Z and C, inscribed precisely in a square. The architect Jan Wils, who belonged to De Stijl from the very beginning, signed his drawings from 1916 on with a geometric monogram consisting of rectangular blocks. In 1920, his then collaborator Piet Zwart used the Wils monogram in a design for a letterhead; this was the beginning of Zwart's career as a typographic designer.[10] Piet Zwart who happened to be Huszar's neighbor, collaborated with him in designing furniture and interiors. The lettering of the drawings followed a pattern of squares, linked together, according to Wijdeveld's system; Zwart followed the same principle in his designs for bookplates and printed matter for the Haagse Kunstkring (Hague Art Circle),[11] and in his geometric logos for the LAGA/IOCO Company (fig. 133).

Wils, Huszar and Zwart lived in Voorburg, a suburb of The Hague, which was also the residence of Cornelis Bruynzeel, founder of a woodworking industry, who was rather sympathetic to the young new art. He commissioned interior designs and exhibition stands from Huszar, Zwart, Klaarhamer and van der Leck, and supported the first six issues of *De Stijl* with a full-page advertisement designed by Huszar (fig 134). In a letterhead for Bruynzeel, Huszar used a geometric alphabet, and also for a cover of a portfolio of architectural drawings, published by the Haagse Kunstkring (fig. 135). This time the letters on the cover are solidly constructed and the abstract composition consists of distinct elements, just the opposite of the *Stijl* cover. These letters are comparable to the basic, upper-case alphabet which van Doesburg made for his own use, on a basic pattern of 5 x 5 units. He maintained that one could arbitrarily distort the basic shape of a letter horizontally or vertically. This was absolutely contrary to classical typography in which the proportions of the basic shape are inviolate and wherein the letter can only be scaled up or down without distortion. His design for the cover of the periodical *Klei* (Clay), 1919 (fig. 136), and the poster for the exhibition *La Section d'Or* (fig. 127), were based on this fundamental alphabet. By changing the basic square framework sometimes to a 2 x 3 rectangle and at other times to one of 5 x 4, he could squeeze long and short lines within a rectangular frame and at the same time construct a visually cohesive picture. Clear legibility was evidently relegated to secondary importance.[12]

Later, van Doesburg experimented very little with letter shapes themselves. When, in 1927, he designed type for the Café Aubette directory in Strasbourg (fig. 138), he reverted to his basic alphabet from 1918-19.[13] Van Doesburg's alphabet, as distinct from the letters in the title of *De Stijl*, consists of letters which are compact, self-contained constructions.

The manner in which the image of the letters of the *De Stijl* title can be separated into elements is found most consistently in the work of Bart van der Leck. In 1919 he designed a poster for the Nederlandse Olie Fabriek (Netherlands Oil Manufacturing Company) at Delft, in which the destruction of the letter shape parallels completely what he was doing in his paintings. The round elements in the classic letter shape are reduced to linear shapes in his letters, but—and here he differs from Huszar—the diagonal is accepted as a matter of course, and the white background is much more prominent than in the more compact shapes of Huszar's letters.[14]

Although the client who commissioned the design did not have it printed, van der Leck continued to use this alphabet; at first in a poster for an exhibition of his own work at Utrecht (fig. 139) and later—a lighter

12. *Haagse Kunstkring: Collected Works* (The Hague: exh. cat. Haags Gemeentemuseum, 1977), p 34. The Golden Section exhibition came from Antwerp in 1920 to the rooms of the Haagse Kunstkring.
13. In 1922 his letters appear on a poster design for the "Kölner Messe" (Cologne Fair), which was reproduced in *De Stijl*, V, 12, 1922, under the name of Egon Engelien.
14. R.W.D. Oxenaar, *Bart van der Leck 1876-1958* (Otterlo: exh. cat. Rijksmuseum Kröller-Müller, 1976), fig. T163. Bart van der Leck had previously employed geometrically styled letter shapes on the poster for the Batavierlijn (1915-16), designed for the shipping firm Wm. Müller & Co., Rotterdam (fig. 37).

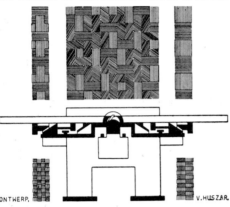

 C. BRUIJNZEEL & ZONEN
ROTTERDAM
PARKETVLOEREN
EIKENVLOEREN MET KOPSCHE GROEF EN MESSING
OM DIRECT OP DE BINTEN TE SPIJKEREN

ONTWERP. V. HUSZAR.

134. Vilmos Huszar
Ad for Bruynzeel Furniture
as reproduced in *De Stijl*, I, 1, 1917, p 2

135. Vilmos Huszar
Portfolio cover for *Volkswoningbouw
Kunstkring*(Artists' Group for Public Housing)
no date
letterpress on paper
17 x 12⅝
42 x 32
Collection Haags Gemeentemuseum

15. The Belgian periodical *Het Overzicht* (The Survey) used the same kind of geometric letters on the cover, designed and cut in linoleum by Jozef Peeters (see numbers 7/8, 1921; 13, 1922; 19, 1913). He wrote about this work and the work of his colleagues Jos. Leonard, Karel Maes and Alf. Francken under the heading "Constructive graphics:" "Whenever a graphic artist is asked to design the letter, he will need to adapt its form to the atmosphere of the literary work." (*Het Overzicht* 19, 1923, p 111). The constructivist periodical *De Driehok* (The Triangle), 1925-26, the successor of *Het Overzicht*, also uses letters that are a crossbreed between van Doesburg's and Wijdeveld's alphabets.
16. Herbert Bayer, "Typographie und Werbsachengestaltung" (Typography and Advertising Design), in *Bauhaus, Zeitschrift für Gestaltung* (Design Journal), II, 1, 1928, p 10.

Josef Albers, "Zur Schablonenschrift" (On Typesetting), in *Offset, Buch und Webekunst* (Offset, Book and Advertising Design), 7, 1926, p 397.
Kurt Schwitters, "Anregungen zur Erlangung einer Systemschrift. I-II" (Attempt to Achieve a Letter System), in *Der Sturm* (The Storm) XIX, 1, 2/3, 1928.
In a letter dated 27 June 1927, Schwitters asked van Doesburg to publish some of his "letter systems" in the next issue of *De Stijl*. Van Doesburg did not comply.
Kurt Schwitters, *Wir Spielen, bis uns der Tod Abholt* (We Play Until Death Takes Us), (Frankfurt/Main, Berlin, Vienna: Ullstein Verlag, 1974), p 116.
17. Examples of such a "commercial" letter type in architecture are Café De Unie (fig. 19) (Rotterdam, J.J.P. Oud, 1924) and the store, Zaudy (Wesel, G. Rietveld, 1928). Vilmos Huszar

version—for wrapping and advertising material for the Amsterdam store Metz & Company. As late as 1941 he designed a bibliophile edition of one of Andersen's fairytales in this way. Van der Leck's letter shapes are not constructed according to a rigid pattern, but distilled from common letter shapes and subsequently interwoven into a homogeneous texture. The resulting loss in direct legibility is amply compensated for by the strong poetic element gained effortlessly through the artless childlike manner in which they are drawn.

Experiments with letter shapes that suggest a parallel with the principles of De Stijl remained few and far between. Gerrit Rietveld applied beautiful geometrically stylized letter shapes to some storefronts (G. & Z.C. jewelry shop, Amsterdam, 1920-22, among others), and as late as 1929, Huszar designed a cover for an issue of *Wendingen,* dedicated to Diego Rivera, in which he used his square letters from the Huszar/Zwart period. But eventually the geometric deformation of the letter image was abandoned, perhaps because this was too reminiscent of Wijdeveld's typography in *Wendingen.*[15]

The potential for the development of new letter shapes from a geometric basis was not realized in The Netherlands; in Germany it was to a certain extent: Herbert Bayer ("Universal," 1925), Josef Albers (Schabloneletters from three basic geometric shapes, 1925) and Kurt Schwitters (Systemschrift, 1927) made a few attempts in this direction, with varying degrees of success.[16] The visual artists and architects belonging to the Stijl group reverted to using existing unrestrained letter types, which, though dating from the 19th century, were nevertheless very well suited to the requirements of legibility and applicability to diverse media. Starting with the fourth volume, the cover of *De Stijl* was constituted once more of existing "grotesques," but now in a new manner that considered the letter as a constructive element in the plane.[17]

In a short article about Rietveld's furniture, in the third volume of *De Stijl,* van Doesburg for the first time used existing type in an unusual manner: he employed different letter sizes in order to emphasize the meanings of his words.[18] In the next issue he went even further and published, in collaboration with Mondrian and Kok, a manifesto about literature in three languages. He wanted to ". . . give a new meaning and new power of expression to the words" and to ". . . create a constructive unity of content and form." Typography was one of the means he wanted to use to this end.[19] In the next issue his meaning was explained, when he published a series of poems, entitled "X-Images" under the pseudonym, I. K. Bonset (fig. 141). These poems had been created some years earlier under the title "Cubistic Verses," but here for the first time

also reverted to an ordinary unrestrained letter in his advertisement for Miss Blanche in *De Stijl,* VII, 79/84, 1927, p 30.
De Stijl's new cover, with its open center and a composition constructed from the edge, deliberately deviates from axial typography in favor of a dynamic solution. The same thing happens in De Stijl's stationery: the title shifts from top center to the left, and is balanced by a vertically placed text in the lower left. The change over to a two-column format was explained by van Doesburg in *De Stijl,* IV, 2, 1921, p 17, on purely practical grounds: the magazine could now be folded for mailing.
18. Theo van Doesburg, "The paintings of Giorgio de Chirico, and a chair by Rietveld," in *De Stijl,* III, 5, 1920, p 46.
19. Theo van Doesburg, Piet Mondrian, Antony Kok, "Manifesto II of De Stijl, 1920—The Literature," *De Stijl,* III, 6, 1920, p 49.

HLEI

15 FEBRUARI 1919.

12e JAARGANG No. 4.

ORGAAN
VANDENBONDVAN
BAKSTEENFABRIKANTEN
ENDENBONDVAN
DAKPANNENFABRIKANTEN

136. Theo van Doesburg
Magazine cover for *Klei*, 1919
pencil, ink on tracing paper mounted on
cardboard
34½ x 24
87.5 x 61
Dienst Verspreide Rijkskollekties

137. Piet Zwart
Rubbervloeren (Rubber Floor), 1922
lithograph on paper
35⅞ x 25½
91 x 65
Collection Haags Gemeentemuseum

138. Theo van Doesburg
Directory for Café Aubette, 1927
pencil, ink, gouache on tracing paper
36¼ x 10⅝
92.2 x 27
Collection State of Holland, on loan to the Musée
National d'Art Moderne, Centre Georges
Pompidou
(not in exhibition)

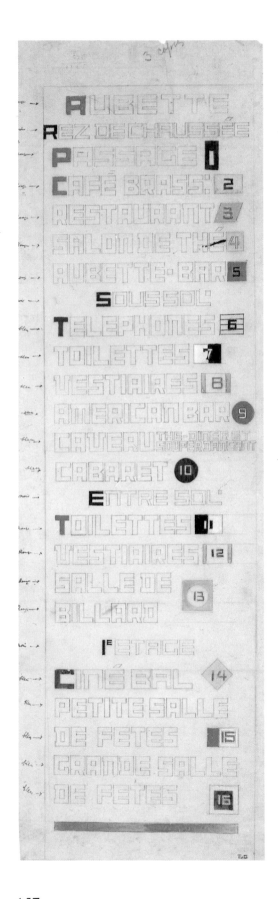

139. Bart van der Leck
Poster for *Tentoonstelling v.d. Leck,*
12 Jan.-9 Feb. 1919 (Exhibition v.d. Leck)
lithograph on paper
45⅝ x 22
115.9 x 55.9
Collection Stedelijk Museum, Amsterdam

20. I.K. Bonset, "X-Images," *De Stijl,* III, 7, 1920, p 57. Van Doesburg's poems have been reprinted—partly in manuscript, partly in their definitive typographical form—in I.K. Bonset, *Nieuwe woordbeeldingen. De gedichten van Theo van Doesburg. Met een nawoord van K. Schippers.* (New Word Images. Poems by Theo van Doesburg. With an epilogue by K. Schippers). (Amsterdam: Em. Querido, 1975). See Hannah L. Hedrick, *Theo van Doesburg, Propagandist and Practitioner of the Avant-garde, 1909-1923* (Ann Arbor: University Microfilms International Research Press, 1980), for an English translation of some of the poems, and an evaluation within the literary tradition.

21. Van Doesburg reviewed Paul van Ostaijen's volume *Bezette stad* (Occupied City) (Antwerp: 1921) very harshly; "Literary: empty, hollow and inflated—a gross imitation of the French sport of literature," in *De Stijl,* IV, 12, 1921, p 179, after he had already panned it in *Het Getij* (The Tide), VI, 1921, p 25-29, as an imitation of Blaise Cendrars. Gerrit Borgers, *Paul van Ostaijen* (The Hague: Bert Bakker, 1971).

22. Til Brugman, "R," in *De Stijl,* VI, 3/4, 1923, pp 55-56.
Antony Kok, "Nachtkroeg" (Nightclub), in *De Stijl,* VI, 3/4, 1923, pp 55-56.

23. El Lissitzky, "Van twee kwadraten" (Of 2 Squares), in *De Stijl,* V, 10/11, 1922.
Yve-Alain Bois, "El L. didactique de lecture" (El L. teacher of reading), in *Avant-Guerre 2,* 1981, p 57.

24. The translation of the Russian text into Dutch naturally forced van Doesburg to change Lissitzky's typography in some places. He also changed the original vertical format of the publication in Russian (Berlin, 1922) to the oblong format in which *De Stijl* was published from the fourth volume on. This change caused

they assumed a typographical form. It was no longer the individual letter that created an "atmosphere" or "association," but rather the organization and scale of the letters and words on the page that accentuated the contents of the text and the meaning of the words. Thus the "X-Images" fit into a literary tradition that traces back to the "calligrammes" of Guillaume Apollinaire by way of futurist poetry to the concrete poetry of our time.[20]

Van Doesburg was aware that similar experiments with visual typography were underway in Belgium. The Belgian poet Paul van Ostaijen achieved even more fascinating results with his "rhythmical poetry" than had van Doesburg, but he was criticized ungraciously in *De Stijl*.[21]

So far, autonomous typography emphasized *form* and *meaning*. However, van Doesburg had, in his manifesto about literature, postulated that in poetry the word should be posed according to its meaning as well as according to its sound. In van Doesburg's work the *sound* element also assumes a shape through typographic means. He published his "Letter-Sound Images" in the fourth volume of *De Stijl*, with directions for correct performance (fig. 142). Here, too, he realized earlier ideas about the role of sounds in poetry, and gave a form to free, elementarist verse through his typography. These ideas related to those of Raoul Haussmann and Kurt Schwitters. In the second issue of his periodical *Mécano* (1922) van Doesburg published a sound poem by Haussmann and his "Manifesto on the laws of sound;" a "Sonata" by Kurt Schwitters appeared in *Mécano* 4/5. In his turn, Schwitters published van Doesburg's "Letter-Sound Images" in the first issue of his magazine *Merz*. Later, van Doesburg published sound poems by Til Brugman and Antony Kok in *De Stijl*.[22]

the relation between text and illustrations to be drastically altered in some places. Lissitzky was clearly least happy with the addition, on the inside of the cover, of van Doesburg's own typographical composition of the words "Voor Allen" (for everyone). This change was undoubtedly unavoidable, because it was practically impossible to translate Lissitzky's drawing, constituting p 3, into Dutch. In any case, Lissitzky's widow expressed herself in the following negative terms: "By his changes, van Doesburg made the cover more commercial than Lissitzky's design had been."
Sophie Lissitzky-Küppers, *El Lissitzky: Painter, Architect, Typographer, Photographer* (Dresden: VEB Verlag der Kunst, 1967), p 21. See also: Camilla Gray, "El Lissitzky's Typographical Principles," in *El Lissitzky* (Eindhoven: exh. cat. Stedelijk Van Abbemuseum, 1966), p 20.

De Stijl's truly important contribution to typography came from abroad. It was the special issue "Of 2 Squares," van Doesburg's adaptation for the Dutch public of the children's book by El Lissitzky, which had just been published in Berlin (fig. 143). This book gave an unequalled survey of all visual, associative, meaningful and auditory possibilities that word and image—juxtaposed in tension—could bring out on the page.[23] Although the Dutch version was not as strong as the original in Russian, it did burst upon the scene like a thunderclap in a clear sky; it made a powerful impression by simultaneously breaking through many conventions because of its revolutionary and convincing notions about the visual potential of the printed book.[24] El Lissitzky's typographical version of Mayakowsky's volume of poems *For Reading Aloud* (Berlin, 1923), which demonstrated even more forcefully the creative use of existing letters and linear materials, resulted in enthusiastic support for his work among the European avant-garde.

140. Vilmos Huszar
Poster for *Tentoonstelling van Hedendaagsche Kunstnyverheid*
(Exhibition of Contemporary Industrial Arts),
1929
lithograph on paper
27½ x 23½
69.9 x 59.7
Collection Stedelijk Museum, Amsterdam

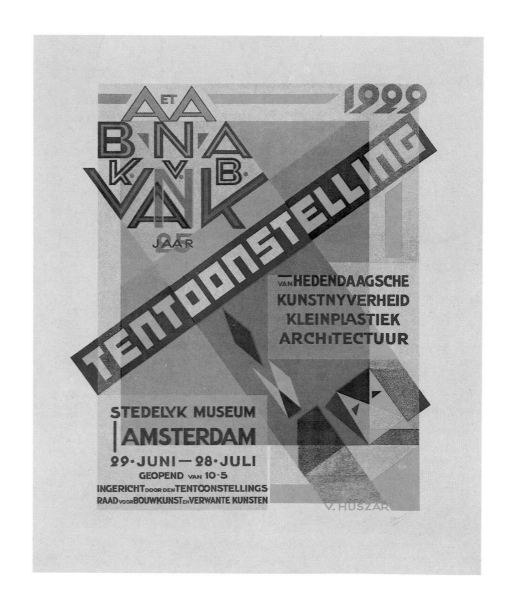

141. Theo van Doesburg
"X-Images" as reproduced in *De Stijl*, III, 7, 1920,
p 57

142. Theo van Doesburg
"Letter-Sound Images" as reproduced in *De Stijl*,
IV, 11, 1921, p 163

X-BEELDEN [1]

DOOR I. K. BONSET.

'k word doordrongen van de kamer waar de tram doorglijdt
ik heb 'n pet op
orgelklanken
van buitendoormijheen
vallen achter mij kapot
kleine scherven
BLIK BLIK BLIK
en glas
kleine zwarte fietsers
glijden en verdwijnen in mijn beeltenis
+ LICHTn
de ritsigzieke trilkruin van den boom
versnippert het buitenmij
tot bontgekleurd stof
de zwartewitte waterpalen
4× HORIZONTAAL
ontelbare verticale palen
en ook de hooge
gekromde blauwe
RUIMTE
BEN IK

---

[1]   Deze „*x*-Beelden" zijn uit de reeks „Kubistische verzen" (1913—1919).

Blikken trommel
Blikken trommel
Blikken trommel
RANSEL
BLikken trommel
Blikken trommel
Ransel
Blikken trommel
Ransel
Blikken trommel
RAN

Rui   schen
Rui   schen
Rui   schen
Rui   schen
Ruischen
Ruisch . . .
Rui . . .
Ru . . .
Ru . . .
R . . .
R . . .
r . .

143. El Lissitzky
Single page from "Of 2 Squares," 1922
(one of 12 pages from *De Stijl*, V, 10/11
letterpress on paper
8½ x 11
21.6 x 27.9
Collection Haags Gemeentemuseum

144. Kurt Schwitters/Theo van Doesburg/
Käthe Steinitz
Cover for "Die Scheuche" (The Scarecrow), *Merz*,
14/15, 1925
letterpress on paper
8¹⁄₁₆ x 9⅝
20.5 x 24.5
Collection Stedelijk Museum, Amsterdam

25. L. Leering-van Moorsel, "The Typography of El Lissitzky," in *The Journal of Typographic Research*, II, 4, 1968, p 323. Jan Tschichold, "Werke und Aufsätze van El Lissitzky" (Works and essays by El Lissitzky), in *Typographische Monatsblätter* (Typographic Monthly), Dec. 1970, p 1.

26. *Ibid.*

27. L. Leering-van Moorsel, in "Annotations on Theo van Doesburg's Typography," *op. cit.*, is of the opinion that the typography of *Die Scheuche* can be attributed completely to van Doesburg, because of a letter from van Doesburg to Käthe Steinitz, dated 16 April 1925. In this letter he proposes detailed typographic corrections. However, from a letter from Schwitters to van Doesburg, dated 22 April 1925, we can conclude that those corrections were not incorporated into the book: "Mrs. Steinitz has departed. I have read your letter to her with the corrections, my dear Does. They came too late, the volume is ready. I hope to be able to send you the first copy today." (Schwitters, *Wir spielen bis uns de Tod Abholt*, *op. cit.*, p 94.)

28. Jan Tschichold, *Die neue typographie* (The new typography), (Berlin: Verlag des Bildungsverbandes der deutsche buchdrucker, 1928).
Kees Broos, Flip Bool, *Domela: Paintings, Reliefs, Sculptures, Graphic Work, Typography, Photographs* (The Hague: exh. cat. Haags Gemeentemuseum, 1980).

When he visited The Netherlands in 1923—on 23 May he gave a lecture for the Haagse Kunstkring on New Russian Art—he met a younger generation, with whom he could discuss his typographical ideas: "The design of the book. . . must be in accordance with the strains and stresses innate in the contents."[25] Soon afterward we can see in the typographical work of Piet Zwart new dynamics and a more spontaneous use of letter and image; and van Doesburg too could not stand aloof from the strong effect of Lissitzky's visual typography. When he visited Kurt Schwitters in Hannover in 1925, he also met Käthe Steinitz, with whom Schwitters had previously collaborated on the children's books *Der Hahnepeter* (The Rooster) and *Die Märchen vom Paradies* (Fairytales of Paradise). She recollects that van Doesburg said, "Couldn't we make another picture book, an even more radical one, using nothing but typographical elements? Lissitzky had once designed a book of poems in a new typographical style. We would try the same method but make it entirely different."[26] Thus *Die Scheuche* (The Scarecrow) was born, the most sympathetic typographical experiment on which van Doesburg collaborated (fig. 144).[27] Schwitters realized the possibility of making these typographical experiments more commercially appealing through group publication. In 1927 he founded the Ring neuer Werbegestalter (Circle of new Advertising Artists). Four of the committed staff of *De Stijl* became members (Friedrich Vordemberge-Gildewart, César Domela, Werner Graeff and Hans Richter). They were joined by Jan Tschichold, Piet Zwart, Hans Leistikow and Walter Dexel. Van Doesburg refused to join. The new ideas found a wide and penetrating distribution through many exhibitions and the publication of Jan Tschichold's book, *The New Typography*.[28]

De Stjil had been in part the source of inspiration for these ideas, in part their incubator, and finally, it had played a crucial role as irritating antagonist.

Kees Broos is Director of the Department of Modern Art, Haags Gemeentemuseum, The Hague.

Translation by Charlotte I. Loeb

The Abstract Environment of De Stijl

> For the pure revelation of painting, what is necessary in the first place is an *atmosphere*. And who is in a better position to bring this atmosphere into being than the architect?. . .
>
> [W]e are in need of a new interior. And who brings the new interior about? The Architect. Therefore we must do business with the architect and achieve with him a spiritual equilibrium. . . . Thus it should not surprise you that I very much desire a collaboration with you. Around our realized emotions you can create a space, an atmosphere, which shall do justice to our artistic expression. We can bring your emotion, realized by means of space and atmosphere, to its full independence, precisely through our coloristic and formal projects.[1]

Nancy J. Troy

With these words, written to the architect J.J.P. Oud in June 1916, Theo van Doesburg expressed the aspirations of a great many artists who came to professional maturity during World War I. The momentous events of the war years coincided with radical developments in the realm of aesthetics, in particular with the genesis of abstract painting, to create a situation in which artists and architects even in neutral Holland felt a need to establish a new environment that would join the arts in a constructive harmony heralding the reintegration of post-war society. Their aim was to work through the arts to achieve an ideal atmosphere, a spiritual equilibrium, in concrete form. To reach that goal, many painters and architects sought to combine their efforts in collaborative endeavors that would bring their respective modes of expression to fulfillment through a process of mutual interaction and aesthetic development. The founding of the magazine *De Stijl* in October 1917, was part of this drive to establish a formal vocabulary, a stylistic credo, to which architects, painters and other artists who shared a common set of ethical and aesthetic principles could all subscribe. The fundamental nature of the magazine, intended to foster ". . . closer contact between artist and public and between the practitioners of the various artistic professions,"[2] was itself reflected in the collaborative environmental projects of those who contributed to the pages of *De Stijl*. Often working together, they produced dozens of coloristic designs destined for both

145. Designed by van Doesburg and painted by Jean Arp, this 1928 stairway in the Café Aubette is reminiscent of the radical, 1917 Oud/van Doesburg-designed stair in "De Vonk" ("the spark"), the Noordwijkerhout holiday residence. Vintage photograph

1. Theo van Doesburg, letter to J.J.P. Oud, 1 June 1916, Institut Néerlandais, Paris. This and subsequent translations by the author unless otherwise stated.
2. Redactie, "Ter Inleiding," *De Stijl*, I, 1 (Oct. 1917), p 1. Facsimile reprint, 2 vols. (Amsterdam: Athenaeum and Polak & Van Gennep; The Hague: Bert Bakker, 1968).

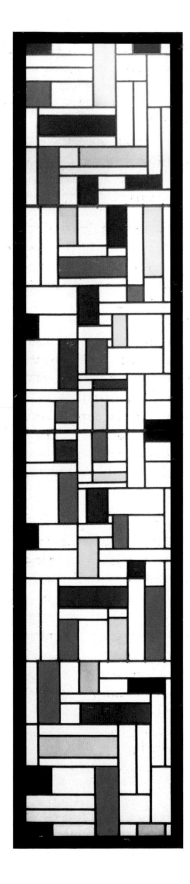
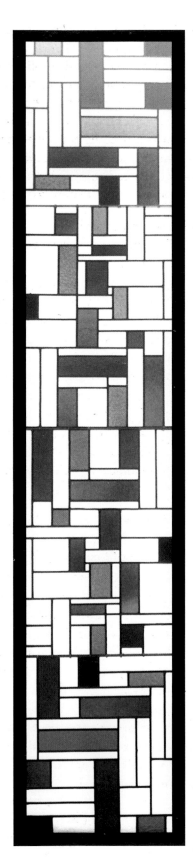
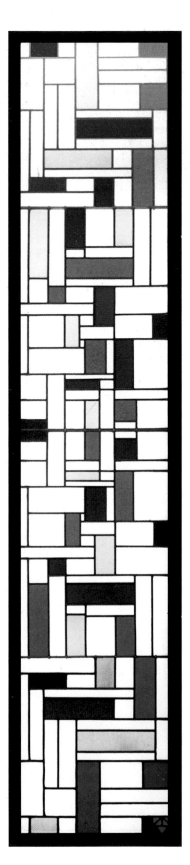

146. Theo van Doesburg
Composition IV (in three parts), 1917
stained glass
112¾ x 22¼ each panel
286.5 x 56.6
Collection Dienst Verspreide Rijkskollekties

147. Jan Wils's townhouse for Mr. de Lange in
Alkmaar, Berlagian in its brick exterior,
contained this extraordinary van Doesburg
stained-glass window, executed by Vennootschap
Crabeth, The Hague. Recently removed from the
now abandoned building, this window was saved
by the Dutch government from imminent
destruction.
Vintage photograph

private and public spaces ranging from houses to café interiors. Furthermore, the interiors of their own ateliers often functioned as both personal dwellings and quasi-public exhibition spaces, and actual exhibitions also provided a locus for this kind of design activity. In such situations it was possible to realize a temporary setting which could serve as a microcosmic model for the environment at large—the city, for example. It was especially the modern urban environment that the De Stijl artists hoped would one day be transformed into an abstract, aesthetically balanced composition at once embodying and providing an appropriate setting for the new social era they envisioned.

The utopian inclination of the De Stijl enterprise as a whole was directly reflected in environmental projects in which color and architecture were merged to form total works of art. Given the radically abstract character of these designs, it is not surprising that relatively few were actually carried out and that of those realized, only two have survived more or less intact to the present day. The rest are known to us only through drawings, descriptions or photographs, or through reconstructions that have been made on the basis of documentary evidence. Ironically, the artists themselves were in part responsible for the disappearance of the work they produced. Unwilling to adapt to inherited traditions or existing conventions, they created designs of uncompromisingly severe stylistic purity that demanded adaptation on the part of those who would inhabit them. When these ideas were broadened to environmental scope, they called for changes in society as a whole. Small wonder, then, that most of their environmental work has been destroyed.

In view of this paradoxical situation, it is important to understand that the De Stijl synthesis of ethics and aesthetics, the effort to achieve a pure art form that would function in a social context, was not a superficial attitude, but one that stemmed from the essential nature of the designs themselves. The collaborative work upon which the moral basis of De Stijl was founded was the immediate consequence of the stylistic purity which characterized De Stijl's aesthetic principles. In calling for a return to the fundamentals of design, the De Stijl program implied that every type of art required systematic study and that once they had mastered their own professional spheres, the painter and the architect, for example, could work together to produce a harmonious environment where their individual contributions would be unified in a common vocabulary of forms. Thus the design process itself would forge a kind of community analogous to that which the abstract environment was meant to bring about.

That, at least, was the theory. In practice, however, it was rarely possible to achieve the ideal of a harmonious collaboration. For in spite of the fact that we have come to think of De Stijl as a monolithic entity—as a community of artists whose work seems on the whole to be very much alike—it was in fact principally in the review that gave the group its name that an image of cohesion was conveyed, and even that seems to have been short-lived, if not actually an illusion. No single body of work bears this out more clearly than the colored environments made by the artists associated with De Stijl. In them and in the circumstances surrounding their creation it is possible to study the working relationships which changed with time and with the varying backgrounds and interests of those who were themselves involved. Indeed, the history of De Stijl as a whole might best be understood in terms of the collaborative efforts which gave rise to these environmental designs.

That history can be roughly divided into three periods, the limits of which correspond to changes in the nature of the collaborative endeavor, changes brought about by the implications of the designs that were produced. During the initial period, from 1916 until about 1921, painters and architects played essentially different roles, the painters in practice, if not in theory, subordinate to the architects. These collaborations resulted in designs in which color was limited to discrete, architecturally predetermined surfaces.

Although a basic continuity can be discerned between the designs that were made in the early years and those that followed in the 1920s, nonetheless significant differences emerged when painters began to recognize and exploit the potential power of color to effect a new kind of abstract spatial experience. Thus, in the second phase, lasting through the mid-1920s, both in word and deed painters demanded authority equal to or even exceeding that of architects in determining spatial design. Architects, on the other hand, were anxious to preserve the efficacy of their work, which was increasingly directed toward the solution of pragmatic social problems, and they ultimately proved unwilling to concede to what they came to regard as the abstract, purely aesthetic considerations of painters.

Finally, the evolution of De Stijl's environmental concerns ended in the disavowal of the validity of collaborative work. By the end of the 1920s, architects and painters were alienated from one another; architects emphasized the rational functionalism of their work, often prohibiting the inclusion of color altogether, while painters tended to disregard physical structure and looked instead to color as a means of achieving their increasingly abstract conception of environmental design.[3]

The first instances of collaboration among De Stijl artists occurred in 1916 and 1917, when Theo van Doesburg produced stained-glass windows and color schemes for buildings designed by J.J.P. Oud and Jan

3. There are, of course, a number of tremendously important projects that cannot be completely assimilated in the schema outlined here. Piet Mondrian's atelier and Gerrit Rietveld's Schröder house are exceptional works in many respects, only one of which is the fact that they did not result from the kind of collaborative endeavor I have described. Nevertheless, I hope to show that even the special qualities of these works can be illuminated and more clearly understood when they are considered in the context of De Stijl's collaborative ideal.

Wils. In their general characteristics these projects were similar to others produced by Bart van der Leck and Vilmos Huszar in collaboration with architects who were not directly associated with De Stijl, and it is possible to consider them all as a group that exemplifies the early phase of the history outlined above.[4] In each case the painters designed color schemes that were strictly defined by the architectural settings in which they were placed. Color was used primarily as a means of reinforcing or highlighting architectural surfaces or structural divisions of those surfaces that had already been determined by the architects.

In the interior of Oud's "De Vonk" vacation house for working women run by the Leiden Community Center, van Doesburg's designs were restricted to the colors of the floor tiles and the doors (fig. 149). In the hall on the first floor above ground level, for example, the ten doors were painted in different sequences of black, white and gray, each color defining a different structural element of a given door, that is, its central flat plane and several layers of surrounding frames. Van Doesburg wanted to release the color planes, to make them free-floating by means of a contrasting light color. He was perhaps better able to realize this idea in his design for a stained-glass window in the stairwell of Wils's townhouse in Alkmaar (fig. 147). Its flat planes of color seem to hover in space, barely confined within the rectangular framework. This monumental work, each of its three sections more than six feet high and just over 21 inches wide, was composed as a triptych on the theme of a fugue by Bach, whose music van Doesburg appreciated for what he felt was its scientific, mathematically precise mode of expression corresponding to the constructive character of his own rectilinear style. The two outer sections of the window are made up of black, yellow, red, blue and clear glass rectangles; these primary color panels flank the middle portion in which the secondaries—violet, green and orange—are employed. In each panel van Doesburg used two basic patterns in inverted and mirroring configurations, working out repetitions and modifications so that the design as a whole creates a stable sense of symmetry, although absolute symmetry does not exist, and there is sufficient compositional and coloristic variation and contrast to suggest the measured rhythmic movement of the fugal theme. Van Doesburg himself described how "[T]he whole comes out against the air. The composition stands completely free in space."[5] Nonetheless, there is a sense in which the window conforms to a fundamental characteristic of easel painting, which is similar in its restriction to an area bounded by a frame. In this respect both the window and the glazed brick mosaics that van Doesburg designed for the exterior of De Vonk (fig. 66) may be described as functioning somewhere between easel painting and architecture, not quite free of the restrictions imposed by the conventions of either practice.

4. Here again it is worthwhile to state that rigid limitations should not be applied to the definition of De Stijl as a group. As we shall see, several crucial developments that informed the De Stijl concept of environmental design involved works produced by or in collaboration with artists who never contributed to the magazine.

5. Theo van Doesburg, letter to Antony Kok, 9 September 1917, quoted by Jean Leering in "De Architectuur en Van Doesburg," in *Theo van Doesburg 1881-1931* (Eindhoven: Stedelijk Van Abbemuseum, 1968-1969), p 20.

169

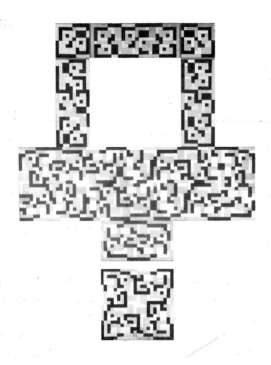

"Through the consistent carrying forward and development of this complementary combination of architecture and painting, it will be possible to achieve in the future, on a purely modern basis, the aim of monumental art: to place man within (instead of opposite) the plastic arts and thereby enable him to participate in them."
Theo van Doesburg, 1918

148. Theo van Doesburg
Design for tile floor, "De Vonk," 1917
watercolor on graph paper on cardboard
38½ x 28⅞
98 x 73.5
Dienst Verspreide Rijkskollekties

149. Van Doesburg provided the designs for the colors of the floor tiles and hallway doors in "De Vonk."
1980 photograph

150. Bart van der Leck
Color study for Villa Kröller-Müller, "Groot Haesebroek," Wassenaar, 1916-17
gouache on paper
27½ x 30⅜
70 x 77
Collection Rijksmuseum Kröller-Müller

The limitations imposed by architecture can be discerned as well in Bart van der Leck's color scheme for an interior designed by H.P. Berlage, a room in which art appreciation courses were to be taught in Helene Kröller-Müller's home (fig. 150). Here van der Leck's color applications respected the structural divisions of Berlage's design and even took into account the nature and placement of the furniture Berlage had made for the room. Color was restricted to surfaces defined by the architectonic considerations of ceiling, floor, door and individual wall surfaces. The white portion of each wall plane, for instance, was separated from those on either side by a thin line of black. The band of red near the ceiling was broken in a way that echoed the lateral dimensions of the cabinets positioned below, to which van der Leck also referred in establishing the height of the black plinth.

Van der Leck's notion of color in architecture was based on the premise that painter and architect perform essentially different functions in creating a harmonious interior. He shared van Doesburg's belief that modern painting and architecture are basically opposed to one another in that painting involves opening, unbinding and extension, in contrast to the enclosing, joining and confining functions of architecture. In the interaction of these characteristics, of movement on one hand and stasis on the other, lay the possibility of their successful combination. In his collaboration with Berlage, however, van der Leck felt that the architect had included too many controlling elements in his design, which thus infringed upon the freedom of van der Leck's own color scheme, forcing the painter to subordinate it to Berlage's architecture and massive wooden furniture. Van der Leck attributed this problem, which he saw as a widespread if not universal dilemma, to a fundamental inequality in the levels of stylistic advancement that had been achieved by painters and architects respectively. He felt that this was exemplified in the disparity between the elemental purity of his own easel painting style and what he believed to be *retardataire* aspects of the practice of architecture embodied in Berlage's designs. Van der Leck saw the domination of the architect over the painter as a direct reflection of this formal inequality and he therefore wanted to avoid any future need to collaborate with architects. In fact, when, contrary to his initial understanding, he learned that architects would be invited to participate in *De Stijl* magazine, he immediately severed all ties with the review, and thus became the first "victim" of what would eventually prove to be the widely acknowledged failure of De Stijl's collaborative ideal.[6]

During the mid-teens, both van der Leck and van Doesburg had made stained-glass windows, and their work in applied design was intimately related to concurrent developments in their easel painting styles.[7] Vilmos Huszar was another De Stijl painter whose applied designs, particularly in stained glass, paved the way for his involvement with interior design

6. Van der Leck explained his reasons for leaving De Stijl to Michel Seuphor who included the account in *Piet Mondrian: Life and Work* (New York: Harry N. Abrams, n.d.), p 138.
7. The relationship between van Doesburg's applied designs and his contemporaneous easel paintings becomes especially apparent when the tripartite window is compared with *Rhythm of a Russian Dance* (fig. 27); the more regularized grid structure of paintings such as *Composition XVI in Dissonance* may be indebted to the De Vonk floor and mosaic designs where the grid was a natural result of the materials employed. Two of van der Leck's gouache studies for *Composition 1917 (Donkey Riders)* (fig. 41) appear to have been designs for a stained-glass window, and several objects visible in his 1918 interior design for J. de Leeuw can be identified with paintings or drawings he executed in the same year.

171

and collaborative work. Like his colleagues, Huszar too believed that everyone engaged in a collaborative effort, even the patron, had a particular role to play in the realization of a total work of art. In the broadest context, he stated, "All this will take on a social significance which will work both ethically and aesthetically on the masses. Thus shall art come to be *in* life."[8] Unfortunately, the designs Huszar was actually able to carry out could hardly approach this goal. In fact, his first extensive color schemes were made for the bedroom of the two sons of Cornelis Bruynzeel, Jr., Huszar's neighbor in Voorburg, near The Hague (fig. 151). An architect named P.J.C. Klaarhamer designed furniture for the room which Huszar painted wine-red and black, adding a blue cushion with black accents to the seats of the several small chairs (fig. 152). In comparison to Rietveld's red/blue chair (fig. 84), designed at about the same time—although apparently not colored until later—Klaarhamer's and Huszar's chairs seem more conventional; despite their plain, rectilinear shape, they lack the sense either of simplified, machine-oriented construction or of loosely interlocking planar elements that make Rietveld's chair so striking.

Although the individual elements in the Bruynzeel bedroom may be of less interest than Rietveld's extraordinary design, the overall coloristic treatment of the interior, in which those elements were entirely assimilated, was nevertheless of major importance in the evolution of De Stijl's abstract, environmental design concerns. Huszar himself wrote that he and Klaarhamer endeavored to plasticize the bedroom space according to the means appropriate to their respective professions: "Plasticizing is arranging the functions rhythmically and at the same time practically."[9] Huszar's color schemes included not only red and black applied to the furniture, and blue and black in the rug, but also yellow, blue, white and gray rectangular planes painted on the walls and ceiling of the room. The large, unbroken planes of color were oriented in such a way as to render more apparent the size and extent of the surfaces to which they were applied. Color application took the placement of furniture into account, but was not limited as in an easel painting enclosed by a frame. Instead, the reversal of color combinations in repeated compositions, over the sides of each bed for instance, made associations across space in a manner analogous to a sitting-room design produced by van der Leck in the same year for J. de Leeuw. There too the painter employed variations of color in a fairly constant configuration in order to bind the four separate walls—and the furniture placed in front of them—into a single, harmonious whole.

This experience of the total space, where each wall and the furniture in front of it formed a separate composition but also interacted with the adjacent surfaces, helped to bring about a new attitude toward the role

151. Vilmos Huszar (furniture by P.J.C. Klaarhamer)
Color study for Bruynzeel bedroom, Voorburg, 1918
A second view of this interior was published in *De Stijl*, V, 5, 1922, p 78.
Vintage photograph

8. Vilmos Huszar, "Over de organisatie in de ambachts-kunst," *Bouwkundig Weekblad*, 41 (1920), p 75.
9. Vilmos Huszar, "Over de moderne toegepaste kunsten," *Bouwkundig Weekblad*, 43 (1922), p 75.

152. P.J.C. Klaarhamer/Vilmos Huszar
Chair for Bruynzeel bedroom, 1918
painted wood with fabric cushion
35½ x 16 x 16½
90.2 x 40.6 x 41.9
Collection Haags Gemeentemuseum

153. Piet Zwart/Vilmos Huszar
Design for chair, 1920
ink, watercolor on paper
20¼ x 13⅜
51.3 x 34
Collection Haags Gemeentemuseum

of color in an environmental context. In the future, color would still be understood as a counterpart to architecture, but it would no longer be intended simply to accent elements of function or construction. Painters felt increasingly free to exploit color as a means of integrating discrete architectural surfaces, disguising doors so that they appeared to be part of the walls which they in fact pierced, and painting around or across corners to undermine the character of each wall as a distinct, individual plane (fig. 154). Thus the holistic effect of interlocking continuity seems to have developed at this point into a conscious goal of the De Stijl painters but, because many architects felt that this use of color compromised the integrity of their designs, it upset the original conception of collaborative work, tipping the scales in favor of painters.

The powerful impact produced by this less restrained use of color can be seen in Piet Zwart's definitive design for an exhibition stand—actually a room with four walls—produced in 1921 (fig. 155). A comparison of that design with Zwart's initial plan for the interior (fig. 156) demonstrates the artist's evolution away from a kind of design that conformed to the architectural character of the floor and walls, which are juxtaposed in the first drawing as discrete, flat planes, the colors of which are reminiscent of Huszar's scheme for the Bruynzeel bedroom furniture. In fact Zwart and Huszar collaborated on furniture designs in 1920 and 1921 (fig. 153), and both artists worked with Jan Wils in those years; although Zwart was not a member of the De Stijl group, he was closely associated with others who were. The evolution of his ideas in connection with the exhibition stand, which had at first demonstrated the influence of De Stijl, eventually came to anticipate later developments in De Stijl coloristic design. Indeed, Zwart's work may in its turn have acted as a catalyst to the development of certain De Stijl ideas.

Zwart can, for example, be credited with the introduction of a new concept of exhibition design that found its ultimate expression in El Lissitzky's Proun rooms and in an exhibition space designed (but probably not realized at full scale) by Huszar together with Gerrit Rietveld for a 1923 exhibition in Berlin (fig. 157). Those later interiors shared with Zwart's *Celluloid Manufacturer's Stand* not only an awareness of the special character of the exhibition space as temporary and intended to be moved through, but also an emphasis on the potential of abstract forms to affect the viewer's experience of spatial continuity. In all three interiors, forms and/or colors were arranged in a manner that denied the discreteness of individual surface planes, crossing the boundaries between them and confounding the viewer's perception of where those boundaries actually were. The result in each case produced an experience of space made active, fused in a dynamic, abstract whole.

173

(facing page)
154. Theo van Doesburg
Design for flower room, Villa de Noailles,
Hyères; architect: Rob Mallet-Stevens,
1924-25
ink, pencil, gouache on tracing paper
21¼ x 24
54 x 61
Collection Stedelijk Van Abbemuseum

155. Piet Zwart
Definitive design for *Celluloid Manufacturer's
Stand*, 1921
ink, gouache on paper
18 x 25½
45.7 x 64.7
Collection Haags Gemeentemuseum

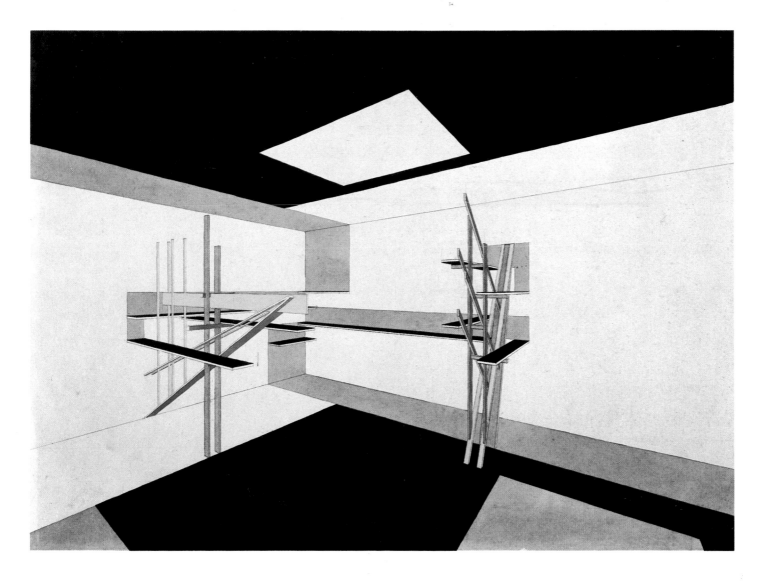

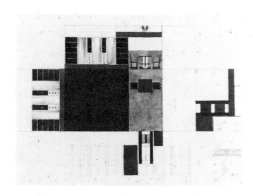

156. Piet Zwart
Exploded box plan, *Celluloid Manufacturer's Stand*, 1921
ink, watercolor on paper
10⅞ x 10⅜
27.5 x 26.5
Collection Haags Gemeentemuseum

These interiors suggest that the increasing demands of painters to make designs in which color could be totally integrated with rather than merely applied to architecture had an impact on De Stijl's collaborative ideal. In claiming greater responsibility for the spatial potential of coloristic design, painters were in effect attempting to insure that their contribution—color—would not be subject to the prerogatives of architects. That this was, indeed, perceived as an ever present danger is made clear by the circumstances that led to Oud's break with van Doesburg and his consequent departure from De Stijl in the fall of 1921.

At issue was a series of color schemes that van Doesburg made for the exterior of two municipal housing blocks, Spangen VIII and IX, being built by Oud in Rotterdam. In several letters to the architect, van Doesburg described how he developed his designs according to a principle of contrasts: "As you know, I always begin with the working out of contrasts; because the street wall already has a predominantly horizontal character. . . I always want to achieve verticality as much as possible by means of color." Since horizontality would be expressed by the red color of the long brick walls, van Doesburg said that for Spangen IX he would use blue and green ". . . to achieve sharp dissonance. . . . Thus I believe the horizontal is not pronounced because [the color scheme] interacts as follows. . . ." He then drew a diagram showing how the interaction of vertical and horizontal accents would produce a dynamic diagonal rhythm which, he stated, would enable him systematically to control the whole side of the building by means of color.[10] Van Doesburg also wanted to use color to mitigate the three-dimensional massiveness of Spangen VIII's principal facade, whose central portion was set back slightly behind two lateral wings (fig. 158). His diagram of the color scheme of houses at Potgieterstraat (fig. 159) was intended to show how the various colors of the window lattice-work would coalesce into planes and converge around a central point. According to van Doesburg the colors, when used in this way, would make the center of the building appear to project outward toward a viewer standing opposite, and the whole facade would therefore seem to stand on a single, continuous plane.

Van Doesburg envisioned color as a means of camouflaging certain elements of Oud's buildings that he found displeasing, such as their predominantly horizontal aspect, and their weighty, sculptural appearance, expressive of mass rather than volume. In view of van Doesburg's desire to work through color contrasts "to control the whole space,"[11] it is not surprising that Oud, in turn, might have felt that the architectural character of his buildings was threatened. In fact, Oud found the color schemes lacking in unity and too much in conflict with

10. Theo van Doesburg, letter to J.J.P. Oud, n.d. [circa Sept.-Oct. 1921], Institut Néerlandais, Paris.
11. *Ibid.*

176

the architecture, and he tried to convince van Doesburg to modify his designs. Outraged by the suggestion that he relinquish his right as an artist to control the totality of the designs he had created, van Doesburg responded with characteristic vehemence in an angry letter that marks the end of his collaboration with Oud: ". . . given the fact that the execution of the whole was assured; given the fact that I am no house-painter but take these things seriously; given the fact that I am van Doesburg, *I have, I seize* the right to cry: *No—No—No;* Entweder so—oder Nichts [Either this way—or not at all]."[12] As it turned out, Oud chose the latter alternative. Van Doesburg's designs were never used and on the few occasions that color was applied to later buildings by Oud, the architect was responsible for those color schemes himself.

The rupture with Oud came at a delicate moment in the history of De Stijl because, by the fall of 1921, van Doesburg had already been negotiating for a year with Léonce Rosenberg, a Paris art dealer who wanted to introduce De Stijl to the French public by sponsoring an exhibition devoted to De Stijl architecture and applied design. The idea for the exhibition had developed out of Rosenberg's commission, offered in October 1920, for a house and gallery to be designed jointly by all the De Stijl artists. Eventually realizing that he did not have sufficient means to build the house, Rosenberg proposed instead that van Doesburg organize an exhibition including floor plans and executed stained glass designed for the house that would itself be shown in model form as the focus of Rosenberg's presentation of De Stijl as a group. That the objects shown in the exhibition should manifest themselves as the work of a unified group of artists, rather than of diverse individuals, was apparently of critical importance to Rosenberg and to van Doesburg from the start. Van Doesburg had written this to Oud when describing the project in April 1921, and it is clear from correspondence of the same period between Oud and Piet Mondrian that van Doesburg had gone to great lengths to assure Rosenberg that De Stijl was indeed a viable group. But although van Doesburg could count on the participation of several De Stijl painters, Mondrian included, by the middle of 1921 Oud was the only experienced architect still associated with De Stijl.[13] This explains Mondrian's reservations about the possibility of carrying out what he referred to as ". . . the big Rosenberg plan. It seems rather impossible to me because there is not yet a Stijl group as a unity or really there is no Stijl group. Rosenberg spoke of several architects to me, of v[an] 't Hoff also. He seems to think all these fellows are still with De Stijl."[14]

In fact, both Wils and van 't Hoff had already broken with De Stijl, and even before Oud followed suit later that year he had decided not to collaborate in the designs for Rosenberg's house. As Municipal Architect

12. Theo van Doesburg, letter to J.J.P. Oud, 3 Nov. 1921, Institut Néerlandais, Paris.
13. By the spring of 1921 both Robert van 't Hoff and Jan Wils had left the De Stijl circle. Gerrit Rietveld had become involved with De Stijl in 1919, the year of his first architectural commission to redesign a shop facade. However, Rietveld was principally a furniture designer and manufacturer in those years; he did not design an entire building until 1924.
14. Piet Mondrian, letter to J.J.P. Oud, 9 April 1921, Institut Néerlandais, Paris.

157. Vilmos Huszar/Gerrit Rietveld
Three views of model room proposed for the
Greater Berlin Art Exhibition, 1923. This
unrealized project was illustrated in
L'Architecture Vivante, 1924, plates 10/11.
Rietveld's Berlin chair (fig. 89) was designed for
this interior.

(facing page)
158. Theo van Doesburg/J.J.P. Oud
Color scheme for facade, Potgieterstraat,
Spangen, October 1921
ink, pencil, watercolor on tracing paper
14 x 21
35.6 x 53.3
Collection Fondation Custodia,
Institut Néerlandais

159. Theo van Doesburg/J.J. P. Oud
Diagram of color scheme for houses in
Potgieterstraat, Spangen, October 1921
pencil, ink, watercolor on tracing paper
11½ x 12¾
29 x 32.3
Collection Fondation Custodia,
Institut Néerlandais

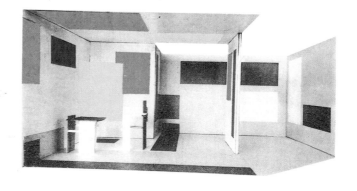

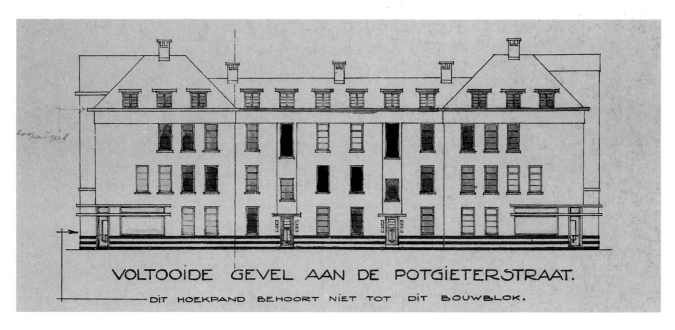

VOLTOOiDE GEVEL AAN DE POTGiETERSTRAAT.

DiT HOEKPAND BEHOORT NiET TOT DiT BOUWBLOK.

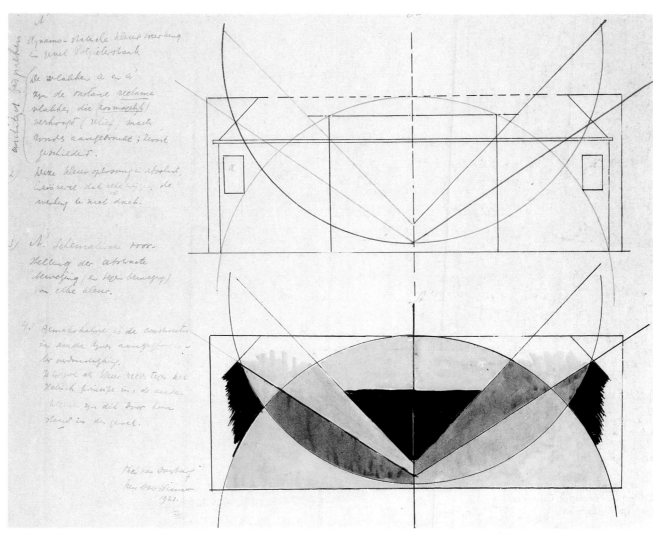

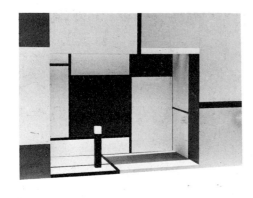

160. Reconstruction (1963) from original documentation after a 1926 model by Piet Mondrian for the set design of *L'Ephémère est Eternel* cardboard, wood
21 x 30⅛ x 10½
53.3 x 76.5 x 26.5
Collection Stedelijk Van Abbemuseum

The Belgian painter Michel Seuphor wrote *L'Ephémère est Eternel* while living in Rome in 1926. Some months later, he took the play to Mondrian in Paris, who responded with this design. The set had three movable elements, one for each act of the play. The original model was lost during Mondrian's moves from Paris to London to New York between 1938 and 1940. The play was performed for the first time in Milan in May 1968.

15. Hans L.C. Jaffé, *De Stijl, 1917-1931: The Dutch Contribution to Modern Art* (Amsterdam: J.M. Meulenhoff, 1956), p 166.
16. Piet Mondrian, "The Realization of Neoplasticism in the Distant Future and in Architecture Today," in Hans L.C. Jaffé, *De Stijl*, trans. R.R. Symonds (London: Thames and Hudson, 1970), p 168.
17. *Ibid.*, pp 169-170.

of Rotterdam, Oud's concern for the solution of practical problems was paramount and he refused to become involved with the Rosenberg project because ". . . there was no 'terrain' to build on and Oud was opposed to 'utopian building' which did not start from given facts. . . ."[15] For the De Stijl painters, on the other hand, it was precisely its utopian aspect that made the Rosenberg project particularly appealing. Mondrian, for example, saw the commission as an opportunity to contribute in an advisory capacity to the development of a free architecture, one that he envisioned beyond the limits of contemporary building practice. In an essay published in *De Stijl* in 1922, he wrote, "*Absolute freedom for continuous experimentation* is necessary if art is to be achieved. How can this come about within the complex limitations of conventional building in our society?"[16]

Mondrian's conception of architecture as art was bound up with the development of his neoplastic easel-painting style, the principles of which he felt could be adapted to architecture. In both cases the flat plane was seen as the essential element. "Thus," he stated, "[Neoplasticism] sees architecture as a *multiplicity of planes:* again the *plane*. This multiplicity is composed abstractly into *plane plastic. . . .* To be a *plastic of the plane* in this way, neoplastic architecture requires *color*, without which the plane cannot be a vital reality for us."[17] At least since 1920, Mondrian had been working to realize these principles by making his own studio into a neoplastic environment (figs. 44-52). Beginning with the division of the interior by the arrangement of the furniture it contained, Mondrian proceeded to plasticize the space with color. He applied pasteboard rectangles of red, yellow, blue, black, white and gray to the studio walls and to some of the furniture, reinforcing the planar character of the surfaces, enlivening them and making the whole space function as an abstract composition of color and planar forms.

The studio was a private space that served as an arena in which Mondrian was entirely free to experiment with coloristic design. He was not bound by the conditions of a commission, nor by the limitations that a collaborative endeavor might impose. For him the studio was a utopian environment, an example for the future, one that he was for practical reasons unable to realize in any other context. Yet, despite his willingness to design a stage set (fig. 160) and a library-study for a private home (fig. 161) in 1926, environmental design never became a central concern for Mondrian, as it did for the other De Stijl painters. Unlike van Doesburg, van der Leck and Huszar, Mondrian did not make stained-glass windows or other kinds of individual applied designs. He considered himself first and foremost to be an easel painter and it was his insistence on the flat plane in painting that was reflected in his notion of architecture and coloristic design. Furthermore, his understanding of

161. Piet Mondrian
Design for the *Salon de Mme. B..., à Dresden,*
1926, as illustrated in Pierre Chareau's article
"Meubles," *L'Art International d'Aujourd'hui,*
VII, circa 1928, plate 50.
Collection Stedelijk Museum, Amsterdam

An unrealized commission, this library-study was,
like the set designed for *L'Ephémère est Eternel,*
conceived as a total neoplastic environment by
Mondrian. His atelier in Paris was undoubtedly
the prototype for this space.

162. Theo van Doesburg
Color design for middle-class housing, Drachten;
architect: C.R. de Boer, 1921
ink, gouache, pencil on paper
11¾ x 20¼
29.8 x 51.4
Collection D. Rinsema

163. Theo van Doesburg
Study in secondary colors for an agricultural
school facade and sides, Drachten;
architect: C.R. de Boer, 1921
ink, watercolor on tracing paper
11 x 44¼
27.9 x 112.5
Collection Museum "'t Bleekerhûs"

164. Theo van Doesburg
Schematic rendering of colors of the facade
for an agricultural school, Drachten;
architect: C.R. de Boer, 1921
ink, watercolor on tracing paper
11 x 36⅝
27.9 x 93
Collection Museum "'t Bleekerhûs"

18. Theo van Doesburg, "Notes on Monumental Art," trans. in Jaffé, *De Stijl,* p 103.

architecture as a multiplicity of planes that relate to one another in a conceptual rather than a material manner is the primary reason why Mondrian never allowed color to deny the character of a planar surface by joining it to adjacent surfaces. Indeed, in this respect, his conception of color in space was fundamentally different from that developed in the early 1920s by van Doesburg and Huszar. Unlike Mondrian, these painters produced designs in which color functioned to propel the viewer through space. Instead of using color to reinforce planes perceived individually and then fused in the mind of the viewer, their aim was to tap the dynamic potential of color by moving it across surfaces and compelling the viewer himself to move in order to experience space in terms of time in an abstract realm made possible by color.

The beginnings of this trend can be seen in van Doesburg's unrealized coloristic designs of 1921 for a block of middle-class housing and an agricultural school that stand opposite each other in the small Friesian town of Drachten. Here for the first time van Doesburg was able to experiment with color in a truly environmental context and, as he was doing concurrently for Oud's buildings in Rotterdam, he proceeded to work out his color schemes on the basis of contrasts. In this case one building was given primary colors (fig. 162) while secondary colors were applied to the other (fig. 163). His sequential rendering of three sides of the agricultural school demonstrates that van Doesburg envisioned planes of color that would be perceived as moving across the surfaces and around the corners of the building. He drew a schematic rendition of the color design (fig. 164), using lines to show how the planes of color were linked not simply by juxtaposition, but in a complex series of arching and diagonal relationships extending across and joining all three surfaces. Unlike his design for the principal facade of Oud's building in Rotterdam, here the color scheme was not focused around a central point or directed toward a stationary viewer standing opposite; instead, it involved the movement of the viewer who would be led by the development of the color scheme itself to proceed around the building and experience it as a whole and in relation to its counterpart across the street. Had the designs been carried out, van Doesburg would have been able to achieve the aim of monumental painting that he had described in 1918: ". . . to place man within (instead of opposite) the plastic arts and enable him to participate in them."[18] Unfortunately, however, the citizens of Drachten were appalled by van Doesburg's plans to transform their quaint little town into a brightly colored De Stijl environment. The designs remained on paper, as did those for Oud's buildings in Rotterdam, and van Doesburg was forced to find other opportunities to develop his conception of coloristic architecture.

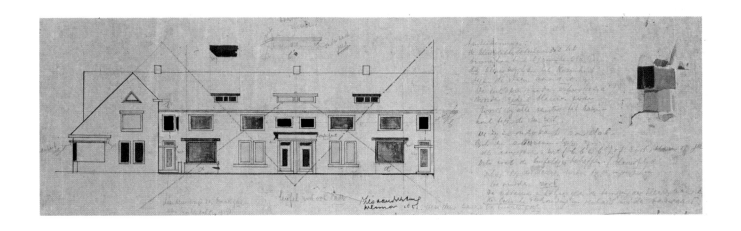

1

With his recent designs rejected and Oud no longer part of his circle, van Doesburg became acutely aware of the need to enlist new members for De Stijl, particularly architects. In Weimar during the winter and spring of 1922, he taught a controversial course on De Stijl theory and practice which was attended mostly by Bauhaus students whom he hoped to convert to De Stijl. Although his ideas did indeed have a considerable impact on the Bauhaus, as far as De Stijl itself was concerned the most important result of van Doesburg's activity in Weimar came about as a consequence of his meeting there with a young Dutch architect named Cornelis van Eesteren, who had attended several of van Doesburg's lectures.

During the next few years van Doesburg and van Eesteren worked closely together and it was a number of their designs that eventually became the focus of Léonce Rosenberg's 1923 De Stijl exhibition. Of the 52 entries in that exhibition, well over half were listed as products of their collaboration, which began with van Doesburg's color scheme for a university hall designed by van Eesteren as his final student project (fig. 165). Van Doesburg's contribution consisted not only of color schemes for the exterior, but also a design for a vast stained-glass skylight, as well as planes of primary color, black and gray, loosely arranged across the floor, walls and balconies of the interior. The colors on the walls and balconies were to be applied in the form of large enameled plaques whose literal materiality would declare the independence of color from architecture and thus reinforce the sense of colored planes hovering free in space which van Doesburg tried to convey in a drawing where only the color and no architectural supporting structure is shown (fig. 167).

The sense of floating planes of color is conveyed even more powerfully by van Doesburg's counterconstructions (fig. 55), a series of drawings he made on the basis of van Eesteren's axonometric projections for two of the three model houses included in Rosenberg's exhibition. In the counterconstructions, color itself functions as an architectural material identical to the plane it defines. In this respect the counterconstructions seem to embody Mondrian's conception of architecture as a multiplicity of planes. But instead of a sequential perception of planes that are then fused intellectually, van Doesburg's counterconstructions posit a new notion of space in relation to time. The two are experienced simultaneously because, van Doesburg wrote, "The new architecture calculates not only with space but also with time as an architectural value. The unity of space and time will give architectural form a new and completely plastic aspect, that is, a space-time aspect." And, he went on, it is color that makes the viewer aware of this new dimension: "The new architecture *employs color organically* as a direct means of expression of relationships in space and time. . . . The task of the modern painter is to integrate color into a harmonic whole (by placing it not on a plane surface of two dimensions, but within the new realm of four-dimensional space-time)."[19] Whether or not they achieve this vision, van Doesburg's counterconstructions can certainly be understood as images of an ideal coloristic architecture which makes no concessions to the realities of function, construction, material, or any other technical considerations. This is essentially a painter's conception of architecture, and it is hardly surprising that van Doesburg almost immediately transposed it into a series of paintings he called countercompositions.

Like Huszar's and Rietveld's exhibition space, van Eesteren's and van Doesburg's designs were created in a special context that allowed the artists to disregard issues of rational functionalism and to avoid the problems presented by conventional building practices. Moreover, it is possible that van Doesburg wanted to provide color schemes for van Eesteren's university hall—even though he knew it would never be executed—in order to be able to include the designs as a collaborative project in the De Stijl exhibition held in Paris in the fall of 1923. The fundamental premise of the exhibition was borne out especially by their designs, which demonstrated the collaborative effort supposedly required for the creation of coloristic architecture. In the exhibition as a whole, which included work by Oud and Wils, as well as Ludwig Mies van der Rohe and Willem van Leusden, who were at most only tangentially related to De Stijl, every effort was made to present all the objects shown as the work of artists united behind a common set of aesthetic principles. To that end, a manifesto entitled, "Towards Collective Construction," was distributed to visitors to the exhibition when it was reassembled at the Paris Ecole Spécial d'Architecture in 1924. When van Doesburg and van Eesteren published the text in *De Stijl*, they introduced it by proclaiming that the exhibition ". . . had as its aim the demonstration of the possibility of collective creation on [a] universal basis."[20]

Over the years van Doesburg wrote repeatedly about the need for collaboration in order to achieve an abstract, coloristic architecture. But for him the collaborative ideal remained a goal that he was unable to achieve to any marked degree. When for example, he discovered that Rietveld had joined Oud and Wils in contributing to an exhibition organized by the Bauhaus in 1923, he virtually accused Rietveld of collaborating with the enemies of De Stijl and wrote, "I have completely given up the desire to work toward a collective goal."[21] Van Doesburg's volatile personality made it impossible for him to tolerate a situation in which he could not exercise total control over a design of his own, or indeed over the activities of his colleagues.[22] Nonetheless, it was principally because of his constant promotion of De Stijl that the idea of the group's unity was maintained, despite the defection by 1925 of most of its original members.

19. Theo van Doesburg, "Towards Plastic Architecture," trans. in Joost Baljeu, *Theo van Doesburg* (New York: Macmillan Publishing Co., 1974), pp 144-145. For a discussion of van Doesburg's concern with notions of the fourth dimension, see Joost Baljeu, "The Fourth Dimension in Neoplasticism," *Form* (9 April 1969), pp 6-14; and Linda Dalrymple Henderson, "The Artist, 'The Fourth Dimension,' and Non-Euclidean Geometry 1900-1930: A Romance of Many Dimensions," Yale University, PhD diss., 1975, pp 423-443.
20. Theo van Doesburg and Cornelis van Eesteren, "Towards Collective Construction," trans. in Jaffé, *De Stijl*, p 191.
21. Theo van Doesburg, letter to Gerrit Rietveld, 10 August 1923, trans. in Theodore M. Brown, *The Work of G. Rietveld, Architect* (Utrecht: A.W. Bruna & Zoon, 1958), p 31.
22. Even today the nature of the collaboration between van Doesburg and van Eesteren is still a volatile issue. The fact that van Doesburg has often been credited with sole responsibility for aspects of the Rosenberg projects—the most important designs they produced together—has contributed to van Eesteren's seemingly protective attitude toward the drawings and documentary material for these projects. He himself made the decision not to allow a number of these designs to be included in the 1982 Walker Art Center exhibition, apparently fearing that his role in their creation would be misrepresented or misunderstood.

In view of the fact that by the mid-1920s both painters and architects were expressing serious doubts about the collaborative ideal that had once been fundamental to De Stijl theory and practice, it is understandable that the major monument of De Stijl coloristic architecture produced in that period was the work of an architect who chose not to seek the advice or contribution of any painter. Rietveld's Schröder house, designed in 1924 (figs. 94-125), was his first large-scale architectural project and it clearly demonstrates his assimilation of the novel aspects of van Eesteren's and van Doesburg's extraordinary houses, models of which had been exhibited the year before (fig. 168). Strongly influenced by the interpenetrating spaces and planar color schemes of those designs, in the Schröder house Rietveld managed to produce an effect of openness and movement in the constructive forms themselves, and he was therefore able to employ color to enhance his structure by delineating individual architectural elements. This is particularly evident in the exterior of the house, composed of what

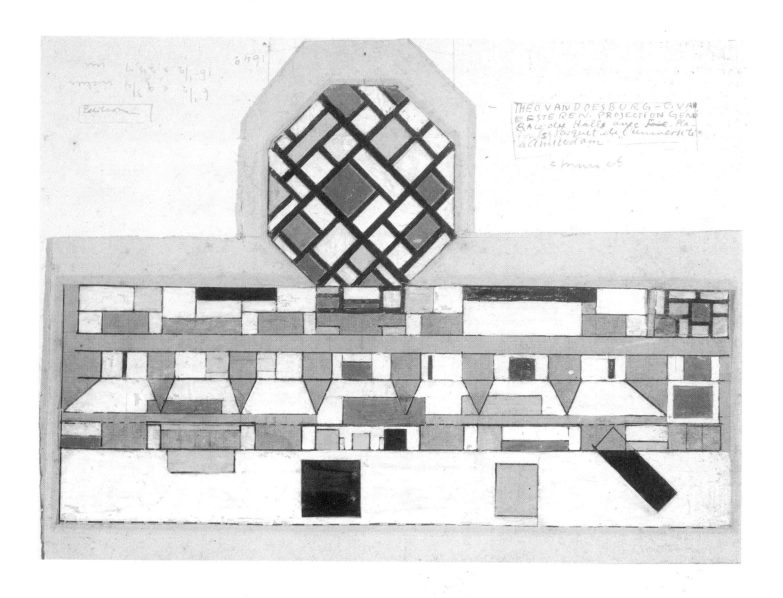

THÉO VAN DOESBURG – C. VAN
EESTEREN. PROJECTION GÉNÉ-
RALE du Hall avec Pla-
fon(s) parquet de l'université
à Amsterdam

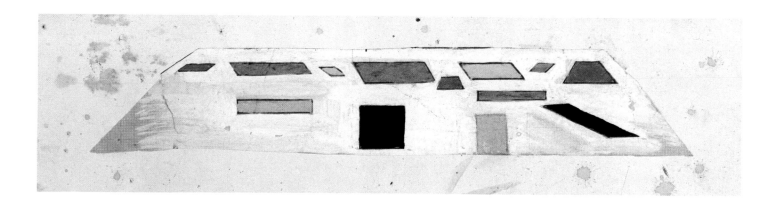

Theodore Brown has described as "visually weightless elements" that suggest volume rather than closed mass.[23] As a result, Rietveld was not obliged to use color in contrast to his architecture, to give it a sense of extension and movement. The sophisticated, stylistically advanced nature of the architecture made it ideally suited to Rietveld's relatively conservative use of color, which was unlike the highly dynamic color schemes that Huszar and particularly van Doesburg resorted to in their efforts to produce similar coloristic spatial effects.[24]

If the Schröder house exemplifies the independence of the architect from the painter in producing a successful coloristic design, one of the last De Stijl abstract environments, the Café Aubette in Strasbourg, demonstrates even more dramatically, from the point of view of painters, the ultimate breakdown of De Stijl's collaborative ideal (figs. 169-182). Designed between 1926 and 1928 by van Doesburg together with Jean Arp and Sophie Taeuber-Arp, the Aubette was intended to be the definitive expression of van Doesburg's aesthetic principles. He himself was responsible for the overall coherence of the various interiors, including ten public rooms, among which were several different bars and cafés, a billiard room, and two dance halls. Arp and Taeuber-Arp designed roughly half of the interiors, although van Doesburg exercised control over the project as a whole. The large, centrally located cinema-dance hall on the first floor above ground level was the most important of all the Aubette interiors and, not surprisingly, van Doesburg chose it as the arena in which he would make his most effective statement with a dynamic use of color designed to activate an otherwise bland architectural space (fig. 182).

Van Doesburg's designs on the walls and ceiling of the cinema-dance hall involved broad compositions of dissonantly colored, rectangular planes oriented at 45-degree angles in contrast to the architecture. As van Doesburg himself explained, ". . . since the architectural elements were based on orthogonal relationships, this room had to accommodate itself to a diagonal arrangement of colours, to a countercomposition which by its nature, was to resist all the tension of the architecture." Clearly based on the countercomposition paintings that were in turn indebted to his work with van Eesteren, the color scheme was intended ". . . to oppose to the material room in three dimensions a super-material and pictorial, diagonal space."[25] The very language in which van Doesburg described his purpose highlights the extremely abstract character of his conception of the colored environment, totally opposed to the actual physical properties of architecture as well as to its practical, functional requirements. When, shortly after its inauguration in February 1928, van Doesburg learned that in response to complaints by their patrons, the owners of the Aubette had already made changes in the interiors, he

23. Brown, p 62.
24. The suggestion that Rietveld's color scheme for the Schröder house may be characterized as being in any way conservative is made only in this comparative context where it serves to emphasize the difference between Rietveld's use of color and that of Huszar and van Doesburg, whose coloristic designs grew out of the collaborative process that Rietveld generally avoided. (His work together with Mrs. Schröder was not a collaboration of the kind I have been discussing here, and his contribution to the Berlin exhibition space of 1923 was probably limited to supplying the furniture it was meant to contain.) To clarify this point further, one might refer once again to Mondrian's studio interior, as it shared with the Schröder house a use of color to enhance architecture by delineating structure rather than contrasting with it. Like Rietveld, Mondrian too refrained from direct collaborations with other artists.
25. Theo van Doesburg, "Notes on L'Aubette at Strasbourg," trans. in Jaffé, De Stijl, p 236.

168. Cornelis van Eesteren/Theo van Doesburg Models (since destroyed) for Maison d'Artiste and Maison Particulière for exhibition at Galerie L'Effort Moderne, Paris, 1923.
Vintage photographs

26. Theo van Doesburg, letter to Adolf Behne, Nov. 1928, quoted in Ulrich Conrads and H.G. Sperlich, *The Architecture of Fantasy*, trans. and expanded by George R. Collins (New York: Praeger Publishers, 1963), p 155.

Nancy J. Troy is an Assistant Professor in the Department of the History of Art, The Johns Hopkins University, Baltimore, Maryland.

was bitterly disappointed to discover that the public was not ready to accept this most advanced of De Stijl's colored abstract environments. "Let the architect create for the public," he wrote, "the artist creates beyond the public and demands new conditions diametrically opposed to old conventions. . . . Constant values are only contained in 100-percent art. This is now my firm conviction."[26]

With these words of profound disillusionment, van Doesburg registered the ultimate failure of De Stijl's collaborative ideal. Despite his aspirations to become a designer on an environmental scale, he was finally compelled to acknowledge that what he strove for was a utopian, aesthetic image of the new environment into which practical demands could not be assimilated. His experience with the Aubette shows how, because of changes in the collaborative relationship between painter and architect, the predominance of the painter had gradually emerged in the abstract environment, which consequently evolved away from and in reaction against the rational, practical concerns of the architect. The kind of environment that van Doesburg and the other De Stijl painters strove for was primarily a painterly vision of a colored, abstract space that was, in the end, unacceptable even to those architects who were originally associated with De Stijl. In rejecting that vision, men like Rietveld and Oud chose to work in a more strictly architectural idiom that they believed was more responsive to existing social conditions. The buildings they produced around 1930 were composed of simple, flat, white, rectangular surfaces; in short, they were precisely the kinds of structures that the De Stijl painters had called for when they began to consider the application of color to architecture more than ten years earlier. Ironically, however, there was no longer any talk of collaboration. Painters like Mondrian and van Doesburg retreated to their private realms where "100-percent art" was still possible, while architects including Rietveld and Oud directed their attention to issues of rationalization and standardization in an attempt to arrive at what they felt must be purely architectural solutions to the problems of housing in modern society. Others, such as van der Leck, Huszar and Zwart, became engaged in activities that were only tangentially related to their earlier coloristic design work. All of them abandoned the ideal of collaboration that had so often been the primary motivating force in creating the colored abstract environments of De Stijl.

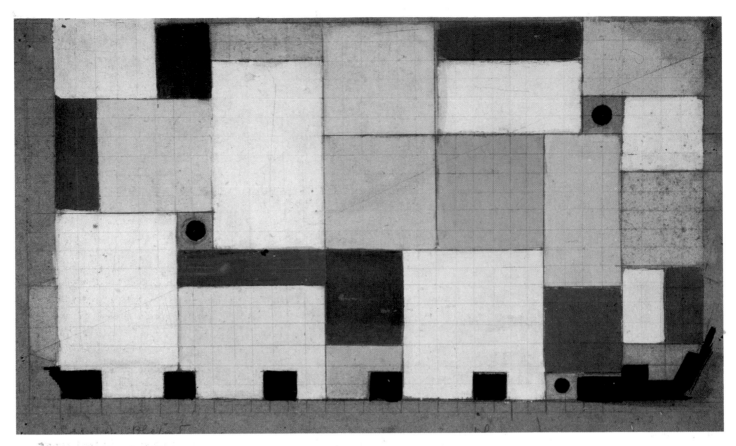

169. Theo van Doesburg
Project for the ceiling of the café-restaurant,
1927
gouache, pencil, india ink on cardboard
9⅜ x 14⅞
23.8 x 37.6
Collection Musée National d'Art Moderne,
Centre Georges Pompidou

170. The Café Aubette was designed for this
opulent 18th-century structure on the Place
Kléber, Strasbourg. Since 1928, the interior has
been completely changed and all traces of the
van Doesburg/Arp/Taeuber-Arp designs have
been destroyed.
1981 photograph

Café Aubette

171. The salon de thé under construction.
Vintage photograph

172. Sophie Taeuber-Arp
Project for the Aubette bar, 1927-28
(Aubette 186)
gouache
8⅝ x 28½
21.9 x 72.39
Collection Musée d'Art Moderne de Strasbourg

In 1926, Theo van Doesburg, Jean Arp and Sophie Taeuber-Arp were commissioned to redecorate the interiors of a large restaurant-nightclub, the Café Aubette, in Strasbourg. The project took nearly two years to complete, involving the design of ten public rooms and their furnishings. For van Doesburg, who maintained overall control of the project, this endeavor was especially significant, for it was his first opportunity to implement his theories of abstract interior design.

Interestingly, the Aubette interiors reflect a fundamental revision in De Stijl theory, a revision that can be described as a shift away from Mondrian's Neoplasticism, based on strict adherence to a horizontal/vertical orientation, toward van Doesburg's new theory of Elementarism, that allowed the use of diagonal elements. Van Doesburg's designs for the grande salle de fêtes (large party room) and café-restaurant, and Sophie Taeuber-Arp's salon de thé (tea room) follow the neoplastic conception of interior design: color planes are aligned with the horizontal/vertical elements of the architecture and do not cross boundaries established by corners. Each wall is treated as a separate composition, thus reinforcing the integrity of discrete surfaces and subordinating color to

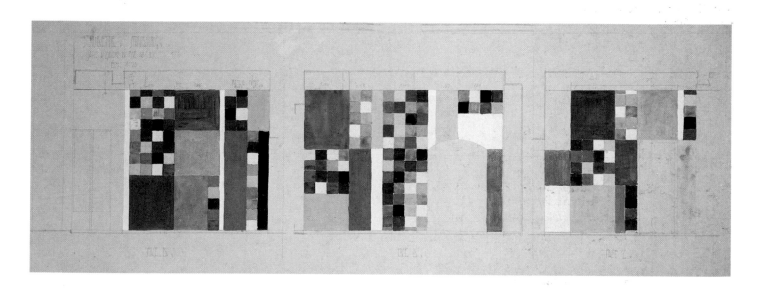

173. Jean Arp's elaborate design for the cave (cellar) included this large wall mural. Totally unlike the other Aubette rooms in which the patterning is rectilinear and abstract, in this unique space, Arp painted biomorphic forms (reminiscent of his sculptures) in yellow, black and blue-gray. Two heads come out of a wave-like band of color and a sun appears to be rising from the wainscot line.
Vintage photograph

174. The salon de thé designed by Sophie Taeuber-Arp in 1926-28, was divided into three areas: the tea room proper, a pastry shop with counters at the Place Kléber side and a more intimate room divided into small cubicles at the rear. The walls and ceiling were divided with asymmetrical squares and rectangles of varying dimensions. These squares were painted in several tones of gray, separated by bands of white. The gray patterns were interrupted at irregular intervals by small rectangles comprised of black, gray and red squares on white grounds. The design originally was to be executed in ceramic tiles, but in the end, it was painted. An axonometric view of this space is seen below in the photograph of Jean Arp.
Vintage photograph

175. Jean Arp and Sophie Taeuber-Arp are seen in their studio surrounded by sketches for the Aubette, circa 1927.
Vintage photographs

architecture. In other designs, such as Sophie Taeuber-Arp's for a foyer-bar on the first floor, the interior space is given greater pictorial continuity by having the color planes traverse corners. Here, color and architecture play equal roles, approaching the De Stijl ideal with their fusion in a total work of art.

As Troy and Frampton have stated, van Doesburg reserved the definitive expression of his ideas on abstract interior design for the most important room in the Aubette, the cinema-dance hall. It is this room that most embodies his elementarist theory by employing color planes oriented at a 45-degree angle to the walls and ceiling. According to van Doesburg, the diagonal placement of the planes creates a "countermovement" that negates the physical presence of the architecture: "If I were asked what I had in mind when I constructed this room, I should be able to reply: to oppose to the material room in three dimensions a super-material and pictorial diagonal space."

That the Aubette interiors proved to be unpopular among patrons in no way detracts from their historical significance. Along with Rietveld's Schröder house, the Aubette can be regarded as one of the crowning achievements of De Stijl architecture. In the all-encompassing scope of the designs, van Doesburg came close to realizing his goal of creating a "total" environment.

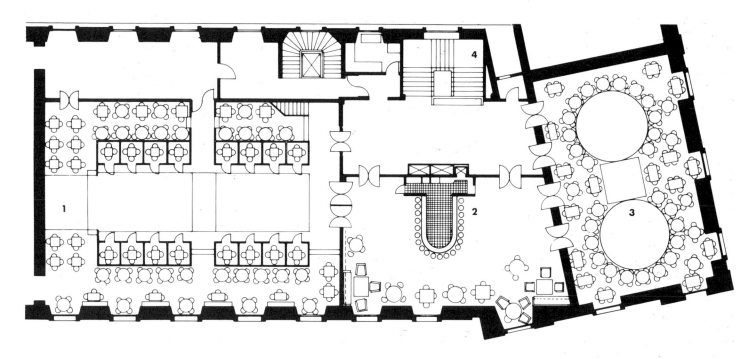

176. First floor plan
Redrawn in 1981 from the 1926 design of
Theo van Doesburg

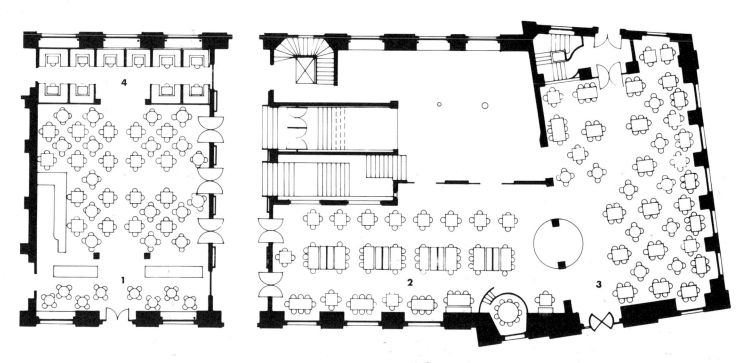

177. Ground floor plan
Redrawn in 1981 from the 1926 design of
Theo van Doesburg

178. Theo van Doesburg
La grande salle de fêtes (large party room), 1926
gouache, ink, pencil on cardboard with collage
bands of paper
20¾ x 11¾
52.6 x 29.8
Collection Musée National d'Art Moderne,
Centre Georges Pompidou

This composition was preliminary to the realized
design. The collage strips are similar to the
colored tapes used much later by Mondrian in
his New York paintings.

179. Sophie Taeuber-Arp
Foyer-bar, 1927-28
(Aubette 63)
gouache
21⅝ x 18⅞
54.9 x 47.9
Collection Musée d'Art Moderne de Strasbourg

A color study for a trapezoidal room that was
situated between the large party room and the
cinema-dance hall. Seated at the bar in the room's
center, one could see a film projected on the
cinema-dance hall screen. The "Greek key"
design was apparently inspired by an Italian trip
taken by Taeuber-Arp in 1926.

180. The grande salle de fêtes was the purest of van Doesburg's neoplastic designs for the Aubette. Its large-scale multi-colored squares and rectangles are surrounded by uniformly sized, raised white bands. The two round dance floors indicated on the floor plan are an oddly discordant note in the otherwise orthogonal pattern of the walls and ceiling.
Vintage photograph

181. In this photograph of the cinema-dance hall, the room is seen as it existed in 1928. The huge obliquely placed rectangles set up a strong diagonal rhythm that contrasts sharply with long vertical windows overlooking the Place Kléber.
Vintage photograph

182. Theo van Doesburg
Color study for the cinema-dance hall, 1926
gouache on cardboard
17 x 29⅜
43 x 74.5
Collection Antonina Gmurzynska

183. Amsterdam, 1928
Collection Nederlands Documentatiecentrum
voor de Bouwkunst, Stichting
Architectuurmuseum

184. C. van Eesteren/Th. K. van Lohuizen/
L.S. Scheffer
General Expansion Plan for Amsterdam (AUP),
1928-34
Collection Nederlands Documentatiecentrum
voor de Bouwkunst, Stichting
Architectuurmuseum

De Stijl and the City

Manfred Bock

Sigfried Giedion, in his celebrated history of modern architecture, *Space, Time and Architecture*, described the pre-history of modern architecture as the growth of a new tradition that came of age at the Weissenhofsiedlung, a 1927 exhibition of housing that took place in Stuttgart. Under the supervision of Mies van der Rohe—one of the 1923 participants in the De Stijl exhibition in Léonce Rosenberg's Paris gallery—German representatives of modern architecture collaborated with such foreign architects as Le Corbusier, J.J.P. Oud and Mart Stam. They designed free-standing houses that constituted the first group expression of what was to become International Style. The new architecture manifested itself as an international movement that would acquire an official basis with the founding of the C.I.A.M. (International Congress of Modern Architecture), whose initial meeting took place in June 1928 at the Chateau de la Sarraz in Switzerland; Gerrit Rietveld represented De Stijl.

The C.I.A.M. functioned as a medium for public relations, as a forum for the exchange of ideas and as a flywheel in the development of the history of architecture and city planning. The congresses created an awareness among architects that the future of architecture cannot be considered separately from city planning. Giedion states that the urban plan demonstrates the level of development of architecture in a given period and demonstrates the ability of a period to manage its own existence. And he continues: "Town planning, always the last branch of architecture to reach full growth, has begun to arrive at new conceptions only quite recently—since about 1925."[1] When Giedion wanted to exemplify the development of this new concept as publicized internationally by the C.I.A.M., he chose Amsterdam as his example, because this city ". . . is one of the few cities of our time that shows a continuous tradition in town planning, unbroken since 1900."[2]

The city plan of 20th-century Amsterdam clearly shows five distinct concepts of urban design (fig. 183). The medieval core is surrounded by

1. Sigfried Giedion, *Space Time and Architecture* (Cambridge: The Harvard University Press, 1941), p 27.
2. *Ibid.*, p 517.

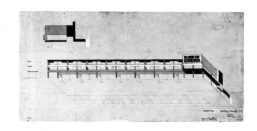

185. Cornelis van Eesteren with color by Theo van Doesburg
Axonometric from below, Winkelgalerij shopping mall, The Hague, 1924
tempera on photostat
13¾ x 28½
35 x 72.5
Collection van Eesteren-Fluck and van Lohuizen Archive

3. Hans L. C. Jaffé, *De Stijl* (New York: Harry N. Abrams, Inc., 1971), p 32.

its regular 17th-century expansion; in turn it is surrounded by the 19th-century quarters—not planned, not cohesive—arbitrarily adhered to the existing city. H.P. Berlage's southern expansion of 1915 is strongly contrasted with that of the previous period. The image of the new western and eastern quarters was determined by the shape of Berlage's expansion. These picturesque and at times impressively monumental residential regions gave Amsterdam, in the 1920s, a reputation as the mecca of public housing.

The Berlage plan remained incomplete; it was modified and incorporated into a larger entity: the General Expansion Plan of Amsterdam (AUP) (fig. 184), that was developed between 1928 and 1934 by the triumvirate L.S. Scheffer, Th. K. van Lohuizen and Cornelis van Eesteren. One can scarcely imagine greater contrast than exists between these two plans. Two worlds collide: the layout of the street versus its use; image versus structure; the private space of street and square, carved out of the city, versus continuous space subdivided and determined by the opened masses, the surfaces and lines of modern architecture. The desire for a geometrical city plan opposes the harmonious spatial order of urban elements in time. Between these concepts—between Berlage, architect of the Amsterdam Stock Exchange and designer of the Expansion Plan of Amsterdam South and van Eesteren, chairman of the C.I.A.M. and designer of the AUP—we find De Stijl.

It is tempting to postulate, as did Giedion and Hans Jaffé, that van Eesteren's experience during his De Stijl period may be considered the foundation of his later development. Jaffé concludes:

> In the early years of De Stijl the modern city was a major source of inspiration to the artists; now it was remade according to De Stijl's principles by one of the group members. Van Eesteren applied De Stijl ideas to the organization of space in larger units—cities or whole provinces; his designs for areas within cities, such as Unter den Linden in Berlin and the Rokin in Amsterdam, were forerunners of designs made many years later for the expansion of Amsterdam. In this, van Eesteren brought to fulfillment one of De Stijl's major concerns, the harmonious ordering of space embodied in the forms of structures of a city, equilibrium of function and form. In this way De Stijl changed contemporary surroundings according to the principles which had come to the fore in the group over the years, and made a lasting impression on many different areas of the human environment.[3]

Although Jaffé makes a distinction between early (Oud) and late (van Eesteren) De Stijl architecture, drawing a parallel with van Doesburg's development from the Nieuwe Beelding (New Imagery) to Elementarism, he nevertheless refers to Stijl principles and to a Stijl group. However, when the application of these principles gives rise to such essentially

186. Cornelis van Eesteren with color by The
van Doesburg
Perspective of Winkelgalerij shopping mall, The
Hague, 1924
pen, ink, tempera, collage mounted on
cardboard
20¾ x 20⅛
52.7 x 51.3
Collection van Eesteren-Fluck and van Lohuizen
Archive

different and formally distinct results as Oud's double working-class
dwelling, 1918, Jan Wils's Papaverhof complex of 1920 (fig. 61),
Rietveld's Schröder house, 1924 (fig. 94), and van Eesteren's study for
a commercial district of 1926, then De Stijl principles must be susceptible
to a very wide range of diverse interpretations.

As has been stated previously, considering De Stijl architects and painters
as a group must be problematical. Perhaps Oud, Wils and van 't Hoff
might be viewed as a group of architects; however, they were not very
cohesive and the club did not exist for long. After the first year, Wils
ceased his collaboration on *De Stijl*. Van 't Hoff's last contribution dates
from August 1919; after a row with van Doesburg, Oud terminated his
active participation early in 1920; Rietveld was not very active, limiting
his contributions to only three short articles in ten years. Finally, van
Eesteren did not publish his manifesto, "Vers une construction
collective" (Towards a Collective Construction) with van Doesburg until
1924. The Stijl architects could not be considered a group analogous to
the Amsterdam School, or the later de 8 (The 8), or Group 32. The only
bonds between Wils, van 't Hoff, Oud, Rietveld and van Eesteren were
the influences they had absorbed from van Doesburg and Mondrian.
However, the ways in which they applied these influences in their

199

architecture were strictly personal and one cannot speak of a common style. Differences of opinion regarding form, space and color, the function of architecture and the visual arts, and in particular, the interaction between architect and painter, characterized ongoing De Stijl conflicts. Finally, Oud, Mondrian and van Eesteren found a periodical in which they could publish their ideas regarding the new imagery, architecture and urban design, ideas not shared by van Doesburg as artist or as editor of *De Stijl*. This journal was Arthur Müller Lehning's *i-10*, 1927-29.

The subjects and articles that Oud and van Eesteren did publish in *De Stijl* represent two phases of development in the architectural and urban design aspects of that periodical. Their collaborations with van Doesburg are consistently lacking in common principles. Not only formally, but in particular in their relation to the interaction between architecture and the visual arts, these architects had disagreements with van Doesburg that proved insoluble. Furthermore, what Oud wrote in 1917 about "The Monumental Image of the City," repeats and summarizes what Berlage had already stated in 1893. Oud's "About Architecture and Normalization in Mass Construction," of 1918, was inspired by a Berlage lecture published in the same year under the title, "Normalization in Residential Architecture." Oud never denied his relationship to this most influential opponent of De Stijl; his constant purpose was to revitalize the design principles of Berlage through new architectural forms. Van Eesteren's adherence to the principles of an anti-monumental and anti-aesthetic New Functionalism, on the other hand, severed any connections he might have had with the history of architecture as an art form and caused him to explore entirely new directions in urban design. Oud, however, who retained the attitudes associated with being an artist, used urban design only in the service of architecture, as demonstrated in his schematic building plan for the Stuttgart Weissenhof and in his expansion plan for Rotterdam-Blijdorp.

Between Berlage's Expansion Plan for Amsterdam South and the AUP there is not De Stijl as such, but the young van Eesteren. During his collaboration with van Doesburg, impressed with Mondrian's art and shaped by the ideas of French and German urban designers, van Eesteren developed a philosophy that would be applied to education, to expansion and reorganization plans for Amsterdam, Berlin, Paris, Lucerne and others, and finally to the functioning of the C.I.A.M., whose chairman he was to become in 1930. Van Eesteren and his allies in the architectural association, The 8, and the Dutch C.I.A.M. group, viewed the road from De Stijl to modern urban design not as a gradual replacement of Berlage with De Stijl, or as a reproduction of De Stijl motifs in the form of development plans, but rather as a realization of De Stijl in urban design: De Stijl becomes the city.

Even though van Eesteren as well as his critics always group the AUP and Mondrian together, I should repeat once more that the aim of the C.I.A.M., a functional city, should not be thought of as a Mondrian painting in three dimensions. Van Eesteren considers De Stijl not only as Mondrian and van Doesburg, but also as Dada and Kurt Schwitters. Unlike Mondrian, Schwitters did not intend to wait until the visual arts and reality (the reality of practical constructions, of grain silos, bridges and factories) would meet each other in "direct and pure imagery;"[4] he represented reality visually. In his collages, Schwitters ordered the fragments of chaos by exclusively aesthetic methods, by applying color and by juxtaposing the objects within the composition according to their aesthetic qualities. These interrelationships between objects and their relationship to the whole divulge a meaning, or, as is frequently stated in De Stijl, their essence, whatever may be the essence of a railroad ticket, a newspaper clipping or another found object.

The structure of the AUP and its subdivisions do not clash with topographical and socio-economic realities. On the contrary, the AUP is designed to make this reality cohesive. The realities of water and soil, of industrial development, of speculation and the need for good, inexpensive dwellings, the inexorable expansion of private transport and of recreational demands, are visually represented in the plan and ordered—sometimes by means of surprisingly slight modifications of the status quo, and sometimes by means of minor adjustments of various elements and relationships.

The AUP is not a stroke of genius of a single individual, but results from the long-term collaboration of Scheffer, van Lohuizen and van Eesteren. The plan was worked out without external disturbances on the basis of the governance and political constellation of Amsterdam around 1930. In 1935 it was confirmed by the Amsterdam City Council without significant opposition. The AUP was, as it were, the collective work of researcher, designer, civil servant and politician:

> The contemporary designer has the task of arranging the plan in such a way that if it proves necessary or desirable to make modifications, this can be accomplished at any time without violence to the framework which determines the structure of the city. *Urban design in the modern sense aims not only at spatial, but also at temporal order.* . . . the eventual form has to evolve gradually in successive stages, and in every period of growth the harmonious relationship between social functions will be maintained.[5]

4. Piet Mondrian, "De schilderkunst en haan practische 'realiseering'" (The art of painting and its practical realization), *De 8 en Opbouw*, 9, 1938, p 73.

5. *Algeen Uitbreidingsplan van Amsterdam. Nota van Toelichting* (General Expansion Plan of Amsterdam. Explanatory Notes) (Amsterdam: Department of Public Works, 1934), pp 29, 167.

187. Cornelis van Eesteren
Axonometric bird's-eye view of contest entry for
the Rokin B: situation with layout of existing and
future buildings
ink, pencil, watercolor, glued to carboard
39⅛ x 39⅛
99.5 x 99.5
Collection van Eesteren-Fluck and van Lohuizen
Archive

6. Cornelis van Eesteren, "De functioneele stad.
Ter inleiding" (The functional city. Introduction),
De 8 en Opbouw, 6, 1935, p 105.
7. Cornelis van Eesteren, excerpts from an address
at the opening of the exhibition "De functioneele
stad" (The functional city), ibid., p 163.
8. Ibid., pp 106, 108.
9. Theo van Doesburg, "Tot een beeldende
architectuur" (Toward a Visual Architecture)
De Stijl, VI (1924) p 79.
10. Cornelis van Eesteren, op. cit., p 106.
11. cf. Clara Weyergraf, Piet Mondrian und Theo
van Doesburg, Deutung von Werk und Theorie
(Munich: Wilhelm Fink Verlag, 1979).

Van Eesteren's and van Lohuizen's point of departure was the city as it existed. They observed a chaos of mutually intertwined and inconsistent functions, evidenced through concentration and relaxation, noise and silence, motion and quiet, billowing chimneys and clear skies. The designers propose to cancel out the negative effects of these chaotic contrasts by providing spatial order.

Van Lohuizen's survey, his urban exploration, served as the basis for the AUP design. As much as was then feasible all functions were analyzed and coordinated. Facts rather than aesthetic axioms constituted the foundation of the plan. Van Eesteren compares the concept of function in urban design with its meaning in mathematics: "Here the function is a variable which depends in its changes on one or more other variable." Van Eesteren declared that the functional city ". . . offers every opportunity to create in harmonious proportions a wholesome physical and psychological environment for man."[6] In addition it guarantees ". . . the necessary equilibrium between the common good and individual freedom."[7] The reality of urban design is very complex. The designer cannot take each and every detail into account; he has to be able to comprehend, to abstract and to restrict himself to the essentials. Moreover, the expansion plan, ". . . needs to be sufficiently flexible to permit architectural growth, and the development of the residential quarter."[8] Accordingly, in van Doesburg's words, the new architecture is ". . . amorphous, yet determinate, i.e., it does not recognize any preconceived formal framework; it is not a mold into which the functional spaces that originate in practical living needs are poured."[9] Van Eesteren expands on this as follows: "The expansion plan serves as a foundation to the architect in determining the situation and essential plan of his building." However, it is the architect ". . . who determines the final form of the plan, its physiognomy."[10] The designers of the AUP were not concerned with decorative effects, the street facade, the shape of the square, the closure of the street by some significant building. Rather, their concern was to create the conditions for future form development. In this sense the plan is a catalyst for the creation of "architectural imagery."

The AUP is thus connected to De Stijl through these 1935 explanations by van Eesteren. The AUP appears to be the embodiment, in urban design, of ideas dating back to 1923 and published in De Stijl in the following year, even though these ideas were originally intended to be specifically architectural and were characterized by van Doesburg's formalism.[11] The AUP planning group was consciously regarded as a collective, for it could only exist on a cooperative basis: the collaboration of van Doesburg and van Eesteren of 1922-23 was the model. Their manifesto, "Vers une construction collective" (Towards a Collective

Construction), containing some experiences from their work on the so-called "Parisian models" and the university hall contains the following statement: "Until now the field of human creativity and its constructive laws have never been explored scientifically. They cannot be imagined. They exist. They can only be determined by collective work and by personal experience." Van Doesburg and van Eesteren formulated one of these fundamental laws as follows: ". . . the modern builder (by means appropriate to the particular art form) makes visible the relationship of its characteristics, not the relationship of objects in themselves."[12] Van Eesteren was evidently impressed with the importance of this law, for in 1955 he stated in a discussion on the location of public buildings within urban space: "Special buildings possess their own particular being. Their total character determines their. . . location with respect to surrounding dwellings. One may compare this to modern compositions. . . in which various materials and colors are used so that each displays its own peculiar essence resulting from its relationship to the others."[13] When in 1943 van Eesteren was asked about the interdependence between the residential quarter and the urban complex, his reply contained the following statement: "Cézanne, Braque, Picasso, Mondrian. Painting is a collection of tensions which recognizes rest as the equilibrium of tensions or as the silence or the absence of tensions. Our cities are an integral entity, comprising action and rest, plants and blacktop, production and consumption. . . . ."

In the same interview, in reply to a question regarding the organization of the city plan, he said:

> Every method of creating order focuses on a purpose. This purpose is the critical factor. We are not interested in the purpose of a dead formalism. The visual arts have preceded architecture. Architecture must adopt the visual potential that has already come to fruition in contemporary art. When we are ready, we shall be able to order, normalize and build in the fashion of our time, which will lead us to beauty.[14]

During their collaboration, van Doesburg and van Eesteren occupied themselves exclusively with problems of form, color and space; the 1923 architectural models, in particular the Maison d'Artiste (fig. 168), were entirely remote from material, construction and function. Aesthetic innovation had to bring about new attitudes and the invention of new materials. The manifesto of 1924, "Tot een beeldende architectuur" (Towards a Visual Architecture), which, although solely signed by van Doesburg, betrays van Eesteren's influence, expresses a slightly more realistic and practical architectural point of view. Van Doesburg states: "The new architecture is elementary, economical and functional, that is to say, it originates in a precise statement of the practical requirements expressed in a clear ground plan."[15]

12. Theo van Doesburg and Cornelis van Eesteren, "Vers une construction collective" (Towards a Collective Construction), *De Stijl*, VI, 6/7, 1924, pp 89-91.
13. Quoted in *Forum*. Maandblad voor architectuur en gebonden kunst (Monthly periodical for architecture and related arts), 9, 1955, p 297. (With thanks to Paulien Houwink for this citation.)
14. Questions E4 and B12 posed by the "Study-Group for Post-War Residential Architecture," typed manuscript, Van Eesteren Archives, Amsterdam.
15. Theo van Doesburg, "Tot een beeldende architectuur," *op. cit.*

Van Eesteren systematized the functionalism which made its appearance in that statement and elaborated it further to make it the basis of his "visual architecture." Van Doesburg, however, changed his mind in that very same year. In "Architecture Diagnosis," his concluding remarks regarding the Stijl exhibition in the Galerie L'Effort Moderne, he writes:

> Architecture must be functional, above all economic and constructive. Many have repeated this statement without realizing that rationalism, extreme economy of means and functionalism cannot fulfill the aesthetic longings originating in a new consciousness. Let us not forget that the progress to functionalism signified the protest against arbitrary decorations in architecture, but that nevertheless, the non-functional, the irrational, the uneconomical, are also functions essential to life and frequently constitute the living source of a creative consciousness."[16]

Van Doesburg writes to Walter Dexel on 21 October 1925: "In my entire mentality I am too independent to become a slave to architecture and to share my future with building authorities and contractors. For a long time I have not belonged with those who have made a deity out of usefulness. . . and in my opinion we should stop anointing creative man with a 'usefulness' lotion."[17]

Van Eesteren developed his concept of visual functionalism in the same year in which van Doesburg reverted to his formalistic point of view. In his comments on his competition entry for the design of a shopping mall with upper-story dwellings in The Hague, 1924—the last project with a color solution by van Doesburg—van Eesteren revealed his design theory (fig. 185). Spatial forms are determined by diverse functions: shopping, living, meeting and other functions have to become abstractions for the designer, in order to fuse them into a single, integrated visual concept. The designer also considers the elements of construction as abstractions, as the embodiment of active and static functions—a support as a line and a wall as a surface. Van Eesteren explains: "The functions of space and construction, so abstracted, can now be managed and controlled simultaneously and contained in forms encompassing these functions as clearly as possible."[18] The eventual architectural forms do not depict their functions, do not translate statistics into aesthetics, but are the "direct and pure" (Mondrian) embodiment of the function: the functions are portrayed.

With his entry in 1924 for the reorganization of the Rokin (Amsterdam's central canal) (fig. 187), based on the principles of Elementarism, van Eesteren takes the next step and he continues in this vein in his designs for Unter den Linden, 1925, using the principle of "gleichgewicht" (equal weight), and for a commercial district in Paris of 1926. To the

16. Theo van Doesburg, "Architectuur—Diagnose" (Architecture Diagnosis), *Architectura*, weekblad van het Genootschap 'Architectura et Amicita,'(weekly periodical of the Society 'Architectura et Amicita'), 28, 1924, p 62.
17. Theo van Doesburg, letter to Walter Dexel, 21 October 1925 (with thanks to Jean Leering, who provided a photocopy of this letter).
18. W. C. V. [W. C. Verschoor], "Prijsvraag Winkelgalerij," *Bowen*, tijdschrift voor Holland en Indie (periodical for The Netherlands and The Netherlands Indies), 2, 1924-25, pp 53-58.

problem of filling in the Rokin Canal in Amsterdam, van Eesteren posed the following theorem in his introduction: "The modern city plan needs a clear division of function;" and he concludes that, "The Rokin's function as a principal access road for traffic must be central to every solution."[19]

The location of the Rokin in the still partly medieval texture of the city obviates the design of a wide highway. However, the street is central to Amsterdam, and visitors to the city need parking facilities; accordingly, van Eesteren fills in a portion for parking. After analyzing and determining the functions, the designer proceeds to their portrayal. Once more he starts with a theorem: "Urban beauty originates in a visual equilibrium between the components that constitute the city or the quarter under examination. A change in one of the components results in a disturbance of the overall equilibrium."[20] Van Eesteren projects a permanent change in scale. The height of the buildings is increased to the maximum permitted in order to make more intense use of space; lots are merged and the varied profile of the Rokin will, after it is filled in, be homogenized by a uniform ground-level surface. Van Eesteren states that, "The designer must sanction this change."[21]

Van Eesteren introduced the third building line in order to re-determine the changed proportions of the district. It is an imaginary line in the sky that aesthetically determines the maximum building height. By inserting a high-rise element, a skyscraper in the concave side of the Rokin where the Spui River interrupts the building line, he attempts to offset the strong horizontality of the facades and the ground plane. Architect W. van Tijen said later: "Van Eesteren attempted, as an urban designer, to determine the character of the third dimension."[22]

The plan was by no means unrealistic. "Determining the destiny of the Rokin," in Mondrian's terms, was, although global in its outlook, financially feasible. The costly modifications of the building facade line could be paid for with proceeds from the sale of the lots; and the use of the corner lot for a skyscraper would greatly increase its value.

Van Eesteren himself stated in an article on the Rokin design in *i 10*: "Highway, automobiles, parking lots, streetcars, offices, warehouses, asphalt. This is the reality, the sole basis for the solution of the Rokin puzzle. I called the design 'elementary' because it is comprised of elements of the city quarter involved. The entire expansion and renewal of Amsterdam should be studied in a similar way."[23] He was to start this study within the next year.

19. Cornelis van Eesteren, "Moderne stedebouwbeginselen in de practijk" (Modern Principles of City Planning in Practice), *De Stijl*, VI, 10/11, 1925, pp 163-164.
20. *op. cit.*, p 166.
21. *op. cit.*, p 167.
22. "Vraaggesprek met W. van Tijen" (Interview with W. van Tijen), *Plan*, 9, 1970, p 523.
23. Cornelis van Eesteren, *Over het Rokin-Vraagstuk (Regarding the Rokin Problem)*, *Internationale Revue, i-10*, I, 3, 1927, pp 84-85.

Manfred Bock is an architectural historian, Kunsthistorisch Instituut der Universiteit van Amsterdam.

Translation by Charlotte I. Loeb

Echoes of De Stijl ■

Martin Friedman

De Stijl has not always been perceived here as a major collective movement and the American artist's knowledge of it has come mainly from Piet Mondrian's painting. But even that association is tenuous, since Mondrian's New York residency began in 1940, well after he had formally dissociated himself from De Stijl. Recently I asked several artists in the United States and Europe, whose work in theme or form might allude to De Stijl, for their thoughts on this movement. Their responses could be taken to represent attitudes of most painters and sculptors today—respectful, but not particularly aware of the full range of its manifestations.

For Americans, the symbol of De Stijl remains Mondrian, though as some of the interviews reveal, feelings about his role are often ambivalent. There was certainly no such equivocation among the group of American abstract artists that initially coalesced around him in New York. They were the true believers. Mondrian's unique position here was as a formidable theorist for whom painting combined spiritual and aesthetic significance, and the quiet force of his personality attracted acolytes whose utilization of De Stijl's basic syntax—rectangles of primary color—rapidly resulted in a number of American dialects. Not only were such native formalists as Leon Polk Smith, Charmion von Wiegand and Burgoyne Diller enamored of its forms and mystique, so were a number of transplanted Europeans. Among the latter, the Swiss-born Fritz Glarner performed what would have been an unthinkable act in De Stijl orthodoxy by organizing clusters of red, blue and yellow rectangular planes within circular "tondo" paintings (fig. 189) and Ilya Bolotowsky, who came to the United States from Russia in 1923, adapted De Stijl's geometry to metal reliefs and columnar sculptures.

But it was the American, Burgoyne Diller, who employed De Stijl imagery in the most original, dramatic manner. In his paintings its familiar red, yellow and black rectangles metamorphosed into large, ritualistic configurations, and his painted wood and formica covered

In conjunction with the De Stijl exhibition, Walker Art Center organized *Echoes of De Stijl*, in which a number of works discussed in this essay were shown.

188. Richard Hamilton
Putting on De Stijl, 1979
collotype on screenprint
19⅝ x 26
50 x 66
Courtesy Charles Cowles Gallery, Inc., New York

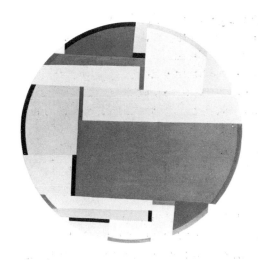

189. Fritz Glarner
Relational Painting, Tondo 40, 1956
oil on masonite
42 diameter
106.7
Collection Walker Art Center,
Gift of the T. B. Walker Foundation

constructions—models for works to be realized in stone—would have fit perfectly within De Stijl's nexus (fig. 190). With the exception of Georges Vantongerloo's modestly-scaled cubistic constructions, purely abstract sculpture was not a dominant aspect of De Stijl. True, Gerrit Rietveld's chairs, tables and cabinets constructed of intersecting and layered color planes can be considered sculpture as well as furniture—but he did not intend to make non-utilitarian forms. To speculate a bit, Diller's symmetrical sculptures, made in the United States at least 30 years after the official demise of the movement, can be regarded as felicitous, if belated, additions to the De Stijl spirit.

Beyond the elaborations on Mondrian's vocabulary by his American followers, De Stijl's influence resonated in less doctrinaire ways and, for many, its emphasis on uncompromising, rigorous abstraction rather than its finite vocabulary of shapes, was the important issue. So responsive were American artists to European post-cubist systems of abstraction that Mondrian's quiet proselytizing during his all-too-brief New York residency had the effect of a match tossed into a huge pile of tinder. The conflagration lasted well past his death here in 1944. In addition to the faithful band that adhered closely to his teachings, a larger artist-audience responded enthusiastically to the geometric theme of which Mondrian was the undisputed master. His influence extended well beyond painting and his by then familiar imagery was widely borrowed and exploited. Through no fault of his own, he was the powerful *éminence grise* behind an insatiable American fascination with modular motifs and rectangular shapes that rapidly found their way into industrial design and fashion. Dress designers freely cannibalized his ideas, as did linoleum and wallpaper manufacturers. Ironically, an aspiration of De Stijl's Dutch founders was to create a universal visual language whose elementary forms would permeate and elevate all aspects of daily life, but this sudden co-opting and mass marketing of De Stijl's motifs in an alien environment was an unanticipated variation of its utopian dream.

Though this early obsession with geometry in American art would eventually give way to more intuitive and expressionist modes, the rationale of Mondrian's art, which sought equilibrium through interaction of rectangular shapes, persisted. A reaction, however, set in and by the late 1950s geometry was overwhelmed by the primal force of Abstract Expressionism. This was a deliberate campaign waged by a new generation of feisty American artists whose objective was to replace all premeditated approaches to painting with one rooted in pure feeling. A unifying aspect of their effort was a general rejection of all things and ideas European; they were determined to create a new American art in which emotion and form would be fused. Spontaneous gesture, not logic, would prevail! For Mondrian, the undisputed genius whose life's work

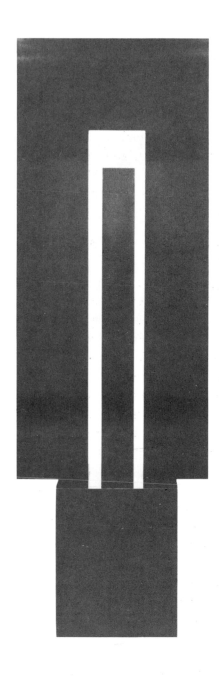

190. Burgoyne Diller
Project for Granite #5, 1963
formica over wood
85½ x 28¼ x 18
217.2 x 71.8 x 45.7
Collection New Jersey State Museum
Gift of the Grad Foundation and Museum
Purchase, 1965

1. Nancy J. Troy, for *Art and Space*, New York,
Washburn Gallery, July-August 1980.

represented the essence of spiritualized geometry, the Abstract Expressionists had only admiration, yet his influence, many felt, was stultifying. As Nancy J. Troy has written, "Indeed, the salient characteristics of Mondrian's style—straight lines and rectangular planes of primary color and non-color—became so pervasive, and his relational mode of composition assumed so much authority that in the 1960s Barnett Newman felt compelled to declare his independence from this tradition while rendering tribute to the power of Mondrian in a series of monumental paintings entitled *Who's Afraid of Red, Yellow and Blue?*"[1]

If, however, geometric painting—and the purist attitude it symbolized—was no longer perceived as a cohesive movement, its rigorous attitudes, after a seemingly dormant period during the Abstract Expressionist heyday, assumed vital new form a generation later in the uncompromising asceticism of minimalist sculpture and hard-edge painting during the 1960s. These latter-day manifestations have a decidedly American cast, with more allusions to industrial and technological forms than to De Stijl's relatively small-scale variations on the rectangle theme.

Unlike American artists who in the early 1940s embraced Mondrian with such fervor as the giver-of-all-truths, the cooler 1960s generation tempered its admiration, for despite his wizardry in converting form to essence, his images seemed to them inhabited by the specter of subject matter. For example, the titles of Mondrian's New York grid-like paintings, *Broadway Boogie-Woogie*, *Victory Boogie-Woogie*, reflected boundless infatuation with American urban themes. Though these proceeded from an entirely abstract basis, their complexes of scintillating lines and tabs of color could be read as neon-lit street grids, lines of traffic and building outlines, especially by a particularly doctrinaire group of young artists determined to purge abstraction of any associational qualities.

Even worse, subject matter aside, there remained the suspicion that just below De Stijl's pristine geometry lurked a traditional approach to picture-making! Those early 20th-century Dutch abstractionists had produced elegant aesthetic equations in which color planes were asymmetrically deployed over a white field; their working method was one of delicate adjustment. Within their rectangles, harmonious microcosms of black lines and blocks of color occurred in indeterminate space, yet forms were always placed in careful relationship to the edges of the canvas. This studied, "relational" approach to pictorial composition was viewed by minimalist hard-liners as yet another manifestation of backsliding, a return to cubist painting ideas, despite De Stijl's austere abstract vocabulary.

By contrast, the imagery of the American purists during the 1960s was radically simple, consisting of large-scale unitary rather than complex shapes. The hard-edge paintings of Ellsworth Kelly, composed of layered geometric color planes, seemed to radiate beyond their borders and the sculptors Don Judd, Sol LeWitt and Carl Andre fabricated metal cubes and grids that dominated the walls and floors of the spaces they occupied. In minimalist sculpture and in the new geometric painting, however, there was none of the complex orchestration of disparate elements typical of De Stijl form. Formally, the minimalists were closer to Russian Suprematism, whose premier painter, Kazimir Malevich, had carried abstraction to what seemed its irreducible limit—a black square on a white field. Nevertheless, Mondrian cast a long shadow on American art and his presence helped immeasurably to create an atmosphere for abstract art here.

But how *is* De Stijl regarded by artists today? The answer: with ambivalence. It is accorded the respect due an important but philosophically distant episode in contemporary art. Few artists I spoke with were particularly interested in De Stijl's social idealism, which seems ingenuous today. Its role in the evolution of Modernism is not questioned but subsequent purist tides have swept it further into history. Nevertheless, the minimalist object-makers feel special kinship with one of its leading figures, Gerrit Rietveld. In fact, these moralists of pure form, Don Judd and Sol LeWitt, collect examples of Rietveld's planar furniture whose exquisitely balanced configurations are the essence of reductiveness. His objects, with their carefully fitted components, reveal the sensitivity of a master cabinetmaker and the straightforward use of uniform wooden slats as structural elements in his tables, chairs and desks anticipated the minimalist sculptors' reliance on available industrial materials and fabrication techniques.

Don Judd began acquiring examples of Rietveld's chairs and other furniture some 15 years ago. These days, most of Judd's work is done in the comparative seclusion of Marfa, Texas where, in addition to producing variations on his basic hollow cube (fig. 191), he recently began making furniture for his children. The unpainted wooden plank construction of his desk and chair, he admits, is somewhat reminiscent of Rietveld's planar designs as well as of "down-home" California mission style (fig. 192). Judd came to Rietveld's work well after his own sculpture had assumed its distinctive form, finding virtues in it that reinforced his own views. A salient aspect of Rietveld's objects, he says, is directness. Their form is ". . . intuitively right, the approach is basic and earthy, uncluttered by ideology."[2] Like most artists of his generation, Judd's first contact with De Stijl was through the clear color and geometry of Mondrian. As a young artist he was also interested in the

2. This and all succeeding statements by the artists were gathered in interviews with the author in spring and summer, 1981.

sharply outlined shapes of Léger and Matisse, but concedes that some of his early paintings might reflect a Mondrian bias. However, under the increasing force of Abstract Expressionism, he says, "Mondrian's art began to appear small-scale and domestic." Like so many of his contemporaries, he turned away from classical European Modernism to the livelier activity on the home front. His new interests were the vaporous radiance of Rothko, and Pollock's heroic transformations of form to energy. Next to these adventurers in *terra incognita*, most European art appeared exhausted and Mondrian seemed "idealistic and remote." Strong views, but understandable if we recall that Judd's sculpture—whose element is the cube—is the antithesis of relational composition.

Notwithstanding such personal reservations, his opinion about De Stijl is decidedly positive and he credits it and Russian Constructivism as more important than Cubism in advancing the cause of abstraction. Cubism, says Judd, could never fully escape the object. By contrast, the Dutch and the Russians fully committed themselves to non-objective form and he is certain that ". . . if they hadn't taken Cubism to its logical conclusion, there would never have been an abstract art."

In 1967, while having some sculptures fabricated in Holland, Sol LeWitt learned that Rietveld's furniture was still being produced in Utrecht and he arranged to trade some of his works for a few Rietveld examples. He was surprised to discover that G.A. van der Groenekan, Rietveld's original cabinetmaker, was still making the celebrated red/blue planar chair—as well as the 1919 armchair, the Berlin chair, and the post-De Stijl zig-zag chair. LeWitt has since become such an avid collector of Rietveld furniture that in 1980 the Wadsworth Atheneum, in Hartford, exhibited his acquisitions. He has made furniture for himself since the 1950s, and a grid table is on the market in a limited edition (fig. 193). Though Rietveld's inspiration is acknowledged, LeWitt's furniture, in its modular tensile structure, is unmistakably related to his own wood and metal sculptures (fig. 194).

In LeWitt's opinion, Mondrian remains De Stijl's chief theorist. LeWitt sees De Stijl's objectives as the pursuit of an ideal order, a characteristic he also values in Russian Constructivism. Because systems play a crucial role in his art, he likes De Stijl's use of methodology but, in true minimalist fashion insists that the philosophy underlying his sculptures is the antithesis of De Stijl's. "De Stijl came out of Cubism," says LeWitt, "but my thinking is opposed to it." Though aware of De Stijl as an aesthetic and social movement, he is more interested in its formal syntax rather than its symbolism. "Forms are only what they are," says LeWitt, "nothing more or less. . . . When I make a triangle, it's only a triangle;

211

191. Donald Judd
Untitled, 1968
stainless steel and blue plexiglass
33 x 68 x 48
83.8 x 172.7 x 121.9
Collection Walker Art Center

192. Donald Judd
Desk and chair, 1979
wood
30 x 48 x 33 and 30 x 15 x 15½
76.2 x 121.9 x 83.8 and 76.2 x 38.1 x 39.4
Collection the artist

a circle is only a circle, with no other significance." Unlike De Stijl's abstractionists, many of whom associated geometry with social and spiritual values, LeWitt deliberately avoids such associations in his work. A perceptible, if nebulous, relationship with De Stijl appears throughout his work. For example, he notes that many of his first wall drawings were elaborate linear configurations, in De Stijl colors—red, yellow, blue and black on white surfaces; now the secondary tones—orange, green and purple, sometimes appear.

De Stijl equals distillation, says the artist and writer Scott Burton, who responds as much to the movement's morality as to its aesthetics. He characterizes it as an early form of conceptual art, primarily because of its idealistic philosophy. He also regards it as the opening chapter of the "utilitarian idea" in modern art, ". . . perhaps the purest phase of the North European 'utilitarian-constructivist' approach which includes the Russian constructivists and the Bauhaus." Burton, more than other artists with whom I spoke, was interested in De Stijl's idealism and social goals. His characterization of the movement is enthusiastic: "Its sparse repertoire of modernist shapes seemed to offer possibilities for all aspects of society; it was the first and the most ingenuous phase of a series of early 20th-century movements that sought to make practical use of abstract imagery. Its efforts toward creating a popular architecture and house interiors that would utilize inexpensive materials represented a revolutionary attitude about art in the service of society."

212

193. Sol LeWitt
Coffee table, 1980
wood and glass
16 x 48 x 48
40.6 x 121.9 x 121.9
Courtesy Multiples, Inc./Marian Goodman
Gallery, New York

194. Sol LeWitt
Cubic Modular Piece #2 (L-shaped Modular Piece), 1966
baked enamel on steel
108 x 55 x 55
274.3 x 139.7 x 139.7
Collection Walker Art Center
Purchased with the aid of funds from the National
Endowment for the Arts and the Art Center
Acquisition Fund

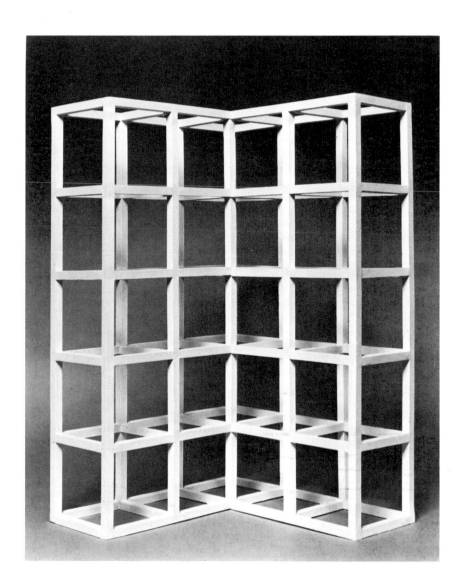

213

195. Scott Burton
Untitled ("Red, Yellow, Blue Cube"), 1979-80
lacquer on particle board
40½ x 30 x 30
102.9 x 76.2 x 76.2
Collection Barry Lowen

214

This concept, however, was only barely tested because, except for architecture, De Stijl utilitarian art was in short supply; few objects other than Rietveld's furniture and children's toys were produced. In contrast, the functional output of the Russian constructivists was more varied—with a larger and more receptive audience—and included architecture, public monuments, theater sets and costumes, spectacular graphics, clothing and pottery designed by such luminaries as Tatlin, Lissitzky, Goncharova and Rodchenko—all in the service of the liberated masses. Their activities had strong support among high officials, until it was determined that the very notion of abstract art was synonymous with the decadence of the West. The most refined phase of European "utilitarian-constructivism" was, of course, the German phenomenon of the Bauhaus in which artists, architects and engineers came together to create objects utilizing the advanced resources of 20th-century technology. Though intended for inexpensive mass production, their elegant appointments for the modular "international style" house—furniture, lamps, fabrics—reflected the aspirations of the high bourgeoisie and were hardly "popular" objects. Today, not surprisingly, these are coveted as expensive classics.

In contrast to the ardently proclaimed social programs of the Russian artists and the Bauhaus's aestheticized technology, De Stijl's idealism was muted. There was no great political cause, such as the Russian revolution, for its artists to serve. Nor were they called upon to raise the populace to new heights aesthetically and morally as the Russians believed their work was destined to do. But it was political reality that ultimately destroyed the Bauhaus. In addition to harboring a collection of freethinkers who were a threat to the totalitarian state, that movement was perceived by Germany's new masters as dangerous because it sought to cross traditional barriers between art and industry, and thus presumed to influence the shape of society. De Stijl, however, was not perceived as a political threat. It was totally non-official, existing almost in a vacuum, with little noticeable effect—and certainly no challenge—to the status quo of a tolerant Holland.

For many artists the totality of De Stijl, its dissolution of boundaries between painting, sculpture and architecture, remains its most positive attribute. One of its saints, the architect Gerrit Rietveld, was as comfortable with fabricating simple, household objects as he was with designing buildings. "Rietveld is my hero!" says Burton, who regards him as the most esoteric yet "populist" of the De Stijl artists, ". . . the one who best understood the concept of a union of the decorative and the plastic arts." He notes that the tension in Rietveld's art results from its being created from the inside outward—as an artist works—rather than from the outside inward—as a designer works. "It is the opposite of form following function." Burton makes a good point because Rietveld's sharp-angled chairs could hardly be characterized as gracious adaptations to the body's contours. The same principle applies to Rietveld's houses; they were created intellectually, following certain idealized proportions and based on subjective distribution of form, color and volume. It was up to the individual to find his place in these structures.

In 1970, Burton began making environments consisting of "found furniture;" and in 1973 he started to design his own furniture. For all his admiration for De Stijl imagery, Burton's own work shows only occasional references to it. He claims that ideas derived from the "utilitarian-constructivist" movement—attitudes shared by Tatlin, Rodchenko, and the De Stijl artists—became important factors in making his objects. Burton has made tables and chairs in steel, bronze, stone and concrete and lately has used raw organic material, one recent result being a chair created from a massive vertical boulder sliced to a right angle to accommodate the sitter. Perhaps Burton's most De Stijl-like object is an ambiguous 1979-80 piece consisting of three primary colored cubes (fig. 195). It has a double existence: a complex of pure and utilitarian forms. With their concealed hinges and pulls, the cubes belie their purpose. Burton says, cryptically, they exemplify the De Stijl spirit because in concealing their contents they are a "negative comment on the idea of conspicuous consumption."

The systems by which De Stijl paintings and furniture are constructed—elementary shapes fitted together by the most economical means—are of particular interest to Frank Stella whose art reflects the full range of geometry. Until a few years ago, his paintings were characterized by straight-edge clarity and virtually anonymous surfaces, their motifs based on such drafting table shapes as triangles, protractors and French curves—symbols of order and precision. In 1976, with a vivid group of three-dimensional paintings, the "exotic bird" series, Stella broke his purist mold in favor of an intense new expressionism, and in the process his formal vocabulary underwent an extraordinary transformation. Its spartan geometry became organic, its triangles and half-circles so stretched and twisted that they literally explode from the picture's surface.

Asked if De Stijl's ideas have in any way influenced his painting, Stella replies affirmatively. Beyond the fact that until the mid-1970s his paintings were finely balanced visual equations, there are other, deeper relationships to the movement that have more to do with attitude than with form. He admires the direct way in which De Stijl artists "went about their business" and discusses the economy of structure so evident in their results. These objects, Stella says, reveal ". . . such elegance of

216

organization and conviction of feeling!" Though De Stijl may seem a distant idiom to us, and may have failed to achieve its social goals, he considers it a model of purity and speculates, "It could easily be reborn if someone liked it well enough to work within its limits."

Like so many other artists with whom I discussed De Stijl, Stella focuses on the matter-of-fact construction of Rietveld's chairs and his ingenious use of the simplest means. Equally, he likes the way Mondrian's paintings are constructed. "It's wonderful," he says, "that painting could be so rich without being complicated." Stella considers the genius of De Stijl artists to have been their ability to put things together in the most objective manner without recourse to virtuosity; they used basic ingredients and "got to the nitty-gritty quickly." When commenting on De Stijl's economy, he is not using the word only to describe a limited number of simple forms favored by its artists, but is also talking about an attitude that produced architecture and furniture of available materials and by simple fabrication processes. "Rich materials," he observes, "do not guarantee important art and can only complicate the issue."

In this respect he even sees an analogy between De Stijl's frugal approach and his own method of working. As an example, he discusses the large black paintings he produced during the late 1950s, noting they were made with the cheapest materials. "With black enamel at $1.39 a gallon and cotton duck, it was possible to go for the big picture." On a more formalistic note, Stella concedes that in many of his paintings parallels exist to De Stijl working methods. He discusses an early rectangular maze painting, the 1962 *Sketch Les Indes Galantes* (fig. 196), which he considers to be within De Stijl's spirit. Although it is not composed of primary color rectangles, but of white, gray and black squares, this does not lessen the relationship. After all, Stella observes, "Value is just the other side of color and both are used as basic means of building form."

Remarking on an aspect of De Stijl painting that seems to trouble other abstract artists of Stella's generation, he does not find its "relational" composition to be disturbing, limiting, or revisionist in any way. Instead, he asks, "Who's to say that De Stijl wasn't just the beginning of a new sense of freedom about putting things together?"

If Mondrian's influence has so affected the tone of American art, what of his influence in Holland today? One of the most important exponents of Dutch purism is the conceptual artist, Jan Dibbets. He is distinguished for elegant interpretations of landscapes and urban vistas presented as sequences of contiguous photographic images. Over a wide arc and from a fixed station point, he isolates segments of his subject and the images that result from this panoramic technique are reassembled in geometric configurations. Some, such as the 1973 *Horizon 1-10° Land* (fig. 199),

217

consist of thin vertical planes that form a procession across a white wall. Others have a comet-like sweep. In their precision and distilled clarity these relate, however tenuously, to the earlier Dutch abstract mode of De Stijl—but to press this analogy makes Dibbets uneasy and he is ambivalent about such associations. Dibbets refutes any notion that his work is predicated on Mondrian's. He stoically observes that, given his geographic and historic circumstances, it would be impossible not to be touched in some way: "To be Dutch is a fact of life!" More central to his artistic development are Giotto, Piero della Francesca, Ingres and Cézanne, he says, and among contemporaries Barnett Newman and Jackson Pollock have had greater sway. Not that he wholly denies native inspiration. The 17th-century Dutch painter, Pieter Jansz Saenredam, master of stark church interiors and loggias, is a spiritual ancestor whose sensitivity in revealing the essence of architectural form Dibbets seeks to achieve in his work (fig. 5).

Though the purity of Dibbets's vision may suggest the spirit of Mondrian, Dibbets acknowledges only one general debt to the master. "Mondrian developed an art that extended beyond the picture frame," he points out, and in his own work he aspires to do the same. "This was a new concept of painting, and even Cubism didn't do this." Thus a relatively small Mondrian painting, he says, ". . . takes the whole wall." (Interestingly, some American minimalists feel otherwise; Don Judd suggests that Mondrian's paintings are self-contained objects rather than forms that seem to extend beyond their borders.) Such domination of space, Dibbets notes, has been the objective of other artists who sought to achieve it through drastically different means. Barnett Newman, for example, ". . . paints or covers the entire wall."

Not only has De Stijl's distinctive vocabulary been influential in the work of two generations of formalist artists here and abroad, but its iconography has turned up, often in affectionately irreverent ways, in the work of artists of other persuasions—primarily Pop Art. Though most Pop imagery is identified with mass culture, a sizeable part deals with art itself. This is not an especially new phenomenon, since generations of painters have cheerfully borrowed themes from illustrious predecessors to recycle in their own idioms, the most esteemed cannibalizer of recent times being Picasso who foraged voraciously through art history. To borrow in art is not necessarily to steal and nowadays can even be considered a form of tribute. This applies to several artists who have worked De Stijl imagery into their own creations.

We begin with the most sober-minded of these distinguished borrowers, George Segal, whose relationship to Mondrian is especially strong. For Segal, Mondrian is the "master of flatness" who, for all his condensation of form, "did not lose profundity." As a young artist he could not ignore Mondrian's unique influence in shaping an energetic abstract art by ". . . pouring natural juices into the structure of abstraction." Segal perceived that a vital naturalism underlay Mondrian's abstract New York paintings and was stirred by the resemblance of his scintillating grid compositions to city forms—an association that disturbed some of his purist contemporaries. In contrast to them, Segal has only kind words for Mondrian's use of relational composition and he utilizes similar principles in his sculpture, emphasizing the exact placement of his plaster personages in their quasi-realistic settings. This is evident in *The Gas Station* (fig. 203), an elongated tableau containing two figures in a skeletal setting that includes a floor-to-ceiling window, a shelf of tires, a Coke machine and a circular clock on a dark, nondescript wall. These forms occupy a shallow space, and the result is virtually a three-dimensional painting. Segal concedes he has used Mondrian-like principles in placing them on an invisible grid. As he tells it, *The Gas Station* went through extensive metamorphosis. Begun in 1963, it was initially extremely complex, ". . . full of collage objects—a blur. . . more like Schwitters's concoctions than Mondrian's precise vision." Dissatisfied with the clutter, he decided to eliminate all forms not crucial to the composition. In the 1964 final version the figures and surviving objects are well-defined elements within an austere, horizontal framework. A similar modular approach characterizes *The Butcher Shop*, an elegiac sculpture made as a memorial to his father. Conceived in 1965, its solitary inhabitant is an elderly woman, posed for by his mother, whose upraised hand holds a meat cleaver. Two gleaming metal crossbars, bristling with hooks, are attached to vertical posts that form a grid. Suspended from the hooks are a hacksaw and a chicken (Segal's only known plaster representation of animal life). The result is a naturalistic variation on a Mondrian composition.

Indeed, Mondrian's spirit inhabits much of Segal's art. He has paid homage to the saint of the rectangle in more overt fashion, in the 1967 *Portrait: Plaster Figure of Sidney Janis with Mondrian's "Composition 1933"* on an easel. Segal and his dealer, the redoubtable Sidney Janis, have had a long, felicitous association and when Janis asked Segal to "do" his portrait, the sculptor agreed only if Janis would pose with his favorite Mondrian which would be included in the final work. It was a deal, and the result is Janis cloned in white plaster, contemplating his treasure. While this unusual art-about-art creation honors the dealer's connoisseurship, it is also Segal's tribute to a painter whose genius he understands. His most recent direct reference to Mondrian occurs in *Hot Dog Stand* (fig. 201), a moody 1978 vignette in which a seedy-looking type is about to make a purchase from a young waitress on the other side of a counter. The simplified elements of the stand are painted black. The

design of the illuminated plastic ceiling has been boldly lifted from a Mondrian. Segal says this sculpture was directly inspired by a hot dog stand he saw in a New Jersey shopping center. "I was flabbergasted to encounter it; someone had seen Mondrian's painting and liked the design, and this was the contractor's version. I was both fascinated and repelled by this rape of Mondrian and proceeded to make my comment on the comment."

Enigma and disorientation characterize Steinberg's arcane observations on politics, manners, mores and—of course—art. It delights him to play with sacrosanct artistic conventions of modern art, and among his delicately perverse commentaries on De Stijl's obsession with flatness are his full-scale variations on Mondrian paintings. In a 1968 work called *The Museum Wall* (fig. 202), we see how Steinberg has created this illusion by using a sequence of five thin vertical trapezoids of diminishing scale. The result is a wonderful perspectival sensation as his "Mondrians" recede serenely into the distance. According to Steinberg, "*The Museum Wall* is about modern art history that found in Mondrian the ideal artist—the master of the Linear, Parallel, Perpendicular and all the paraphernalia of Western order." In his variation on Mondrian's art Steinberg says all of these grand ideas are "strangely subjected to perspective!"

So well known had Mondrian's famous style of rectangular abstraction become, that by the 1950s it symbolized modern art and was frequently the subject of cartoons. The most memorable of these were made by Saul Steinberg for *The New Yorker*. In an especially fine example, we see the stereotypical goateed romantic painter in the act of creation (fig. 204). His opulent surroundings are those of the 19th-century atelier. Palette in one hand, paint brush delicately raised in the other, he works on his latest masterpiece, which rests on a monster easel. He is painting a Mondrian, of course.

The painstaking subdivision of the rectangle was the essence of De Stijl's approach, but for Lichtenstein art is anything but a methodical process. Consequently, his paintings that respond to the De Stijl aesthetic neither laud nor deprecate the movement. Instead, as he puts it, they are his efforts to suggest Mondrian's imagery, devoid of any philosophy that generated it. His evocations are ". . . Mondrians after the fact—obviously fakes." That point is made clear because his Mondrians are rendered in the ben-day dot patterns, the same technique used in his glorifications of newspaper cartoons (fig. 200). In all his re-creations of art history, Lichtenstein explains, his intention is to portray the "bare bones of a style," whether it be classical art, German Expressionism or De Stijl—but without the sense of "discovery and invention" that produced it. It is mode, not motivation that Lichtenstein comments on.

196. Frank Stella
Sketch Les Indes Galantes, 1962
oil on canvas
71½ x 71½
181.6 x 181.6
Collection Walker Art Center
Gift of the T.B. Walker Foundation

220

A teasing relationship with Mondrian's work continues in Lichtenstein paintings of themes that make no direct reference to De Stijl. For example, in the 1973 *Artist's Studio No. 1 (Look Mickey)* (fig. 197), we detect Mondrian's familiar grid, rather freely adapted to describe the back and side walls of the room. Several rectangles layered against the walls contain such familiar Lichtenstein icons as Donald Duck, the reflecting mirror, a classical architectural detail and comic-strip lettering. These appear mainly in brilliant reds, yellows and blues, which the artist likes because they are ". . . the least sensitive colors in the world of product marketing," but for which, it will be recalled, the De Stijl artists had more lofty regard. Such paradoxes delight Lichtenstein.

Those popsters who borrowed Mondrian's syntax understood they were tampering with holy writ, yet found the temptation irresistible. For them modern art's high seriousness was embodied in De Stijl's cosmic rectangles but, as Lichtenstein observes, De Stijl's idealistic vision seemed out of sync with present realities. Pop was in large measure a vigorous reaction against elitist and obscure themes and dedicated itself to the common man's subject matter. Its forms derived from a yeasty consumer culture that celebrated the supermarket, mass communications, movie stars and sports heroes—nothing arcane about those! Yet its artists were anything but blue-collar in their approach to making art. They aestheticized their mundane subjects through processes that revealed sophisticated understanding of form, space and color. In the spirit of the 1960s they were an educated elite playing at proletarian politics, who, for all their rejection of pure abstraction, could never escape its spell.

In Pop Art, references to monuments of art history often question the societal values that produced those hallowed forms. Such gentle probing of our cultural legacies characterizes much of the English Pop movement. More than its hard-hitting American cousin, English Pop is replete with historical, literary and artistic allusions, and the most cerebral of its practitioners is Richard Hamilton, whose small-scale paintings, collages and prints derive their subjects from such diverse areas as politics, literature, middle-class mores and art history.

While Richard Hamilton says De Stijl themes occur periodically in his work, he feels no particular involvement with the movement. "But then," he goes on, "I plagiarize from any and many sources. It may be that I have used De Stijl more often than some other styles because the source is very clear—unmistakable. That is to say, it is very obvious that I am quoting and it is unlikely that any reasonable, well-informed viewer would not recognize the source and, when recognizing, would understand that it was a reference rather than an influence. But I feel no greater rapport with De Stijl than with Watteau, or Francis Bacon, both of whose styles

197. Roy Lichtenstein
Artist's Studio #1 (Look Mickey), 1973
oil, magna on canvas
96 x108
243.8 x 274.3
Collection Walker Art Center
Gift of Mr. and Mrs. Kenneth N. Dayton
and the T.B. Walker Foundation

221

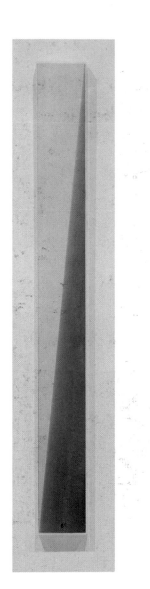

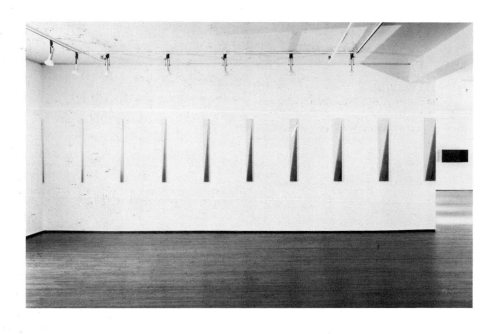

198. Jan Dibbets
Horizon 1-10° Land, 1973
(detail)

199. Jan Dibbets
Horizon 1-10° Land, 1973
10 color photographs
48 high, width variable
121.9
Collection Walker Art Center

200. Roy Lichtenstein
Non-Objective II, 1964
oil on canvas
48 x 48
121.9 x 121.9
Collection Mr. and Mrs. Michael Sonnabend

201. George Segal
Hot Dog Stand, 1978
painted plaster, painted wood, plastic, metal,
electric lights
108 x 72 x 79¼
274.3 x 182.9 x 201.3
Collection San Francisco Museum of
Modern Art
T.B. Walker and Clinton Walker Fund Purchase

202. Saul Steinberg
The Museum Wall, 1968
colored crayon, graphite on wood
five parts
24 x 13½ x ¼, assembled
61 x 34.3 x .6
Collection the artist

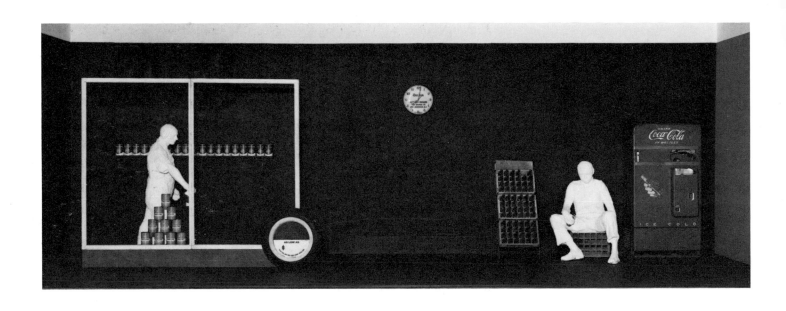

203. George Segal
The Gas Station, 1963-64
plaster and mixed media
102 x 288 x 56
259 x 731.5 x 142.2
Collection National Gallery of Canada, Ottawa

204. Saul Steinberg
Drawing courtesy The New Yorker Magazine,
Inc., 1952, 1980

I have aped—among others." Rapport or not, Hamilton's references to De Stijl reveal a perceptive understanding of its history and forms. He "documents" De Stijl objects—Rietveld's chairs—while simultaneously doing inventive improvisations on the movement's abstract syntax. A recent series of Hamilton prints includes two works, *Interior with Monochromes* and *Putting on De Stijl* (fig. 188), both highly refined and mildly satirical variations on De Stijl composition. Both combine—collage fashion—photographs of Rietveld's famous chairs with photographs of interiors and planes of vivid color. In *Putting on De Stijl*, Rietveld's celebrated red/blue and zig-zag chairs are almost absorbed by an animated background consisting of large-scale red, blue, yellow and black rectangles. All sense of volume is cheerfully destroyed. There is every reason to suspect that Hamilton's title was inspired by a mid-50s "skittle" song whose first line, "Putting on the agony, putting on the style," provides the clue.

Another interested observer, with special capacity to comment—not always so objectively—on the dynamics of 20th-century art movements is the artist Ray Johnson. Through his information-filled collages Johnson conducts a non-stop disquisition on the state-of-the-art of contemporary art and his penchant for combining fragments of history and contemporary symbols in eccentric association reassures us that Dada's spirit is indestructible. His paper rectangles combine newspaper photographs, product advertising, Xeroxes of correspondence and a range of personal symbols, including a double-headed snake and cartoon mouse head. In those Johnson collages that deal with contemporary art, Piet Mondrian remains a favorite subject for arcane comment. Johnson is acquainted with the range of Mondrian's production: the early realistic chrysanthemum paintings, the pioneer "plus and minus" abstractions and New York pictures. He finds "the lightness and grace" of Mondrian's work compelling and has made several collages in appreciation. In a 1967 example, *Mondrian* (fig. 205), that features a photograph of Mondrian turning the knob of a radio, Johnson says he wanted "to show the intervention of the outside world into the severity of Mondrian's studio," with the radio as his primary contact. Johnson, like Richard Hamilton, is able to draw upon such esoterica as pop music lyrics of earlier decades. Knowing of the quiet painter's fondness for jazz and dancing, Johnson in his collage whimsically inscribed a few lines of the "beach culture" nonsense song, IT WAS AN ITSY BITSY TEENY WEENY YELLOW POLKA DOT BIKINI. Johnson admits he was a bit free with chronology, since that little ditty appeared on the public scene well after Mondrian's death in 1944. The collage's three rectangles, arranged vertically, represent "strata" of art history, Johnson says, and thus it functions on three levels: on top is a small tessera that alludes to ancient classical and far-eastern art; Mondrian's photograph symbolizes De Stijl; the

225

rectangle containing ITSY BITSY's deathless prose defines Pop Art's beginnings. In Johnson's cryptic explanation, the tessera that floats over Mondrian's balding cranium, a feature the hairless Johnson especially likes, ". . . establishes the fact that this is a Ray Johnson picture and brings in the art element!"

From reactions of the many artists with whom I spoke, it would appear that De Stijl's spirit is very much with us even if its orthodoxy isn't. To this generation of American artists whose education was as much in the university lecture hall as in the studio, the movement appears as a distant, hazy fusion of social and artistic ideas—strictly an early 20th-century European phenomenon. Artistic collectives, complete with programs and published manifestoes, have had little place in American art even though we have produced a number of identifiable styles, each with its bands of adherents. For example, proponents of social realism in the 1930s and early 40s shared ideological goals but this hardly constituted a formal artistic movement. The same can be said for its nemesis and successor, Abstract Expressionism, which despite its New York locus and emphasis on large-scale gestural imagery, did not represent a communal movement whose objective was the betterment of society.

However lofty De Stijl's philosophy might appear to American eyes, its reality was something less than ideal. To begin with, De Stijl was a loose confederation of painters, architects and graphic designers who, though predominantly Dutch, were hardly in frequent contact. In large measure the movement was held together by the manipulative skills of its prime apologist, Theo van Doesburg, who used its publication to propagandize ardently for the movement. For American artists, De Stijl's ultimate realization was Mondrian's reductive vision and without his brief presence in New York it's doubtful if De Stijl's vocabulary would have gained such a foothold. Its social philosophy was untranslatable to the volatile, multi-textured American scene. Though distinguished figures such as Oud, van Eesteren and van 't Hoff are identified with De Stijl architecture, for most American artists and architects its personification is the work of one man, Gerrit Rietveld, whose reputation abroad is

205. Ray Johnson
Mondrian, 1967
collage on paper
18½ x 14
47 x 35.6
Collection David Bourdon

226

based on a single, much-published house, his 1924 masterpiece for Mme. Schröder-Schräder in Utrecht. Now, as we have seen, Rietveld's multi-hued planar furniture is enjoying a great vogue among artists, and original examples are being avidly collected here and abroad.

The limited quantity of De Stijl painting in the United States has been a negative factor in making the movement better known. Aside from Mondrian's paintings in a few major public collections, De Stijl material is in short supply, virtually all of it on the East Coast, where the largest De Stijl collections are to be found in The Museum of Modern Art, Yale University Art Gallery and The Solomon R. Guggenheim Museum. In most museums, isolated examples of De Stijl art are usually grouped with other cubist-related works, and though these are formally compatible, such well-intended juxtaposition can blur identity. A room of Mondrians, van Doesburgs, van der Lecks, Huszars and Vantongerloos would be awesome but, alas, even in Holland we are denied that experience except on the rare occasion of a special installation.

Small wonder that contemporary artists' knowledge of De Stijl is fragmentary. Lately, a number of the more enterprising have started to research the recent past, perhaps to find precedents for their own directions. In the process, as we have learned from comments of those interviewed for this piece, they have become knowledgeable about the work of certain De Stijl artists and in a few cases have identified with that work. While the minimalists admire the De Stijl artists' revelation of essentials through total abstraction they prefer to accomplish this through their own reductive processes. The "popsters" may borrow a Mondrian motif as a good-natured jest but, secretly perhaps, they would like to incorporate a little of his magic in their earthier pursuits.

From the perspective of the contemporary artist, De Stijl's great accomplishment was the formulation of a visual language that transcends time and geography. It is also a paradoxical syntax; on the one hand stunningly pragmatic in its elemental form and color; on the other, the essence of mystery because its rectangular configurations of primary colors are metaphors of the cosmic order. Despite its simple aspect, De Stijl is not about simplicity. For artists today such levels of meaning are as intriguing as they are unfathomable, and, consequently, the phenomenon of De Stijl remains a bright presence among them.

Martin Friedman is Director of Walker Art Center.

De Stijl Chronology

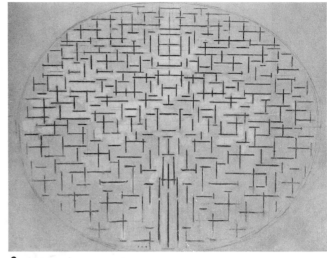

2

1

Many sources have been used in compiling this chronology. The Art Center would like to acknowledge sources that have been particularly significant: Joost Baljeu, *Theo van Doesburg,* 1974; H.L.C. Jaffé, *De Stijl 1917-1931,* 1959; H.L.C. Jaffé, *De Stijl,* 1971; Rudolf W.D. Oxenaar, *Bart van der Leck 1876-1958,* 1976; and Nancy J. Troy, "De Stijl's Collaborative Ideal: The Colored Abstract Environment," 1979.

1911-12
Mondrian settles in Paris and begins cubist period. **1**
Rietveld opens cabinet workshop in Utrecht.
Van Doesburg begins writing art criticism.

1914
Mondrian returns to Holland.
Van Doesburg drafted into army, serves on Belgian frontier. Meets poet Antony Kok and discusses idea of publishing a magazine.

1914-17
Mondrian creates "Pier and Ocean" series. **2** Interpretations of the rhythmic motion of waves against a pier and shoreline, these works are Mondrian's last to take nature as their point of departure. The strict limitation of form to short vertical and horizontal lines introduces an essential element of De Stijl's pictorial vocabulary.

1915-16
Van Doesburg and Mondrian meet.
Theosophist Dr. M.H.J. Schoenmaekers publishes *The New Image of the World* (1915) and *Principles of Plastic Mathematics* (1916), two works which influence Mondrian's theory of Neoplasticism. Adopting the theosophic idea that the essence of reality can be expressed as a series of opposing forces, Schoenmaekers emphasizes the polarity of horizontal and vertical elements, and the importance of primary colors. He also states that the new image of the world presents "a controllable precision, a conscious penetration of reality, and exact beauty."

4

5

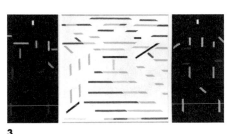

3

6

With the encouragement of van Doesburg, Mondrian begins writing his theoretical ideas that later appear in *De Stijl* in a series of essays entitled "Neoplasticism in Painting." Following the reasoning of Schoenmaekers and other Theosophists, Mondrian defines Neoplasticism as the reconciliation of the opposing forces that constitute the basic structure of the universe. Through the resolution of this duality, the neoplastic work attains a perfect harmony and directly expresses the absolute, the universal. The expression of absolute harmony is achieved through the construction of equilibrated relationships ". . . the position, dimension, and value of the straight line and rectangular (color) plane."

1916
Van Doesburg, after demobilization, settles in Leiden. Meets architects Jan Wils and J.J.P. Oud.
Bart van der Leck moves to Laren where he meets Schoenmaekers and Mondrian. To van der Leck, Mondrian's paintings must seem a far more advanced version of the style he has been pursuing for several years. His change from a fundamentally realist style to one that **3** approaches nonobjectivity is probably due to Mondrian's influence. In turn, Mondrian is influenced by van der Leck: in 1917, he reintroduces color into his paintings, using the flat, almost primary hues that have characterized van der Leck's work.

1917
Mondrian and van Doesburg paint first completely nonobjective works in which forms are not abstracted from nature. **4**
Van Doesburg provides stained-glass windows, mosaics, tile floors and color schemes for Oud's "Villa Allegonda" and "De Vonk." Provides **5** stained-glass windows for a town house by Wils in Alkmaar.
De Stijl group founded. Includes Mondrian, van Doesburg, Huszar, van 't Hoff, van der Leck, Oud, Vantongerloo and Wils. First issue of **6** *De Stijl* appears in October. Van der Leck withdraws from group shortly after publication of first issue, having disagreed with van Doesburg over the inclusion of architects as contributors to the journal.

7

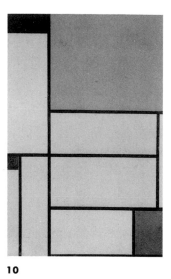

10

8

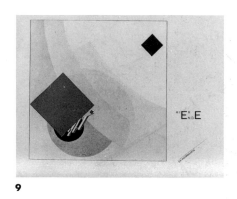

9

1918
Rietveld meets Robert van 't Hoff, Theo van Doesburg and other members of De Stijl. Designs red/blue chair. **7**
November: publication of first De Stijl manifesto, written by van Doesburg, signed by van Doesburg, van 't Hoff, Huszar, Kok, Mondrian, Vantongerloo and Wils.

1919
Van 't Hoff, believing the goals of De Stijl to have little chance of being realized in the immediate future, withdraws from group.
Mondrian moves back to Paris.
Rietveld joins De Stijl.

1920
Van Doesburg undertakes European tour to spread De Stijl ideas. In Berlin, meets Hans Richter and Viking Eggeling and sees their first abstract films. At the home of Bruno Taut, meets Walter Gropius. Begins writing dadaist poems under the pseudonym I.K. Bonset. Van Doesburg's position on Dada's relevance to De Stijl is defined in article, "Is a Universal Plastic Notion Possible Today?" Writes, "Only a radical cleansing of social and artistic life as, in the domain of art, is already done by Dada, . . . can prepare civilization for the New Vision's happiness which is greatly and purely alive in a few people."
Mondrian begins treating his studio as a neoplastic environment, at first by arrangement of the furniture, later by attaching rectangles of primary colors to the walls. **8**
April: second De Stijl manifesto, "On Literature," signed by van Doesburg, Mondrian and Kok.

1921
Van Doesburg publishes dadaist "anti-philosophy" in *De Stijl* using the pseudonym Aldo Camini. Visits the Bauhaus, Weimar.
Rietveld begins collaboration with Truus Schröder-Schräder on interior designs.
August: third De Stijl manifesto, "Towards a New Formation of the World."
El Lissitzky meets van Doesburg and begins association with De Stijl. **9**
Mondrian arrives at mature style: rectangles of primary colors set on white grounds divided by black lines. **10**

12

11

13

1922
Mondrian retrospective at the Stedelijk Museum, Amsterdam, on occasion of his 50th birthday.
Van Doesburg gives unofficial lecture series at the Bauhaus, Weimar. Represents De Stijl at The International Congress of Progressive Artists, Düsseldorf. Here, he delivers statement on the creative demands of De Stijl, calling for the development of a universal means of expression and the end of the separation between life and art. Later hosts International Congress of Constructivists and Dadaists, Weimar. **11**

1923
Van Doesburg moves to Paris and begins collaboration with Cornelis van Eesteren on design of three architectural models. The **12** models reflect van Doesburg's idea that time as well as space is an architectural value. The realization of "space-time" architecture involves using colored planes to articulate interpenetrating volumes that radiate outward from a central axis. The dynamic quality of these designs is evident also in the decision to treat the front, back and sides as equally important, so that continuous movement around the exterior is suggested.
With Kurt Schwitters and Nelly van Doesburg, van Doesburg makes a "Dada" tour of Holland.

De Stijl architecture exhibition held at Léonce Rosenberg's Galerie l'Effort Moderne, Paris. **13** Shown are architectural drawings and models by van Eesteren and van Doesburg, a model for a jewelry shop by Rietveld, interior color applications by Huszar, and a design for a glass skyscraper by Mies van der Rohe. Other participants include Oud, Wils, and W. van Leusden.
Huszar and Rietveld collaborate on the design of an exhibition space for the Greater Berlin Art Exhibition.

14

15

16

1923-24
Rietveld and Truus Schröder-Schräder collaborate on design and construction of the Schröder house, Utrecht, the first house built according to De Stijl principles. **14**

1924
Van Doesburg publishes 16-point program, "Towards Plastic Architecture," on occasion of second De Stijl architecture exhibition, Paris. Point 16 declares architecture as the synthesis of Neoplasticism; it denies the viability of painting and sculpture as separate elements, and asserts the primacy of architecture by stating that it includes all the arts in its very essence. Van Eesteren and van Doesburg collaborate on urban planning projects.
Vantongerloo makes sculptures based on mathematical formulas.

1924-25
Van Doesburg develops new theory of painting called "Elementarism." Conceived "as a radical correction of neoplastic ideas," Elementarism allows the use of diagonal elements in painting in order to create works possessing a greater dynamism than possible with a strict horizontal-vertical orientation. Underlying the new emphasis on dynamics is van Doesburg's desire to realize a more definite expression of time in his work, a goal he also pursues in his architectural projects. **15**

1925
Mondrian withdraws from De Stijl after disagreeing with van Doesburg over the latter's introduction of diagonals into painting.
Kiesler designs and constructs model for *City in Space,* Austrian Pavilion, Exposition des Arts Décoratifs, Paris. **16**
Oud designs Café De Unie, Rotterdam.

17

18

DE STIJL

ND

VAN DOESBURG

1917—1931

INTERNATIONAL MAANDBLAD
VOOR NIEUWE KUNST WETEN-
SCHAP EN KULTUUR
DERNIER NUMERO

19

1926
Van Doesburg, Sophie Taeuber-Arp and Jean Arp begin collaboration on the Café Aubette, Strasbourg. This project provides van Doesburg with the opportunity to apply De Stijl principles to all aspects of design. Over the next two years, he makes over 199 drawings, ranging from designs for a cinema-dance hall to designs for ashtrays and typography.
Van Doesburg outlines his theory of Elementarism in a series of articles in *De Stijl*. Mondrian designs interior *Salon de Mme. B. . . . , à Dresden,* and stage set for Michel Seuphor's play *L'Ephémère est Eternel.*

1927
Van Doesburg prepares ten-year "jubilee" issue of *De Stijl* celebrating the achievements of the group over the previous decade.

1928
Completion of Café Aubette, Strasbourg. **17**

1929
Van Doesburg designs and begins construction of his own house, Meudon, France. Renews friendship with Mondrian. **18**

1931
"Abstraction-Creation" group formed in Paris. Includes many former members of De Stijl. Van Doesburg dies 7 March in Davos, Switzerland.

1932
Last issue of *De Stijl*, edited by Nelly van Doesburg and dedicated to Theo. **19**

Biographies/Bibliographies

Jean (Hans) Arp 1887-1966

1887
Born 16 September, Strasbourg.

1916
Participates in founding of Zurich Dada group.

1917
First abstract wood reliefs.

1925
Publishes *Die Kunst-Ismen* with El Lissitzky.

1926
Settles in Paris. Meets Mondrian and Michel
Seuphor. Begins collaboration with van
Doesburg and Sophie Taeuber-Arp for design
of Café Aubette, Strasbourg.

1931
Joins "Abstraction-Creation" group, Paris.

1966
Dies in Basel, Switzerland.

Jean (Hans) Arp: Bibliography

Arp, Jean. *Arp on Arp: Poems, Essays,
Memoirs*. Edited by Marcel Jean. Translated
by Joachim Neugroschel. New York: The
Viking Press, 1972.

_____ .*On My Way—Poetry and
Essays 1912-1947*. The Documents of Modern
Art. New York: Wittenborn, Schultz, Inc.,
1948.

_____ .*Onze Peintres vus par Arp.
Taeuber, Kandinsky, Leuppi, Vordemberge,
Arp, Delaunay, Schwitters, Kiesler, Morris,
Magnelli, Ernst*. Zurich: Edition Girsberger,
1949.

Arp, Jean and Lissitzky, El. *Die Kunst-Ismen*.
Erlenbach and Zurich: Eugen Kentsch Verlag,
1925.

Cassou, Jean. *Arp*. Paris: Musée National d'Art
Moderne, 1962.

Giedion-Welcker, Carola. *Jean Arp*. New York:
Harry N. Abrams, Inc., 1957.

Read, Herbert. *The Art of Arp*. New York:
Harry N. Abrams, Inc., 1968.

Soby, James Thrall, Editor. *Arp*. New York:
The Museum of Modern Art, 1958.

Theo van Doesburg 1883-1931

1883
Born 30 August, Utrecht.

1912
Writes art criticism.

1914
Joins army, serves on Belgian frontier.
Meets poet Antony Kok and discusses the idea
of publishing a magazine.

1915
Corresponds with Piet Mondrian.

1916
Discharged from army. Settles in Leiden and
meets architect J.J.P. Oud.
Paints geometric abstractions of landscape and
still-life subjects.

1917
Founds De Stijl. First issue of magazine published in October.
Designs color schemes and stained-glass windows for buildings by Oud and Wils.
First neoplastic works using colored rectangles.

1920
Begins publishing dadaist poems.
Travels to Berlin. Meets Hans Richter and Viking Eggeling and sees their first abstract films.

1921
Publishes his dadaist "anti-philosophy" in *De Stijl* using the pseudonym Aldo Camini.
Develops architectural color theories in designs for middle-class housing and agriculture school in Drachten, Holland.

1922
Teaches at the Bauhaus, Weimar. Begins to concentrate on architecture.
Begins publication of dadaist magazine *Mécano*.
Hosts International Congress of Constructivists and Dadaists, Weimar.

1923
Moves to Paris.
Collaborates with Cornelis van Eesteren on architectural drawings and models for the De Stijl architecture exhibition held at Léonce Rosenberg's Galerie l'Effort Moderne, Paris.

1924
Develops theory of Elementarism.
Makes first countercompositions.

1926
Publishes manifesto of Elementarism.
Begins collaboration with Jean Arp and Sophie Taeuber-Arp on interiors for the Café Aubette, Strasbourg.

1929-30
Builds house in Meudon, France.

1931
Participates in the founding of "Abstraction-Creation" group in Paris.
Dies of heart attack on 7 March, Davos, Switzerland.

Theo van Doesburg: Bibliography

Aggis, Maurice and Jones, Peter. "Van Doesburg: A Continuing Inspiration," *Studio International*, March 1969, pp 113-116.

Baljeu, Joost. "Architecture and Art," *Structure*, 1, 1958, pp 46-56.

_____ . *Theo van Doesburg.* New York: Macmillan Publishing Co., Inc., 1974.

Blok, Cor. "Theo van Doesburg," *Art International,* April 1969, pp 21-23.

Brown, Gordon. "In the Galleries: van Doesburg," *Arts Magazine,* May 1970, p 56.

Doesburg, Theo van. *De Nieuwe beweging in de schilderkunst.* Delft: Technische Boekhandel en Drukkerij J. Waltman, 1917.

_____ . *Principles of Neo-Plastic Art.* Greenwich, Connecticut: New York Graphic Society, 1969 (reprint).

_____ . *Wat is Dada??????* English translation in Baljeu, Joost, *Theo van Doesburg.* New York: Macmillan Publishing Co., Inc., 1974, pp 131-135.

_____ . "De betekenis van de kleur in binnen—en buitenarchitectuur," *Bouwkundig Weekblad,* 44, 21, 1923, pp 232-234. English translation in Baljeu, Joost, *Theo van Doesburg,* pp 137-140.

_____ . "Caminoscopy," (Aldo Camini) *De Stijl,* IV, 5, June 1921, pp 65-71; 6, June 1921, pp 82-87; 7, July 1918, pp 97-99; 8, August 1918, pp 118-122; 12, December 1918, pp 180-182.

_____ . "Het einde der kunst," *De Stijl,* VI, 9, 1924-25, pp 135-136. English translation in Baljeu, Joost, *Theo van Doesburg,* pp 149-151.

_____ . "Zur Elementaren Gestaltung," *G,* 1 July 1923. English translation in Baljeu, Joost, *Theo van Doesburg,* pp 140-142.

_____ . "L'Elémentarisme et son origine," *De Stijl,* VIII, 87/89, 1928, pp 20-25. English translation in Baljeu, Joost, *Theo van Doesburg,* pp 166-175.

_____ . "Farben in Raum und Zeit," *De Stijl,* VIII, 87/89, 1928, pp 26-27, 31-34. English translation in Baljeu, Joost, *Theo van Doesburg,* pp 175-180.

_____ . "Manifest I van 'De Stijl ' 1918," *De Stijl,* II, I, November 1918, pp 2-3, signed by Theo van Doesburg, Robert van't Hoff, Vilmos Huszar, Antony Kok, Piet Mondrian, Georges Vantongerloo and Jan Wils.

_____ . "Manifest II van 'De Stijl' 1920," *De Stijl,* III, 6, pp 49-50, signed by Theo van Doesburg, Piet Mondrian and Antony Kok. English translation in Balijeu, Joost, *Theo van Doesburg,* pp 110-111.

_____ . "Manifest III. Tot een nieuwe wereldbeelding," *De Stijl,* IV, 8, August 1921, pp 125-126. English translation in Baljeu, Joost, *Theo van Doesburg,* pp 113-114.

_____ . "Von der neuen Aesthetik zur materiellen Verwirklichung," *De Stijl,* VI, 1, March 1923, pp 10-14. English translation in Baljeu, Joost, *Theo van Doesburg,* pp 127-131.

_____ . "Notices sur l'Aubette a Strasbourg," *De Stijl,* VIII, 87/89, 1928, pp 2-18.

_____ . "Schilderkunst van kompositie tot contrakompositie," *De Stijl,* VII, 73/74, 1926, pp 17-18, 23-27. English translation in Baljeu, Joost, *Theo van Doesburg,* pp 156-161.

_____ . "Schilderkunst en plastiek. Elementarisme," *De Stijl,* VII, 78, 1926-1927, pp 82-87. English translation in Baljeu, Joost, *Theo van Doesburg,* pp 163-166.

_____ . "Schilderkunst en plastiek. Over contra-kompositie en contra-plastiek. Elementarisme," *De Stijl,* VII, 75/76, 1926, pp 35-43. English translation in Baljeu, Joost, *Theo van Doesburg,* pp 156-161.

_____ . "Tot een beeldende architectuur," *De Stijl,* VI, 6/7, 1924, pp 78-83. English translation in Baljeu, Joost, *Theo van Doesburg,* pp 142-147.

_____ . "Vers une construction collective," (with Cornelis van Eesteren). *De Stijl,* VI, 6/7, 1924, pp 89-91. English translation in Baljeu, Joost, *Theo van Doesburg,* pp 147-148.

_____ . "Der Wille zum Stil. Neugestaltung von Leben, Kunst und Technik." *De Stijl,* V, 2, February 1922, pp 23-32; 3, March 1922, pp 33-41. English translation in Baljeu, Joost, *Theo van Doesburg,* pp 115-126.

Feuk, Douglas. "Space Formation in the Work of Theo van Doesburg," *Aris,* I, 1, 1969, pp 2-19.

Georgel, Pierre and de Lillers, Edmée. *Theo van Doesburg: Projets pour l'Aubette.* Paris: Centre Georges Pompidou, 1977.

Gerstner, Karl. "Die Aubette als Beispiel integrieter Kunst," *Werk,* October 1960, pp 375-380.

Giroud, M. "Theo van Doesburg et De Stijl," *Art Press,* October 1977, pp 24-25.

Hedrick, Hannah. *Theo van Doesburg. Propagandist and Practitioner of the Avant-Garde 1909-1923.* Ann Arbor: UMI Research Press, 1980.

_____ . "Van Doesburg's Dream," *The Structurist,* 9, 1969, pp 9-13.

Jeanneret, Charles-Edouard (Le Corbusier) and Ozenfant, Amedée. "L'Angle droit." *L'Esprit Nouveau,* 18, 1923.

Leering, Jean. "Van Doesburg: Stijl and All." *Art News,* March 1969, pp 38-41.

McNamee, Donald. "Van Doesburg's Elementarism," *The Structurist,* 9, 1969, pp 22-32.

Polano, Sergio. *Theo van Doesburg, Scritti do arte e di architettura.* Rome: Officina Edizione, 1979.

Schuurman, K.E. "Theo van Doesburg Compositie 1919." *Museumjournaal,* VII, 1, June 1961.

Seuphor, Michel. "L'Aubette de Strasbourg," *Art d'Aujourd'hui,* December 1953.

Theo van Doesburg 1883-1931. Edited by Leering, Jean. Eindhoven: Stedelijk Van Abbemuseum, 1968.

Welsh, Robert P. "Theo van Doesburg and Geometric Abstraction," *De Stijl,* ed. F. Bulhof. The Hague: M. Nijhoff, 1976.

Zevi, Bruno. "Theo van Doesburg Tomorrow," *Museumjournaal,* XIV, 2, April 1969, pp 58-63.

César Domela b. 1900

1900
Born 15 January, Amsterdam.

1919
Paints naturalistically.

1923
First completely nonobjective works.

1924-25
Meets van Doesburg and Mondrian in Paris. Joins De Stijl.

1927
Moves to Berlin.

1928
Begins constructing reliefs based on neoplastic principles.

1933
Moves to Paris. Joins "Abstraction-Creation" group.

1981
Lives and works in Paris.

César Domela: Bibliography

Bool, Flip and Broos, Kees. *Domela: Paintings, Reliefs, Sculptures, Graphic Work, Typography, Photographs.* The Hague: Haags Gemeentemuseum, 1980.

César Domela: Werke 1922-72. Düsseldorf: Stadtische Kunsthalle und Kunstverein für die Rheinlande und Westfalen, 1972.

Clairet, Alain. *César Domela: Oeuvre Catalogue Raissoné.* Paris: Edition Carmen Martinez, 1978.

Domela, César, "My Conception of Abstract Plastic Art," *Leonardo,* January 1969, pp 21-30.

Ginderstael, Roger van. "Entretien avec César Domela," *Cimaise,* XVII, 99, November-December 1970, pp 42-48.

Jaffé, H.L.C. *César Domela: Paintings, Constructions, Tableaux-Objects 1924-60.* New York: Galerie Chalette, 1961.

Kay, Marguerite. "Domela's Abstractions." *Studio,* October 1949, pp 108-111.

Cornelis van Eesteren b. 1897

1897
Born 4 July, Kinderdijk, The Netherlands.

1917
Receives honors diploma from Academy of Fine Arts and Technical Sciences, Rotterdam.

1921
Wins "Prix de Rome."

1922
On visit to Weimar meets Theo van Doesburg.

1923
Collaborates with van Doesburg on
architectural projects. Participates in De Stijl
architecture exhibition, Galerie l'Effort
Moderne, Paris.

1924-27
Office manager for architect Jan Wils.

1925
Collaborates with van Doesburg on design of
Winkelgalerij, a shopping arcade in The
Hague.

1927-30
Lecturer on town planning, Staatliche
Bauhochschule, Weimar.

1929
Appointed chief architect for Amsterdam.

1930-47
President of International Congress
of Modern Architecture (C.I.A.M.).

1981
Lives in Amsterdam.

Cornelis van Eesteren: Bibliography

Blijstra, Reinder. *C. van Eesteren*. Translated
by Roy Edwards. Amsterdam:
J.M. Meulenhoff, 1971.

Eesteren, Cornelis van. "Moderne stedebouwbeginselen in de praktijk," *De Stijl*, VI, 10/11,
1924-25, pp 161-168; 12, pp 138-140.

_____ . "10 jaar 'Stijl;' kunst, techniek
et stedebouw," *De Stijl*, VII, 79/84, 1927,
pp 93-96.

Jaffé, H.L.C. "Prof. C. van Eesteren 4 Juli 70
jaar," *Bouwkunding Weekblad*, LXXXV,
1927, pp 213-219. Abridged and translated in
Architectural Design, December 1967, p 514.

Robert van't Hoff   1887-1979

1887
Born 8 November, Rotterdam.

1913-14
Travels to United States. Meets Frank
Lloyd Wright.

1914-16
Returns to Holland. Designs and builds houses
at Huis-ter-Heide which are strongly influenced
by Wright.

1916
Meets Theo van Doesburg and J.J.P. Oud.

1917
Participates in founding of De Stijl.

1919
Withdraws from De Stijl.

1937
Moves to England.

1979
Dies 25 April, England.

Robert van 't Hoff: Bibliography

Jonker, Gert. "Robert van 't Hoff maker van
het kleinst denkbare oeuvre." *Bouw*, 12,
6 June 1979, pp 6-8.

_____ . "Een poging tot
reconstructie: de werken van R. van 't Hoff."
Bouw, 13, 23 June 1979, pp 17-23.

Tummers, Nicolas H.A. "Rob van 't Hoff en
het werk van Wright." *Cobouw*, 16, June 1967,
p 25.

Van 't Hoff. Eindhoven: Stedelijk Van
Abbemuseum, 1967.

Vilmos Huszar   1884-1960

1884
Born Budapest, Hungary.

1905
Emigrates to Holland; settles in Voorburg.

1917
Participates in founding of De Stijl. Designs
De Stijl magazine cover.

1918
Designs color applications for bedroom of
Bruynzeel house, Voorburg.

1920-21
Collaborates with Piet Zwart on furniture
designs.

1923
Leaves De Stijl. Collaborates with Rietveld on
exhibition interior for Greater Berlin Art
Exhibition.

1925
Pursues work in graphic design and paintings.

1960
Dies in Hierden, The Netherlands.

Vilmos Huszar: Bibliography

Badovici, Jean. "Entretiens sur l'Architecture
Vivante. Intérieur par V. Huszar."
L'Architecture Vivante, Fall-Winter 1924,
pp 14-15.

Huszar, Vilmos. "Aesthetische
Beschouwingen," *De Stijl*, I, 2, December 1917,
pp 20-23; 3, January 1918, pp 33-35; 5, March
1918, pp 54-57; 7, May 1918, pp 78-84; 12,
October 1918, pp 147-150; II, 1, November
1918, pp 7-10; 3, January 1919, pp 27-31.

_____ . "Ruimte-kleur-compositie
voor een eetkamer," *De Stijl*, V, 1,
January 1922, pp 7-8.

Frederick Kiesler 1890-1965

1890
Born Vienna, Austria.

1922
Designs sets for Karel Capek's play *R.U.R.*

1923
Designs first "endless" house, conceived as a space theater.

1924
Architect and director for Music and Theater Festival, Vienna. Designs "Leger and Träger" exhibition system.

1925
Designs and builds model of *City in Space* for Austrian Pavilion, Exposition des Arts Décoratifs, Paris.

1926
Emigrates to New York. Appointed Director of International Theater Exhibition, New York.

1942
Designs interiors for Peggy Guggenheim's Art of this Century gallery, New York.

1957
Forms architectural firm, Kiesler and Bartos.

1965
Dies 27 December, New York.

Frederick Kiesler: Bibliography

Creighton, Thomas. "Kiesler's Pursuit of an Idea," *Progressive Architecture*, July 1961, pp 104-123.

Goodman, Cynthia. "Current of Contemporary History: Frederick Kiesler's Endless Search," *Arts Magazine*, September 1979, pp 118-123.

Held, Roger. "Endless Innovations. The Theories and Scenic Design of Frederick Kiesler." Bowling Green State University: PhD dissertation, 1977.

Kiesler, Frederick. "Ausstellungssystem Leger und Träger," *De Stijl*, VI, 10-11, 1924-25, pp 138-141.

_____ . *Contemporary Art Applied to the Store and Its Display*. New York: Brentano's, 1930.

_____ ."Erneuerung des Theaters," *De Stijl*, VII, 75-76, 1926, pp 51-52.

_____ . "Manifest Vitalbau-Raumstadt-Functionelle-Architektur," *De Stijl*, VI, 10/11, 1924-25, pp 141-146.

Lawder, Standish. *The Cubist Cinema*. New York: New York University Press, 1975, pp 108-113.

St. Florian, Frederick. *Frederick Kiesler Architekt 1890-1965*. Vienna: Galerie Nachst St. Stephan, 1975.

Yamaguchi, Katsuhiro. *Frederick Kiesler: Environmental Artist*. Tokyo: Bijutsu Shappan-Sha, 1978.

Bart van der Leck 1876-1958

1876
Born 26 November, Utrecht.

1905
Collaborates with P.J.C. Klaarhamer on book illustrations. Contact with H.P. Berlage.

1912
Begins stylizing forms and using flat planes of color.

1916
Moves to Laren. Meets Mondrian, van Doesburg, Huszar and Dr. M.H.J. Schoenmaekers. Designs interior color scheme for Villa Kröller-Müller, Otterlo. Paints nearly abstract *Mine Triptych*.

1917
Participates in founding of De Stijl. Paints nonobjective "compositions."

1918
Leaves De Stijl. Returns to painting abstractions based on observed subjects.

1928
Begins designing textiles for Metz & Co., Amsterdam.

1949
Retrospective exhibition at Stedelijk Museum, Amsterdam.

1958
Dies in Blaricum, The Netherlands.

Bart van der Leck: Bibliography

Bart van der Leck. Amsterdam: Stedelijk Museum, cat. 205, 1959.

Bart van der Leck, a la recherche de l'image des temps. Paris: Institut Néerlandais, 1980.

Feltkamp, W.C. *B.A. van der Leck, Leven en Werken*. Leiden: Spruyt, Van Mantem & De Does, 1956.

Gribling, F. "Het utopistische realisme van Bart van der Leck." *Museumjournaal*, XXI, 5, 1976, pp 212-220.

Leck, Bart van der. "De plaats van het moderne schilderen in de architectuur." *De Stijl*, I, 1, pp 6-7. English translation in Jaffé, Hans, *De Stijl*, 1970, pp 93-95.

Overzicht van het Levenswerk van Bart van der Leck. Amsterdam: Stedelijk Museum, Uitgave 57, 1949.

Oxenaar, Rudolf Willem Daan. *Bart van der Leck, 1876-1958*. Otterlo: Rijksmuseum Kröller-Müller, 1976.

_____ . "Bart van der Leck tot 1920. Een Primitief de Nieuwe Tijd." Utrecht: Rijksuniversiteit te Utrecht, Proefschrift, 1976.

_____ . "Birth of De Stijl, Part Two: Bart van der Leck." *Artforum*, June 1973, pp 36-43.

El Lissitzky 1890-1941

1890
Born 23 November, Smolensk, Russia.

1919
Appointed professor of architecture and graphic arts at Vitebsk Art Labor Cooperative. Meets Kazimir Malevich.
Creates first "Prouns."

1921
Appointed head of the faculty of architecture of the Vkhutemas Art School, Moscow.
First contacts with van Doesburg in Berlin.

1922
Participates in International Congress of Progressive Artists, Düsseldorf and Congress of Constructivists and Dadaists, Weimar.
Publishes in *De Stijl.*

1923
Designs "Proun Room," Greater Berlin Art Exhibition.

1923-25
Lives in Locarno, Switzerland.

1926-28
Designs exhibition interiors: International Art Exhibition, Dresden, 1926; Niedersächsische Landesgalerie, Hanover, 1927-28.

1928
Chief artist for Soviet pavilion, International Press Exhibition, Cologne.

1941
Dies in Moscow.

El Lissitzky: Bibliography

Birnholz, Alan. "El Lissitzky." Yale University: PhD dissertation, 1973.

_____ . "For the New in Art: El Lissitzky's Prouns," *Artforum,* November 1969, pp 68-73.

Bowlt, J.E. "El Lissitzky," *New Lugano Review,* 3, 1-2, 1977, pp 49-55.

Elliott, D. *El Lissitzky 1890-1941.* Oxford, England: Museum of Modern Art, 1977.

Frampton, Kenneth. "The Work and Influence of El Lissitzky," *Architects' Year Book,* 12, 1968, pp 253-268.

Leering, Jean. *El Lissitzky.* Eindhoven: Stedelijk Van Abbemuseum, 1966.

Lissitzky, El. "Proun," *De Stijl,* V, 6, June 1922, pp 81-85.

_____ . "Prounen Raum," *G,* 1, 1923, n.p.

Lissitzky-Küppers, Sophie. *El Lissitzky: Life, Letters, Texts.* Greenwich, Connecticut: New York Graphic Society, 1968.

Lueddeckens, Ernst. "The Abstract Cabinet of El Lissitzky," *Art Journal,* 30, 3, Spring 1971, pp 265-266.

Richter, Horst. *El Lissitzky, Sieg über die Sonne. Zur Kunst des Konstruktivismus.* Cologne: M. Dumont Schauberg, 1958.

Piet Mondrian 1872-1944

1872
Born 7 March, Amersfort, The Netherlands.

1909
Joins the Theosophical Society of Amsterdam.

1910
Takes part in founding of Moderne Kunstkring, Amsterdam.

1911
Moves to Paris.

1912
Beginning of cubist period.

1914
Returns to Holland because of father's illness. Outbreak of World War I prevents return to Paris.
Works in Domburg and begins "plus-minus" series.

1915
Moves to Laren. Comes into contact with Theosophist Dr. M.H.J. Schoenmaekers.
Begins correspondence with van Doesburg.

1916
Meets Bart van der Leck.

1917
First completely non-objective paintings. Participates in founding of De Stijl. Publishes "Neoplasticism in Painting" in *De Stijl.*

1918
First diamond-shaped (lozenge) paintings.

1918-19
Begins to use horizontal and vertical lines as structural elements.

1919
Returns to Paris.

1921
Limits palette to primary colors: red, yellow and blue, with black, white and gray.

1922
Retrospective exhibition of Stedelijk Museum, Amsterdam, on occasion of 50th birthday.

1925
Withdraws from De Stijl after disagreeing with van Doesburg over use of diagonal elements in painting.

1926
Designs *Salon de Mme. B. . . . à Dresden* and a stage set for Michel Seuphor's play, *L'Ephémère est Eternel.*

1929
Renews friendship with van Doesburg.

1931
Joins "Abstraction-Creation" group, Paris.

1938
Leaves Paris for London.

1940
Moves to New York.

1944
Dies 1 February, New York.

Piet Mondrian: Bibliography

Alma, P.; Brugman, Til; van Eesteren, Cornelis; Oud, J.J.P.; and Seuphor, Michel. *Piet Mondrian.* Amsterdam: Stedelijk Museum, 1946.

Baljeu, Joost. *Mondrian or Miró.* Amsterdam: De Beuk, 1958.

Banham, Reyner. "Mondrian and the Philosophy of Modern Design." *Architectural Review,* October 1957, pp 227-229.

Bill, Max; van Doesburg, Nelly; Joosten, Joop; Rowell, Margit; Welsh, Robert; and Wijsenbeek, L.J.F. *Piet Mondrian.* New York: The Solomon R. Guggenheim Museum, 1971.

Blok, Cornelis. *Mondrian in de Collectie van het Haags Gemeentemuseum.* The Hague: Gemeentemuseum, 1968.

Blotkamp, Carel. "Mondrian's First Diamond Compositions." *Artforum,* December 1979, pp 33-39.

Busignani, Alberto. *Mondrian.* New York: Grosset & Dunlap, 1968.

Carmean, E.A., Jr. *Mondrian, The Diamond Compositions.* Washington, D.C.: National Gallery of Art, 1979.

Champa, Kermit. "Piet Mondrian's 'Painting Number II—Composition with Grey and Black'." *Arts Magazine,* January 1978, pp 86-88.

Elgar, Frank. *Mondrian.* London: Thames and Hudson, 1968.

Gay, Peter. *Art and Act: Causes in History—Manet, Gropius, Mondrian.* New York: New York University Press, 1976.

Henkels, Herbert; Holtzman, Harry; Joosten, Joop; Maur, Karin; and Welsh, Robert. *Mondrian: Drawings, Watercolors, New York Paintings.* Stuttgart: Staatsgalerie, 1980.

Holtzman, Harry. *Mondrian: The Process Works.* New York: The Pace Gallery, 1970.

Hunter, Sam. *Mondrian.* New York: Harry N. Abrams, Inc., 1958.

Jaffé, H.L.C. *Piet Mondrian.* New York: Harry N. Abrams, Inc., 1970.

James, Martin. "The Realism Behind Mondrian's Geometry." *Art News.* December 1957, pp 34-37.

Joosten, Joop. "The Birth of De Stijl, Part I: Piet Mondrian—Abstraction and Compositional Innovation." *Artforum,* April 1973, pp 54-59.

Mondrian, Piet. "L'architecture future néoplasticienne." *L'Architecture Vivante,* III, 9, 1925, pp 11-13.

_____ . "De l'art abstrait. Réponse de Piet Mondrian." *Cahiers d'Art,* VI, 1, 1931, pp 41-43. English translation in *Art Students League Quarterly,* 1, spring 1941.

_____ . "Art and Life." English translation by Til Brugman in Jaffé, Hans, *De Stijl 1917-1932.* Amsterdam: J.M. Meulenhoff, 1959, pp 209-254.

_____ . "Het bepaalde en het onbepaalde." *De Stijl,* II, 2, December 1918, pp 14-19. English translation by Martin James and Harry Holtzman in Jaffé, Hans, *De Stijl.* New York: Harry N. Abrams, Inc., 1971, pp 103-106.

_____ . "Dialoog over de nieuwe beelding: zanger en schilder." *De Stijl,* II, 4, February 1919, pp 37-39; 5, March 1919, pp 49-53. English translation in Jaffé, Hans, *De Stijl.* New York: Harry N. Abrams, Inc., 1971, pp 117-126.

_____ . "Documentatie over Mondrian." Edited by Joop Josten. *Museumjournaal voor Moderne Kunst,* XIII, 4, 1969, pp 208-215; 5, pp 267-270; 6, pp 321-336.

_____ . "De huik naar den wind." *De Stijl,* VI, 6/7, pp 86-88.

_____ . "Moet de schilderkunst minderwaardig zijn aan de bouwkunst?" *De Stijl,* VI, 5, May 1923, pp 65-71. English translation in Jaffé, *De Stijl,* 1971, pp 183-185.

_____ . "Natuurlijke en abstracte realiteit." *De Stijl,* II, 8, June 1919, pp 85-89; 9, July 1919, pp 97-99; 10, August 1919, pp 109-113; 11, September 1919, pp 121-125; 12, October 1919, pp 133-137; III, 2, December 1919, pp 15-19; 3, January 1920, pp 27-31; 5, March 1920, pp 41-44; 6, April 1920, pp 54-56; 8, June 1920, pp 65-69; 9, July 1920, pp 73-76; 10, August 1920, pp 81-84. English translation in Seuphor, Michel, *Piet Mondrian: Life and Work.* New York: Harry N. Abrams, Inc., 1956, pp 301-352.

_____ . "Het neo-plasticisme (de nieuwe beelding) en zijn (hare) realiseering in de Muziek." *De Stijl,* V, 1, January 1922, pp 1-7; 2, February 1922, pp 17-23.

_____ . "De nieuwe beelding in de schilderkunst." *De Stijl,* I, 1, October 1917, pp 2-6; 2, December 1917, pp 12-18; 3, January 1918, pp 29-31; 4, February 1918, pp 41-45; 5, March 1918, pp 49-54; 7, May 1918, pp 73-77; 8, June 1918, pp 88-91; 9, July 1918, pp 101-108; 10, August 1918, pp 121-124; 11, September 1918, pp 124-134; 12, October 1918, pp 140-147. English translation in Jaffé, *De Stijl,* 1971, pp 36-93.

_____ . *Plastic Art and Pure Plastic Art, and Other Essays.* The Documents of Modern Art. Edited by Robert Motherwell. New York: Wittenborn, 1945.

_____ . "De realiseering van het néo-plasticisme in verre toekomst en in de huidige architectuur." *De Stijl,* V, 3, March 1922, pp 41-47; 5, May 1922, pp 65-71. English translation in Jaffé, *De Stijl,* 1971, pp 163-171.

_____ . *Toward the True Vision of Reality.* New York: Valentin Gallery, 1942.

_____ . *Two Mondrian Sketchbooks, 1912-14.* Edited by Joop Joosten. Introduction and English translation by Robert Welsh. Amsterdam: Meulenhoff International, 1969.

Ottolenghi, Maria Grazia. *L'opera completa di Mondrian.* Milan: Rizzoli, 1974.

Pleynet, Marcelin. "Mondrian 25 ans après." *Art International,* March 1969, pp 23-26; April 1969, pp 31-33; May 1969, pp 57-58.

Ragghianti, Carlo. *Mondrian e l'arte del XXe secolo.* Milan: Edizioni di Comunita, 1962.

Seuphor, Michel. *Piet Mondrian Life and Work.* New York: Harry N. Abrams, Inc., 1956.

Smith, Brydon. "More About Mondrian: the Search for a Universal Plastic Expression." *Canadian Art,* October 1966, pp 14-17.

Sondag, G. "Couleur/non-Couleur dans la peinture de Mondrian." *Critica d'Arte,* January-February 1976, pp 47-56.

Sweeney, James Johnson. *Piet Mondrian.* New York: Museum of Modern Art, 1948.

Troy, Nancy J. "Piet Mondrian's Atelier." *Arts Magazine,* December 1978, pp 82-87.

Welsh, Robert. "The Birth of De Stijl, Part I: Piet Mondrian—the Subject Matter of Abstraction." *Artforum,* April 1973, pp 50-53.

_____ . *Piet Mondrian, 1872-1944.* Toronto: The Art Gallery of Toronto, 1966.

Wiegand, Charmion von. "The Meaning of Mondrian." *Journal of Aesthetics and Art Criticism,* 2, 8, Fall 1943, pp 62-70.

Wijsenbeek, L.J.F. *Piet Mondrian.* New York: New York Graphic Society, 1968.

Jacobus Johannes Pieter Oud
1890-1963

1890
Born Purmerend, The Netherlands.

1916-17
Collaborates with van Doesburg on the design of two houses: a vacation house "De Vonk" at Noordwijkerhout, and "Villa Allegonda" at Katwijk. Designs Strandboulevard Apartments (unrealized).
Participates in founding of De Stijl.

1918
Appointed City Architect for Rotterdam. Begins designing Spangen housing projects.

1919
Designs factory for Purmerend (unrealized).

1921
Breaks with van Doesburg and withdraws from De Stijl.

1925
Designs the Café De Unie, Rotterdam.

1927
Designs housing for Weissenhofsiedlung Exposition, Stuttgart.

1937-42
Designs office building for Shell-Nederland, The Hague.

1963
Dies, The Hague.

J.J.P. Oud: Bibliography

Badovici, Jean. "Entretiens sur l'Architectures Vivantes. Les possibilities architectoniques de demand," *L'Architecture Vivante,* Spring-Summer 1924, pp 29-32.

Baljeu, Joost. "De Stijl toen en J.J.P. Oud nu," *Forum,* XV, 8, 1961, pp 285-288.

Gruyter, W.J. de *J.J.P. Oud.* Rotterdam: Museum Boymans, 1951.

Hitchcock, Henry Russell. *J.J.P. Oud.* Paris: Editions "Cahiers d'Art," 1931.

_____ . *Modern Architecture.* New York: Museum of Modern Art, 1929.

Joedicke, Jürgen. *Fur eine lebendige kunst.* Stuttgart: Karl Krämer Verlag, 1965, pp 112-124.

Oud, J.J.P. "Kunst en Machine," *De Stijl,* I, 3(4), January 1918, pp 41-43. Translated in Jaffé, Hans. *De Stijl.* New York: Harry N. Abrams, Inc., 1971, pp 96-98.

_____ . "Het Monumentale stadsbeeld," *De Stijl,* I, 1, October 1917, pp 10-11. Translated in Jaffé, Hans. *De Stijl,* 1971, pp 95-96.

_____ . *Mein Weg in 'De Stijl'.* Translated by Kees and Erica de Wit. The Hague: Nijgh & Van Ditman, 1961.

_____ . *Ter Wille van een Levende Bouwkunst.* The Hague and Rotterdam: Nijgh & Van Ditman, n.d.

Polano, Sergio. *J.J.P. Oud Architettura Olandese.* Milano: Franco Angeli Editore, 1981.

Stamm, Gunther. "Het jeugdwerk van de architekt J.J.P. Oud 1906-1917." *Museumjournaal,* 22, 6, December 1977, pp 260-266.

_____ . *The Architecture of J.J.P. Oud 1906-1963.* Tallahassee: Florida State University Art Gallery, 1978.

Wiekart, K. *J.J.P. Oud.* Translated by C. de Dood. Amsterdam: J.M. Meulenhoff, 1965.

Hans Richter 1888-1976

1888
Born 6 April, Berlin.

1916
Joins Zurich Dada group.

1919-21
Collaborates with Viking Eggeling on scrolls and films.

1920
Makes first abstract film. Meets Theo van Doesburg.

1923
Begins publication of the periodical *G*.

1925
Viking Eggeling dies.

1928
Stops painting in order to concentrate on filmmaking.

1941
Emigrates to New York.

1942-56
Teaches film at City College, New York.

1976
Dies 1 February, Locarno, Switzerland.

Hans Richter: Bibliography

Graeff, Werner. "Concerning the So-Called G Group," *Art Journal,* 23, 4, Summer 1964, pp 280-282. Reply by Raoul Hausmann, 24, 4, Summer 1965, pp 350-352.

Habasque, Guy. "Hans Richter." *Quadrum,* 13, 1962, pp 61-74.

Lawder, Standish D. *The Cubist Cinema.* New York: New York University Press, 1975, pp 35-64.

Richter, Hans. "Easel-Scroll-Film." *Magazine of Art,* February 1952, pp 78-86.

_____ . "Film as an Original Art Form." *College Art Journal,* 10, 2, Winter 1951, pp 157-161.

_____ . "A History of the Avant-Garde." In Stauffacher, Frank, ed. *Art in Cinema.* San Francisco: Museum of Art, 1947.

_____ . *Hans Richter.* Edited by Cleve Gray. New York: Holt, Rinehart and Winston, 1971.

Gerrit Rietveld 1888-1964

1888
Born, Utrecht.

1911
Opens cabinet shop in Utrecht.
Begins to study architecture with P.J.C. Klaarhamer. Meets Bart van der Leck.

1918
Constructs the red/blue chair.
Meets Robert van 't Hoff, Theo van Doesburg and other members of De Stijl.

1919
Designs sideboard based on neoplastic principles.
Joins De Stijl.
Establishes independent architectural practice.

1921
Begins collaboration with Mrs. Truus Schröder-Schräder.

1923
Collaborates with Huszar on design for Greater Berlin Art Exhibition.
Participates in De Stijl architecture exhibition at Léonce Rosenberg's Galerie l'Effort Moderne, Paris.

1924-25
Designs and builds house in collaboration with Mrs. Truus Schröder-Schräder.

1928
Participates in the founding of C.I.A.M. (International Congress of Modern Architecture).

1928-64
Receives many international architectural commissions.

1964
Dies 25 June, Utrecht.

Gerrit Rietveld: Bibliography

Badovici, Jean. "Entretiens sur l'Architecture Vivante. Maison à Utrecht (Pays-Bas) par T. Schräder et G. Rietveld," *L'Architecture Vivante,* Fall-Winter 1925, pp 28-29.

Baroni, Daniele. *The Furniture of Gerritt Thomas Rietveld.* Woodbury, N.Y.: Barron's Educational Series, Inc., 1978.

Blotkamp, Carel. *Rietveld Schröder Huis 1925-1975.* Edited by Bertus Mulder and Gerrit Jan de Rook. Utrecht and Antwerp: A.W. Bruna & Zoon, 1975.

Brown, Theodore. *The Work of Gerrit Rietveld, Architect.* Utrecht: A.W. Bruna & Zoon, 1958.

Buffinga, A. *Gerrit Thomas Rietveld.* Translated by Ina Rike. Amsterdam: J.M. Meulenhoff, 1971.

Doesburg, Theo van. "Aanteekeningen bij een leunstoel van Rietveld." *De Stijl,* II, 11, September 1919, p 133.

Kultermann, Udo. "Der Rot-Blau Stuhl von Rietveld." *Alte und Moderne Kunst,* 20, 141, 1975, pp 20-22.

Plantenega, Haro. *Rietveld.* Amsterdam: Stedelijk Museum, 1977.

Rietveld, Gerrit. "Aanteenkening bij kinderstoel," *De Stijl,* II, 9, July 1919, p 102.

_____ . *Rietveld, 1924. Schröder Huis.* Amsterdam: Steendrukkesij de Jong & Co., 1963.

Kurt Schwitters 1887-1948

1887
Born 20 June, Hanover.

1918
Meets Hans Arp and Raoul Hausmann.
Creates first collages.

1918
First "Merz" works.

1920-23
Begins construction of Hanover Merzbau.

1922
Meets Theo van Doesburg.

1922-23
Dada tour of Holland with Theo and
Nelly van Doesburg.

1923
Founds *Merz* magazine.

1927
Founds "Der Ring Neuer Werbegestalter" with
Vordemberge-Gildewart, César Domela and
Moholy-Nagy.

1932
Joins "Abstraction-Creation" group.

1937
Moves to Norway.

1940
Moves to England.

1948
Dies 8 January in Ambleside, England.

Kurt Schwitters: Bibliography

Bolliger, Hans. "Résumé chronologique de la
vie et de l'oeuvre de Kurt Schwitters." In *Kurt
Schwitters, Collages.* Paris: Berggruen & Cie,
1954.

Lach, Friedhelm. *Der Merz Künstler Kurt
Schwitters.* Cologne: M. Dumont Schauberg,
1971.

Schmalenbach, Werner. *Kurt Schwitters.*
New York: Harry N. Abrams, Inc., 1977.

Schmalenbach, Werner and Steinitz, Käthe.
Kurt Schwitters. New York: Marlborough-
Gerson Gallery, 1965.

Schwitters, Kurt; Steinitz, Käthe and Doesburg,
Theo van. *Die Scheuche.* Hanover: Aposverlag,
1925.

Sophie Taeuber-Arp 1889-1943

1889
Born 19 January, Davos, Switzerland.

1916-29
Teaches textile design at School of Applied Arts,
Zurich.

1916
Participates in founding of Zurich Dada group.

1926
Collaborates with Jean Arp and van Doesburg
on design of Café Aubette, Strasbourg.

1931
Joins "Abstraction-Creation" group, Paris.

1943
Dies 13 January, Zurich.

Sophie Taeuber-Arp: Bibliography

Arp, Jean; Bill, Max; Buffet-Picabia, Gabrielle;
Kandinsky, Wassily; Schmidt, Georg; Seuphor,
Michel; Staber, Margit and Taeuber-Arp,
Sophie. *Sophie Taeuber-Arp.* New York: Albert
Loeb Krugier Gallery, 1970.

Arp, Jean; Rossignol, Claude and Weber, Hugo.
Sophie Taeuber-Arp. Strasbourg: Musée d'Art
Moderne, 1977.

Marter, Joan. "Three Women Artists Married
to Early Modernists: Sonia Delaunay-Terk,
Sophie Taeuber-Arp, and Marguerite
Thompson Zorach," *Arts Magazine,* September
1979, pp 88-95.

Schmidt, Georg, ed. *Sophie Taeuber-Arp.* Basel:
Holbein Verlag, 1948.

Sophie Taeuber-Arp. Paris: Musée National
d'Art Moderne, 1964.

Staber, Margit. "Aubette et caetera; Sophie
Taeuber-Arp als Innenarchitektin," *Werk,* April
1977, pp 48-49.

——————— . *Sophie Taeuber-Arp.*
Translated by Eric Schaer. Lausanne: Editions
Recontré, 1970.

Wolters, Theo. "Decorations d'intérieurs crées
et réalisees à Strasbourg par Sophie Taeuber et
Jean Arp," *L'Information de l'histoire de l'art,*
XV, 2, March-April 1970, pp 73-81.

Georges Vantongerloo 1886-1965

1886
Born 24 November, Antwerp, Belgium.

1915
Meets Theo van Doesburg.

1917
Creates first abstract sculptures.
Participates in the founding of De Stijl.

1919-27
Lives in Menton, France.

1921
Withdraws from De Stijl.

1924
Creates first sculptures based on mathematical
formulas.

1927
Moves to Paris.

1931
Member of "Abstraction-Creation" group,
Paris.

1965
Dies in Paris.

Georges Vantongerloo: Bibliography

Burnham, Jack. *Beyond Modern Sculpture.* New York: Braziller, 1968, pp 134-136.

Georges Vantongerloo. London: Marlborough Fine Art Limited, 1962.

Livingston, Jane; Mertons, Phil; Thomas-Jankowski, Angela and Vantongerloo, Georges. *Georges Vantongerloo.* Washington: Corcoran Gallery of Art, 1980.

Staber, Margit. "Georges Vantongerloo." *Art International,* February 1966, pp 13-15.

_____ . "Georges Vantongerloo: Mathematics, Nature and Art." *Studio International,* April 1974, pp 181-184.

Vantongerloo, Georges. "L'Art Plastique [L]² = [s] Neo-Plasticisme." *Vouloir,* 22, 1926, n.p.

_____ . *Paintings, Sculptures, Reflections.* New York: Wittenborn Schultz, 1948.

Wiegand, Charmion von. "Georges Vantongerloo." *Arts Magazine,* September 1960, pp 40-45.

Jan Wils 1891-1972

1891
Born 22 February, Alkmaar, The Netherlands.

1914
Employed in H.P. Berlage's architectural firm.

1916
Meets van Doesburg.

1917
Establishes independent architectural practice, Voorburg.
Participates in founding of De Stijl.
Collaborates with van Doesburg in design of a town house, Alkmaar.

1920
Designs Papaverhof middle-class housing, The Hague.

1928
Designs Olympic Stadium, Amsterdam.

1972
Dies, Voorburg, The Netherlands.

Jan Wils: Bibliography

Hoff, Robert van 't. "Het hotel café-restaurant 'De Dubbele Sleutel' (eerste gedeeltelijke verbouwing) te Woerden. Bijlage 10. Architect Jan Wils," *De Stijl,* II, 5, March 1919, pp 58-60.

Wils, Jan. "De Nieuwe Bouwkunst." *De Stijl,* I, 4, January 1918, pp 31-33.

Piet Zwart 1885-1977

1885
Born 28 May, Zaandijk, The Netherlands.

1919
Meets Vilmos Huszar and Jan Wils. Becomes acquainted with principles of De Stijl.

1920-21
Collaborates with Huszar on furniture designs.

1920-22
Collaborates with Wils and Huszar on architectural projects.

1921
Joins H.P. Berlage's architectural firm.

1923
Begins designing publicity for Dutch Cable Works (NKF).
Meets El Lissitzky and Kurt Schwitters.

1925
Appointed chief assistant to H.P. Berlage.

1925-26
Designs interiors for Leo Faust Restaurant, Paris.

1927
Joins "Ring neuer Werbegestalter" design group.
Leaves Berlage's firm.

1929
Designer for Netherlands postal, telegraph and telephone service (PTT).

1977
Dies, The Netherlands.

Piet Zwart: Bibliography

Althaus, Peter F. *Piet Zwart*. Documents in the Visual Arts, I. Fridolin Muller, editor. Teufen: Verlag Arthur Niggili, 1966.

Broos, Kees. *Piet Zwart*. The Hague: Haags Gemeentemuseum, 1973.

_____ . "Piet Zwart." *Studio International*, April 1973, pp 176-180.

Jaffé, H.L.C. "Piet Zwart, A Pioneer of Functional Typography." *New Graphic Design,* 10, June 1961.

Spencer, Herbert. *Pioneers of Modern Typography*. New York: Hastings House, 1969, pp 110-121.

General Bibliography

Baljeu, Joost. "The Problem of Reality with Suprematism, Constructivism, Proun, Neoplasticism and Elementarism." *The Lugano Review,* I, 1, 1965, pp 105-124.

Baroni, Daniele. "Struttura e linguaggio in De Stijl." *Ottagono*, 43, December 1976, pp 44-49.

Barr, Alfred H. "De Stijl 1917-1928." *Bulletin of the Museum of Modern Art*, 20, 2, pp 3-13.

_____ . *Cubism and Abstract Art*. New York: Arno Press for The Museum of Modern Art, 1936, pp 140-52.

Boorstein, Eli. "The Oblique in Art: Toward the Oblique in Space." *The Structurist*, 9, 1969, pp 32-43.

Bulhof, Francis, ed. *Nijhoff, Van Ostaijen, De Stijl: Modernism in the Netherlands and Belgium in the First Quarter of the 20th Century*. The Hague: Martinus Nijhoff, 1976.

De Stijl. Complete reprint of the magazine (1917-1932) in two volumes. Edited by Ad Petersen. Amsterdam: Athenaeum. The Hague: Bert Bakker; Amsterdam: Polak and Van Gennap, 1968.

Fanelli, Giovanni. *Moderne Architectuur in Nederland 1900-1940*. The Hague: Staatsuitgeverij, 1978, pp 131-166.

Hess, Thomas B. "The Dutch: This Century." *Art News*, January 1953, pp 23-25.

Jaffé, H.L.C. *De Stijl*. New York: Harry N. Abrams, Inc., 1971.

_____ . *De Stijl 1917-1931 The Dutch Contribution to Modern Art*. Amsterdam: J.M. Meulenhoff, 1959.

_____ . "The De Stijl Concept of Space." *The Structurist*, 8, 1968, pp 8-12.

_____ . "The Diagonal Principle in the Works of van Doesburg and Mondrian." *The Structurist*, 9, 1969, pp 14-21.

_____ . *Mondrian und De Stijl*. Cologne: Galerie Gmurzynska, 1979.

Leitner, Bernhard. "Dutch Architecture: 1920-1940." *Artforum*, June 1972, pp 76-78.

Levin, Kim. "Kiesler and Mondrian, Art into Life." *Art News*, May 1964, pp 50-52.

Mansbach, Steven A. *Visions of Totality. László Moholy-Nagy, Theo van Doesburg, and El Lissitzky*. Ann Arbor: UMI Research Press, 1980.

Milner, John. "Ideas and Influences of De Stijl." *Studio International*, March 1968, pp 115-119.

Naylor, Gillian. "De Stijl: Abstraction or Architecture." *Studio International*, September-October 1976, pp 98-102.

The Non-Objective World, Twenty-Five Years 1914-1939. London: Annely Juda Fine Art, 1978.

O'Konor, Louise. *Viking Eggeling 1880-1925: Artist and Filmmaker, Life and Work*. Translated by Catherine G. Sundström and Anne Bibby. Stockholm: Trya Almquist and Wielsell, 1971.

Oud, J.J.P. *Hollandische Architektur*. Bauhausbucher 10. Munich: Albert Langen Verlag, 1926.

Overy, Paul. *De Stijl*. London: Studio Vista; New York: E.P. Dutton, 1969.

Passuth, C. "Kurt Schwitters, Theo van Doesburg et le 'Bauhaus'." *Bulletin du Musée Hongrois des Beaux-Arts,* 40, 1973, pp 69-83.

Phillpot, Clive. "Movement Magazines: the Years of Style." *The Art Press: Two Centuries of Art Magazines*. Edited by Trevor Fawcett and Clive Phillpot. London: Art Book, 1976, pp 41-44.

Ragon, Michel. "The De Stijl Movement and Architecture." *Cimaise*, 17, 99, November-December 1970, pp 66-75.

Richter, Hans. "Viking Eggeling." *Studio International,* March 1972, pp 97-99.

Sers, Philippe. "The Story of De Stijl." *Cimaise,* 17, 99, November-December 1970, pp 12-24.

Sweeney, James Johnson. "Mondrian, the Dutch and De Stijl." *Art News,* June 1951, pp 24-25.

Troy, Nancy J. "De Stijl's Collaborative Ideal: The Colored Abstract Environment." Yale University: PhD dissertation, 1979.

Vordemberge-Gildewart, Friedrich. "Zur geschichte der Stijl-bewegung." *Werk,* November 1951, pp 349-355.

Weaver, Mike, ed. "Great Little Magazines, No. 6: 'De Stijl.'" *Form,* 6, December 1967, pp 29-39; 7, 1968, pp 25-32.

Wescher, Herta. "Art in Europe Around 1925." *Cimaise*, 17, 99, November-December 1970, pp 76-81.

_____ . "An Interview with Nelly van Doesburg." *Cimaise*, 17, 99, November-December 1970, pp 35-42.

Weyergraf, Clara. *Piet Mondrian und Theo van Doesburg, Deutung von Werk und Theorie*. Munich: Wilhelm Fink Verlag, 1979.

Wolter, Theo. "L'Aubette." *Cimaise*, 17, 99, November-December 1970, pp 49-56.

Zevi, Bruno. *La Poetica dell'architettura neoplastica*. Milan: Politecnica Tamburini, 1953.

Acknowledgments

When the De Stijl exhibition was initiated in 1979, we learned that 1982 would be the anniversary of 200 years of unbroken diplomatic ties between The Netherlands and the United States. With that fact in mind, we took the idea for the exhibition to Mrs. Geri Joseph, former United States Ambassador to Holland. Her immediate enthusiasm for the project and the good will she elicited from our Dutch colleagues set us off on the right path. We are grateful for her crucial early support.

This publication and the exhibition of De Stijl masterworks would not have been possible without the guidance, access to collections and generous assistance given to us by staff members of many museums and government collections in The Netherlands, for they have worked with us since 1979 to make the project a reality. Foremost among them: Rudolf W.D. Oxenaar, Director of the Rijksmuseum Kröller-Müller; Edy de Wilde, Director of the Stedelijk Museum, Amsterdam; Theo van Velsen, Director of the Haags Gemeentemuseum; Rudolph de Haas, Director of the Dutch State-Owned Art Collections, The Hague; Rudolf H. Fuchs, Director of the Van Abbemuseum, Eindhoven; and, Dick van Woerkom, Director of the Nederlands Documentatiecentrum voor de Bouwkunst, Amsterdam.

Other staff members of these institutions have given vast amounts of time and expertise to the exhibition. They include: Joop Joosten, Research Curator, Stedelijk Museum, Amsterdam; Wim de Wit, Research Curator at the Nederlands Documentatiecentrum voor de Bouwkunst; Kees Broos, Director of the Department of Modern Art, and Herbert Henkels, Curator, Haags Gemeentemuseum; Evert van Stratten, Curator, Dutch State-Owned Collections; and, Margriet Suren, Curator, Van Abbemuseum. In addition, we have received invaluable assistance from Wil Berteaux, Design Curator, and Ada Stroeve, Department of Applied Arts, both of the Stedelijk Museum, Amsterdam; Auke van der Woud, former Curator of the Rijksmuseum Kröller-Müller, and Wouter van der Horst, Director of "'t Bleekerhûs" Museum, Drachten.

Many other friends in Holland have given advice and assistance in various ways: Gerrit Oorthuys, architect and historian, located materials for us in the Rietveld archive in Utrecht; Bertus Mulder, architect, has permitted our use of his drawings of the Rietveld/ Schröder house; Thil Oxenaar, a board member of the Rietveld/ Schröder Foundation, spent many hours with us interpreting for Mrs. Truus Schröder-Schräder in conversations about the house in Utrecht where she has lived since 1924; and, to the redoubtable Mrs. Schröder, who permitted us to impose on her hospitality so that a series of new photographs of the house could be made for the exhibition, we extend our thanks with particular pleasure. Frank den Oudsten, who made the Rietveld/Schröder house photographs for us, has earned our friendship and admiration. We are grateful to Cornelis van Eesteren, who, with Mrs. Schröder and César Domela (in Paris), is among the last of the De Stijl participants still living, spent many hours working on loans from his archive. Maude van Loon kindly permitted us to tape jazz recordings that had belonged to Piet Mondrian. Hans L.C. Jaffé, in addition to writing the introduction for this publication, advised on loans for the exhibition. Our thanks also to Janny and Harry Hovinga for photo research in Holland.

On this side of the Atlantic, many art historians and curators have given us important assistance. In organizing the exhibition and selecting objects for it, we have progressed with great confidence because our primary consultant has been Nancy J. Troy, Assistant Professor of Art History at Johns Hopkins University. In addition to her vast knowledge of the history of this movement, her familiarity with De Stijl collections and with the Dutch language have been essential to the success of this project. Robert P. Welsh, Chairman of the Department of Art History, University of Toronto, consulted with us at the outset and helped give shape to our earliest proposals.

The exhibition will be shown at the Hirshhorn Museum in Washington, D.C. in the spring of 1982, and for their enthusiastic participation we wish to thank Abram Lerner, that museum's Director, and Stephen Weil, Deputy Director. In order to provide an opportunity for Dutch museum goers to see their familiar De Stijl holdings in conjunction with many superb examples from the United States and from elsewhere in Europe, the exhibition will be divided in half chronologically and thus shown simultaneously in the late summer and fall of 1982 at the Stedelijk Museum, Amsterdam and the Rijksmuseum Kröller-Müller in Otterlo.

An exhibition of this scope could not have been undertaken without financial assistance. For their help in this regard we are indebted to the staffs of the National Endowment for the Arts and the National Endowment for the Humanities. We would particularly like to thank Patricia McFate, former Deputy Director and Cheryl McClenney, Assistant Director, Museums and Historical Organizations Program, of the Humanities Endowment staff. Alice Martin has given much needed assistance in the securing of U.S. government indemnity for the exhibition, a program that insures invaluable works of art from abroad so that they may be seen by American audiences. Edward Russell, of Champion International Corporation, has our deep appreciation for his generous assistance. And we are grateful to Andries Ekker, former Counselor for Press and Cultural Affairs, Dutch Embassy, Washington, D.C., for his invaluable help in securing the financial assistance of the Dutch government for the exhibition.

A number of his vintage photographs of Mondrian's Paris atelier have been loaned to us by the great photographer, André Kertész. Mrs. Lillian Kiesler has kindly permitted the reproduction here of a photograph of Frederick Kiesler's *City in Space*. Harry Holtzman, longtime friend of Mondrian and executor of his estate in the United States, has given permission for the reproduction of Mondrian images in this publication.

Several art dealers assisted with loans, including: Annely Juda, London; Antonina Gmurzynska, Cologne; Alain Tarica, Paris; and Sidney Janis, New York. In Paris, several staff members of the Centre Georges Pompidou were extremely helpful. We wish to thank Pontus Hulten, former Director of that institution, Germain Viatte, Director of Collections, Edmée de Lillers, Assistant Curator, Department of Drawings, and Christian Derouet, Curator of the Department of Drawings. The Belgian painter, Michel Seuphor, friend and biographer of Mondrian, was generous with his time and knowledge. We are grateful to Carlos van Hassalt, Director of the Fondation Custodia, Institut Néerlandais, Paris, for his assistance. We wish to thank Ulrike Gauss, Curator of the Stuttgart State Museum, for her loan of Mondrian atelier photographs. We are also indebted to Greta Ströh, librarian of the Hagenbach-Arp archive in Meudon, for the use of vintage photographs of the Café Aubette. Our thanks as well to Yve-Alain Bois, Paris, for his interest and advice. Mme. Nadine Lehni, Curator of the Musée d'Art Moderne in Strasbourg, was enormously helpful with photographs and models of the Aubette. For advice in regard to the Aubette we are indebted to Theo Wolters and Julien Nussbaum, who was also responsible for the fabrication of the Aubette models.

To the authors of this book we extend our sincere gratitude for their fine essays and their unfailing affability. Our thanks also to the intrepid translators. We have enjoyed working with our co-publishers at Abbeville Press in New York: special thanks are owed to Mark Magowan, Robert Abrams and Dana Cole. We also wish to express our appreciation for his assistance and patience to Andreas Landshoff of Meulenhoff/Landshoff Publishers in Holland.

We cannot properly thank the lenders to the exhibition here and abroad (they are listed on p 248) for they have been willing to part with their superb objects for an entire year in order that a broad public might have the opportunity to see these works in the context of this new view of De Stijl. To the artists who were interviewed for the essay "Echoes of De Stijl," we extend thanks for their concise remarks and their generous loans to our homage to De Stijl exhibition.

To all my colleagues at Walker Art Center go particular thanks. Their complex tasks for the exhibition and publication were carried out with consistent skill, care and good humor. (Art Center staff members who participated directly are listed on p 250.) Finally, I owe a special debt to Martin Friedman, who, in addition to directing many aspects of the exhibition, has given consistently valuable counsel and support toward the realization of this project.

Mildred Friedman

Lenders to the Exhibition

The Art Institute of Chicago, Chicago, Illinois

"'t Bleekerhûs," Drachten, The Netherlands

Busch-Reisinger Museum, Harvard University, Cambridge, Massachusetts

Centraal Museum der Gemeente, Utrecht, The Netherlands

Mr. and Mrs. Arthur A. Cohen

Cincinnati Art Museum, Cincinnati, Ohio

The Cleveland Museum of Art, Cleveland, Ohio

Mr. and Mrs. J. Dibbets

Dienst Verspreide Rijkskollekties, The Hague, The Netherlands

Van Eesteren-Fluck and van Lohuizen Archive, Amsterdam, The Netherlands

Fondation Custodia, Institut Néerlandais, Paris, France

Arnold and Milly Glimcher

Antonina Gmurzynska

Galerie Gmurzynska, Cologne, West Germany

Graphische Sammlung Staatsgalerie Stuttgart, Stuttgart, West Germany

Haags Gemeentemuseum, The Hague, The Netherlands

Herbert F. Johnson Museum of Art, Cornell University, Ithaca, New York

Kay Hillman, New York, New York

Hirshhorn Museum and Sculpture Garden, Smithsonian Institution, Washington, D.C.

Kaiser Wilhelm Museum, Krefeld, West Germany

Sandra Kocher

Kunstmuseum, Basel, Switzerland

The Minneapolis Institute of Arts, Minneapolis, Minnesota

Musée d'Art Moderne de Strasbourg, Strasbourg, France

Musée National d'Art Moderne, Centre Georges Pompidou, Paris, France

Museum Boymans-van Beuningen, Rotterdam, The Netherlands

Museum of Art, Carnegie Institute, Pittsburgh, Pennsylvania

Museum of Art, Rhode Island School of Design, Providence, Rhode Island

Museum of Fine Arts, Houston, Texas

The Museum of Modern Art, New York, New York

Muzeum Sztuki, Lodz, Poland

National Gallery of Art, Washington, D.C.

Nederlands Documentatiecentrum voor de Bouwkunst,
Stichting Architectuurmuseum, Amsterdam, The Netherlands

Mr. and Mrs. Morton G. Neumann

The Pace Gallery, New York, New York

Philadelphia Museum of Art, Philadelphia, Pennsylvania

The Phillips Collection, Washington, D.C.

Portland Art Museum, Portland, Oregon

Rijksmuseum Kröller-Müller, Otterlo, The Netherlands

D. Rinsema

Mrs. Nieuwenhuizen Segaar-Aarse

Sidney Janis Gallery, New York, New York

J.P. Smid, Kunsthandel Monet, Amsterdam, The Netherlands

The Solomon R. Guggenheim Museum, New York, New York

State of Holland

Stedelijk Museum, Amsterdam, The Netherlands

Stedelijk Van Abbemuseum, Eindhoven, The Netherlands

Thyssen-Bornemisza Collection, Lugano, Switzerland

The Toledo Museum of Art, Toledo, Ohio

Wellesley College Museum, Wellesley, Massachusetts

Winston-Malbin Collection (Dr. and Mrs. Barnett Malbin)

Yale University Art Gallery, New Haven, Connecticut

Seven Private Collections

**Walker Art Center
Staff for the Exhibition
and
Board of Directors**

Direction
Martin Friedman

Administration
Donald C. Borrman
Miriam Swenson

Organization and Design
Mildred Friedman

Handling of Works
Carolyn De Cato

Editorial Research and Assistance
Trent Myers

Editorial and Secretarial Assistance
Linda Krenzin
Diane Oelhafen

Graphic Design
Robert Jensen
Nancy Allen
Will Ayres
Don Bergh

Catalogue Index
William Horrigan

Installation Models
Ron Elliott

Installation
Hugh Jacobson
Steve Ecklund
Joe Janson
John King
Mark Kramer
Cody Riddle

Public Information
Mary Abbe Martin
Karen Statler

Photography
Glenn Halvorson
Donald Neal

Related Events
Richard Peterson
Nigel Redden
Steve Sharratt
Melinda Ward
Adam Weinberg

Slide-Tape
Marie Cieri
Jana Freiband
Charles Helm

Tour Coordinator
Benita Geffen

Reproduction Credits

Courtesy Mr. and Mrs. Arthur A. Cohen: fig. 128

Courtesy the Art Institute of Chicago: fig. 6

Geoffrey Clements, courtesy David Bourdon: fig. 205

Joseph Crilley, courtesy New Jersey State Museum: fig. 190

P. Delbo, courtesy Haags Gemeentemuseum: figs. 46, 47, 48, 49, 50, 51

De Stijl, I, 1, 1917: figs. 12, 13, 134

De Stijl, I, 6, 1918: fig. 15

De Stijl, II, 1, 1918: fig. 68

De Stijl, II, 9, 1919: fig. 14

De Stijl, III, 7, 1920: fig. 141

De Stijl, IV, 8, 1921: fig. 69

De Stijl, IV, 11, 1921: fig. 142

De Stijl, V, 1, 1922: fig. 71

De Stijl, VIII, 85/86, 1928: fig. 130

Courtesy Dienst Verspreide Rijkskollekties: figs. 29, 55, 57, 59, 127, 136, 146, 148, 166, 167

Courtesy van Eesteren-Fluck and van Lohuizen Archive: figs. 185, 186, 187

Courtesy Peter Eisenman: fig. 82

Courtesy Gladys Fabre: fig. 19

Courtesy Fondation Custodia, Institut Néerlandais: figs. 158, 159

R. Franz, courtesy Musée d'Art Moderne de Strasbourg: figs. 172, 179, 180, 181

Courtesy Kenneth Frampton: fig. 81

Courtesy The Frank Lloyd Wright Memorial Foundation: fig. 62

Stuart Friedman, courtesy Multiples, Inc./Marian Goodman Gallery: fig. 193

Courtesy Galerie Gmurzynska: figs. 25, 182

Roger Gass, courtesy Daniel Weinberg Gallery: fig. 195

Courtesy Haags Gemeentemuseum: figs. 23, 37, 38, 93, 126, 129, 131, 132, 133, 135, 137, 143, 152, 153, 155

Courtesy Hagenbach-Arp Archive: figs. 171, 173, 174, 175

Courtesy John Hejduk: fig. 83

Thomas J. Henderson: fig. 192

Courtesy Hirshhorn Museum and Sculpture Garden, Smithsonian Institution: fig. 35

André Kertész: figs. 44, 45, 52

Courtesy Mrs. Lillian Kiesler: fig. 7

Levende Kunst, I, 7, 1918, courtesy Nancy J. Troy: fig. 147

Courtesy Mrs. Barnett Malbin: fig. 10

Lázló Moholy-Nagy, courtesy Busch-Reisinger Museum, Harvard University: fig. 70

Courtesy Musée National d'Art Moderne, Centre Georges Pompidou: figs. 138, 169, 178

Courtesy Museum of Art, Carnegie Institute: fig. 8

Courtesy Museum of Art, Rhode Island School of Design: fig. 22

Courtesy Museum Ludwig: fig. 20

Courtesy The Museum of Modern Art, New York: figs. 11, 27, 28, 33, 34, 36, 72, 73, 74, 75, 77, 79

Courtesy Nederlands Documentatiecentrum voor de Bouwkunst, Stichting Architectuurmuseum: figs. 61, 76, 80, 151, 183, 184

Courtesy *The New Yorker Magazine:* fig. 204

Frank den Oudsten: figs. 63, 64, 65, 66, 67, 87, 94, 95, 102, 103, 104, 105, 106, 107, 108, 109, 117, 118, 119, 120, 121, 122, 123, 124, 125, 149

Frank den Oudsten, courtesy "'t Bleekerhûs:" figs. 162, 163, 164

Courtesy Philadelphia Museum of Art: fig. 16

Eric Pollitzer, courtesy Herbert F. Johnson Museum of Art, Cornell University: fig. 4

Courtesy private collector: fig. 42

Courtesy Rietveld Foundation: figs. 98, 99, 100, 101, 113, 114

Courtesy Rijksmuseum, Amsterdam: fig. 5

Courtesy Rijksmuseum Kröller-Müller: figs. 9, 18, 24, 26, 30, 43, 150

Izak Salomons, courtesy Rietveld Foundation: fig. 96

O. Scholl, courtesy Musée d'Art Moderne de Strasbourg: fig. 145

Courtesy Sidney Janis Gallery: fig. 201

Courtesy J.P. Smid: figs. 39, 40, 41

Courtesy The Solomon R. Guggenheim Museum: fig. 7

Courtesy Sonnabend Gallery: fig. 200

Gerald Stableski, courtesy Walker Art Center: fig. 191

Courtesy Stedelijk Museum, Amsterdam: figs. 1, 21, 32, 58, 84, 86, 88, 89, 90, 91, 92, 138, 139, 140, 144, 157, 161

Courtesy Stedelijk Van Abbemuseum: figs. 2, 3, 31, 56, 60, 85, 97, 154, 160

Robin Verhoeven, courtesy van Eesteren-Fluck and van Lohuizen Archive: fig. 165

Walker Art Center: figs. 156, 170, 188, 189, 191, 194, 196, 197, 198, 199, 202, 203

Courtesy Wellesley College Museum: fig. 17

Drawings by Victoria Gibbs: figs. 51, 176, 177

Drawings courtesy Bertus Mulder: figs. 110, 111, 112, 115, 116

Index

Text set in Sabon and Spartan at
Walker Art Center on a Mergenthaler
CRTronic.
Color separations and half-tones by Spectralith.
Chicago.
Printed and bound in Spain
by Heraclio Fournier, S.A. - Vitoria
Design by Robert Jensen.